The Wage under Attack

Employment Policies in Europe

P.I.E. Peter Lang
Bruxelles · Bern · Berlin · Frankfurt am Main · New York · Oxford · Wien

This work is the fruit of a collective research endeavour which was completed within the framework of the Institut Européen du Salariat (European Institute on the Salariat), a project supported by the Maison des Sciences de l'Homme Lorraine (Lorraine Institute for Social Sciences and Humanities).

The following institutions also contributed to financing the present book:

- Universitat Autònoma of Barcelona - Centre d'Estudis Sociólogics sobre la Vida Quotidiana i el Treball (QUIT);

- Université Paris Ouest Nanterre – Laboratoire des Institutions et Dynamiques Historiques de l'Economie (IDHE);

- Université Libre de Bruxelles - Groupe de Recherche sur les Acteurs Internationaux et leurs Discours (GRAID) ;

- Facultade de Economia do Porto – Centro d'Estudios de Economia Industrial, do Trabalho e da Empresa (CETE).

We owe special thanks to Philippe Pochet for his careful reading of the manuscript and precious advice, and to Virginie Vathelet for her professionalism and much appreciated assistance in preparing the manuscript. We are particularly grateful to Merle Shore, our translator, for her close, and affectionate, collaboration and her essential participation in bringing this book to completion.

Bernadette Clasquin & Bernard Friot (eds.)

The Wage under Attack

Employment Policies in Europe

"Work & Society"
No.75

Éditions scientifiques internationales
Brussels, 2013
1 avenue Maurice, B-1050 Brussels, Belgium
info@peterlang.com; www.peterlang.com

ISSN 1376-0955
ISBN 978-2-87574-029-8
D/2013/5678/17

Library of Congress Cataloging-in-Publication Data
The wage under attack : employment policies in Europe / Bernadette Clasquin & Bernard Friot (eds.). pages cm. -- (Work & society, 1376-0955 ; No. 75)
Includes bibliographical references and index. ISBN 978-2-87574-029-8 (alk. paper) 1. Labor policy--Europe. 2. Wages--Government policy--Europe. I. Clasquin, Bernadette. II. Friot, Bernard, 1946-
HD8376.5.W34 2013 331.12'042094--dc23 2013001912

CIP also available from the British Library.

Bibliographic information published by "Die Deutsche Nationalbibliothek".

"Die Deutsche Nationalbibliothek" lists this publication in the "Deutsche National-bibliografie"; detailed bibliographic data is available on the Internet at <http://dnb.d-nb.de>.

Contents

Part III: Back into the Labour Market!

Conclusion

List of Acronyms

AIEE	*Acuerdo Interconfederal para la Estabilidad en el Empleo* (Intersectoral Agreement for Employment Stability)
ANPE	*Agence Nationale pour l'Emploi* (French National Employment Agency)
API	*Allocation de parent isolé* (Single parent allowance)
ARE	*Allocation d'Aide au Retour à l'Emploi* (Return-to-work allowance)
ASSEDIC	*Association pour l'Emploi Dans l'Industrie et le Commerce* (Association for Employment in Industry and Trade).
ASS	*Allocation de Solidarité Spécifique* (Specific solidarity allowance)
CCOO	*Comisiones Obreras* (Trade Union Confederation of Workers' Commissions)
CEOE	*Confederación Española de Organizaciones Empresariales* (Spanish Confederation of Employers' Organisations)
CES	*Consejo Económico y Social* (Social and Economic Council)
ECB	European Central Bank
EPA	*Encuesta de la Población Activa* (Labour Force Survey)
GDP	Gross Domestic Product
INEM	*Instituto Nacional de Empleo* (National Institute of Employment)
NIC	National Insurance Contribution
OECD	Organisation for Economic Co-operation and Development
PES	Public Employment Service
PFEE	*Plan para el Fomento del Empleo Estable* (Programme for the Promotion of Stable Employment)

PSOE	*Partido Socialista Obrero Español* (Spanish Socialist Party)
RMA	*Revenu Minimum d'Activité* (Activity minimum income)
RMI	*Revenu Minimum d'Insertion* (Insertion minimum income)
RSA	*Revenu Solidarité Active* (Active solidarity income)
RWE	Reduced Wage Employment
SMIC	*Salaire Minimum Interprofessionnel de Croissance* (Minimum wage)
UGT	*Unión General de Trabajadores* (General Workers' Confederation)
WTC	Working Tax Credit
WFTC	Working Family Tax Credit

Introduction

Bernadette CLASQUIN
General Secretary, Maison des Sciences de l'Homme Lorraine

Bernard FRIOT
Emeritus Professor, University of Paris Ouest Nanterre; member of the Institut Européen du Salariat

Merle SHORE
Translator

Since 2007, as we are being told, the economy has been in crisis – a crisis of public debt and a crisis of employment. But this so-called crisis serves a particular purpose. It is being used to justify pursuing a process that was launched some 30 years ago under the name of "reform". And that process has fed an economic downturn, which then serves as a pretext for stepping up the same policies that have provoked it – in other words, for administering more of the same toxic remedy that ends up killing the patient. The two targets of this reform policy are the socialised wage (or more precisely, its social contribution component), and the *qualification* system, and the overall aim of the European Union (EU) is to impose the Anglo-Nordic Beveridgean model in both fields. A model which, with regard to social contributions, rests on that famous distinction between a "first pillar" of tax-financed public schemes – distributing either a national solidarity allowance or benefits in the form of a deferred income via a pay-as-you-go (PAYG) provident scheme – and a "second pillar" of funded occupational schemes. In the field of employment, "employability" has become the key word, with reforms advocating lifelong learning, career path security, and such like, all of which serve to reinforce the labour market and weaken the qualification system. These reforms mark a break with internal and occupational markets, civil service systems, and with everything that saves the individual from having to submit to the labour market. These two targets – the social contribution that finances the socialised wage, and the qualification system that emancipates workers from the labour market – are the two major wage institutions created in continental Europe during the 20th century under the influence of the Bismarckian tradition. The socialised wage does not correspond to a state-guaranteed provident scheme, nor does it base pension and unemployment benefits on that contributory principle of "I'm entitled to these benefits because I've paid for them": it changes the definition of economic value by attributing a continued wage to the unemployed and the retired, that is, by asserting the principle that economic value is created independently of employment and the labour market. The present volume thus contests the orthodoxy that Esping Andersen's (1990) typology has come to represent, and which, by disqualifying the continental tradition as "conservative-corporatist", and glorifying the Nordic version of the Beveridgean tradition as "democratic", serves to legitimate the reforms promoted by the EU. Our aim is to demonstrate the emancipatory potential of the continental tradition of the socialised wage, and the negative implications of the reforms aimed at bringing it into line with the Beveridgean model.

Our research[1] seeks to contribute to the sociology of monetary resources, which it analyses not only as the product of social relations, but also as producing these relations: the relations between capital and labour will thus differ depending on whether workers' pay includes a savings component or not (and thus whether or not it feeds financial accumulation); and if it is a price that is negotiated, or if it recognises the qualification attached to the person (and thus whether it supports the labour market or not). The transformations of the nature of workers' resources involve the major institutions of the convention of labour, namely: what activity is considered as producing economic value; the measure of that value; the conditions of its production; and its distribution. Hence the pertinence of developing a grammar of monetary resources (what we call "resource regimes") for our research network, and indeed for all those who are interested in the transformations of the wage brought about by EU-led reforms. The term "wage" is used here to mean the total wage, which comprises the direct wage plus the remuneration of time out-of-work such as sickness, maternity, unemployment and retirement.

Our previous book, *Wage and Welfare* (Clasquin *et al.*, 2004), presented our first attempts to theorise a problematic which would take us beyond the dominant representations and resultant pessimistic hypotheses about the end of work, the absence of a true alternative, and such like. As with the present volume, it presented the results of the research undertaken by a European network to explore different national realities and the influence of European construction. The entry point of the

---

1 This volume is based on the collective research undertaken within the framework of the European project "Employees Resources and Social Rights in Europe" (RESORE), FP 5, Key action "Improving the socio-economic knowledge base" (contract number: HPSE-CT-2002-00104).

analysis was to take the wage as the central institution channelling resource flows, in order to highlight the links between the wage and social protection, and address the question of the construction and transformation of social rights over resources. In contrast to other studies focusing on areas such as public policies, the transformation of employment forms, the cost of labour or the level of resources, the aim was to conceptualise the links between the nature of resources, social protection and employment forms. Adopting a socio-economic approach, we proposed a sociology of resources that enabled us to identify ideal-types of the social statuses created by the transformations observed. The conceptualisation of the combination between the analytical categories of social rights and workers' status laid the basis for the construction of the theoretical framework of resource regimes.

The present volume is a continuation of that first endeavour.[2] It proposes an analysis of the changes affecting the relationship between the nature of resources and forms of subordinated labour, paying particular attention to the impact of European construction. It offers a fresh perspective on the *salariat*, highlighting its emancipatory potential, and critiquing the thesis of its decline. The research presented here has progressed on two levels. Firstly, the role played by the EU, its discourses and institutions has been brought to the fore; and the implications have been clarified using the resource regime analytical framework, which has been revised and further developed. Secondly, the examination of national policies has served to highlight the convergence between the national level and the reforms prescribed for the Union as a whole.

This second volume seeks to show that the waves of reform have been accelerated by the European Union via the succession of treaties signed over the past 30 years, and that the latter have generated or ratified national employment and social protection policies whose primary function is to change the nature of the wage to make it compatible with the model of *flexicurity* (Klammer, 2005) – a process that the current crisis has served to amplify. As a result, as our analysis of transformations in the origin of workers' resources will show, governments as well as the actors in the spheres of the wage and employment have brought about a change in the meaning of employment. The various European research projects conducted by our network have led us to the conclusion that employment in its present form runs counter to the institution of the wage that was progressively established during the last century:

---

2 *Wage and Welfare* remains a useful tool for understanding the development of the approach that produced the results presented here.

> It is our postulate that in the course of the 20th century, through both their union and their political struggles, the workers in the countries currently involved in the construction of the European Union obtained resource regimes which, at the beginning of the 1970s, constituted a potential basis for challenging financial accumulation, capitalism's dominant logic. And that, at the end of that decade, the European ruling classes seized the opportunity of the construction of a single market for capital and the providers of goods and services to launch a counter-revolution aimed at shifting these resource regimes in a direction favourable to financial accumulation. (Friot, 2004, p. 75)

And, precisely, what we have seen in the past five years is the bailing-out of financial-market shareholders thanks to the massive monetary creation undertaken by the ECB. This is what the media and the ruling classes call the "crisis", presenting it as a matter of fate that none can escape, and using it to blackmail the populations with threats of both job loss and debt. But we will show here that this so-called crisis has been used to accelerate and extend the policies pursued over the past 30 years, and which have plunged Europe into an economic recession that cannot simply be explained by the collapse of the financial markets in 2007.

The RESORE research project was a collective endeavour that brought together some 30 researchers from nine European countries. The 14 authors of the present book all participated in the various thematic workshops, and their reports on their findings constituted the first drafts of the bulk of the texts presented here. Our collective research experience, which began in 1997 and continued until completion of this book, was funded by several EU contracts[3] thanks to which we were able to improve our knowledge of our respective national realities, discuss their specificities, and construct a theoretical alternative (Clasquin, 2006). A history of the beginnings of our network can be found in the introduction to our first book. An animated debate then arose within the group, reflecting a split between two intellectual traditions and two models of social protection: the Beveridgean model that originated in the UK and influenced the Scandinavian countries, and the Bismarckian model that is dominant in the continental European countries. The present volume is more specifically the fruit of the work of a sub-group that shares an intellectual style and a continental model of social protection (Austria, Belgium, Spain, France, and Portugal).[4] The

[3] The RESORE project was preceded by a thematic network, the Social Construction of Employment, conducted within the framework of the 4th European Research Programme. It was followed by the integrated CAPRIGHT project (Resources, rights and capabilities: in search of social foundations for Europe) in which the majority of the authors participated.

[4] Special thanks to the colleagues who contributed to our thinking and who are not present in this book, in particular Rahgnild Barbu, Torsten Brandt, Massimo Canarella, Nicolas Castel, Patricia Frericks, Willibrord de Graaf, Enrico Fravega, Mark Harvey,

fact that the EU is seeking to impose a Nordic model of social protection – with the consequences that will be described in the chapters that follow – has strengthened our sense of the importance of contributing to the debate. This is why we have sought to develop a theoretical proposal based on the resource regime framework. This line of thinking has also been pursued in a number of other works (Castel, 2009; Coron, 2006; Dufresne, 2010 and 2011; Friot, 2010 and 2012, Gobin, 2007; Gobin and Dufresne 2010; Higelé *et al.*, 2009).

In Part I of this chapter, we will present our point of view and our reasons for reasserting the value of the continental (Bismarckian) tradition. Some of the key analytical categories used here will then be explained in Part II, in particular, those that present problems with regard to their transposition into English. The last part will present the contents of the book.

I. European Research Highlighting the Advantages of the Continental Model

Two key features constitute the originality of the continental model: first, social protection is based on the wage since it is financed by social contributions proportionate to the direct wage; and second, wage levels are based on grids negotiated collectively at cross-sectoral level (rather than at the enterprise or sectoral level), and that correspond to recognised levels of experience, credentials and skills which, taken together, constitute what is defined here as a qualification system. Although these fundamental characteristics have not been accompanied by the achievement of social democracy (Friot, 2012b), they nonetheless constitute the basis for an emancipatory relationship to work. Emancipatory, because they subvert subordination by creating the possibility for free (non-subordinated) work during periods of unemployment, maternity and retirement, which are not seen as risks to be covered by an insurance system, but as social rights. Because, with this possibility of working freely, the worker is not reduced to simply being the possessor of labour power that will be exchanged for a wage on a market. And finally, because it is the collective forces that negotiate the qualification grid that also define social protection policies (Friot, 2010). Whatever the initial intentions may have been, the legacy of the Bismarckian model proves to be more emancipatory than that of the Beveridgean tradition. The latter has had to base long-term commitments on advanced funding, and maintains the identification between the wage and employment since the labour market is the consecrated form of the relationship to work. In

Ute Klammer, Robert Maier, Ingrid Mairhuber, Luca Queirolo Palmas, Claus Schaeffer and Peter Urwin, with whom we shared this warm and stimulating adventure.

contrast, the socialisation of the wage in the Bismarckian tradition permits work to be disconnected from employment and opens up perspectives for moving beyond the labour market; moreover, it permits long-term commitments to be financed without recourse to savings.

Our collective research strategy, in its initial phase, was to compare our respective countries and learn more about the societal specificities of each national space, with a view to identifying differences and convergences between them in the fields of employment and social protection. Our observation of the interaction between the European and national levels and the propaganda deployed by the EU led us to seek out the participation of researchers with specialised knowledge of the Community level. Their contribution to our thinking was already apparent in our first book. In the next phase of our research, we sought to refine our analysis of the two-way effects that serve to strengthen and legitimate the push to construct a common European "social model" subsumed to economic and financial goals. The articulation between the national and European levels was central to the construction of our line of enquiry (Hantrais, 2009).

The articulation between these two levels thus led us to integrate the process of European construction into our examination of developments in the fields of pension reform and employment policy. It should be noted that with the concept of the "total wage", employment and social protection can be analysed together, and the complementary nature of the changes brought to light, whatever the situation (unemployment, retirement, or employment). We chose to focus on pension reforms and employment policy measures for several reasons. These two fields permitted examination of all the categories of money affecting the nature of resources (the wage, savings, investment income) and of the full range of resource regimes (and their combinations); they also allowed us to investigate transformations in the origin of resources by examining the core and not only the margins of the *salariat*. The issue of pensions offered an entry point to dealing with the primary target of the reforms, that is, non-employment situations covered by social contributions, while the study of employment policies enabled us to look into the ways in which the measures introduced serve to undermine the socialised wage. Furthermore, for the reformers, a labour market and financial accumulation constitute the complementary and indissociable ingredients required to restore the capitalist convention of labour.

Philosophers and anthropologists have shown that communicative and ritual acts are closely related, and how both have served to construct myths in different societies throughout history (Austin, 1962; Accardo, 2006, *inter alia*). Manipulating representations is crucial to the success of the reform undertaking. These concerted policies, in their design and their implementation, disseminate "thinking norms" via national and European discourses which have undermined the socialised wage institutions constructed by the continental experience. We are collectively and individually confronted with mythologies and fetishisms that seek to impose a single system of thinking, even in the social sciences. Analysing the reform argumentation at both national and European level is thus, in our view, essential to an examination of the facts and to the scientific research process. We have sought to develop, through a sociology of resources, a typology that fully recognises all the European traditions, and thereby to propose a conceptual framework which has a powerful critical force with respect to the dominant representations.

II. Questions of Terminology

Wage (salaire)

In French, *salaire* designates the remuneration paid to workers employed under an employment contract, and is said to be direct or net when limited to the pay received by workers from their employer, and total when social contributions are included. It is in this sense that wage(s) will be used to translate *salaire* here. However, there is also a specific meaning that will be given the term "wage" in this book: in the singular form, as a concept developed on the basis of the predominant continental experience, it designates the institution constructed around two fundamental elements: the qualification system (*la qualification*) and social contributions (*la cotisation*). Accordingly, any remuneration that does not recognise a position in a qualification grid, or that is not associated with social contributions, is not considered to be a wage. Conversely, a retirement pension financed by social contributions and based on the qualification system, is defined as a wage.

Wage-earner (salarié)

In French, according to the dominant continental usage, *salarié* designates a worker with an employment contract. However, in this book, we promote the usage of this term to designate any person receiving a wage in the sense defined above (thus including economically inactive persons such as unemployed workers or retirees). We have therefore chosen to translate *salarié* as wage-earner rather than employee.

*Salariat**

In the classical sense, this term refers to the overall population working under an employment contract. However, we wish to promote its usage in a different sense, to denote not only the general body of wage-earners, but also the range of institutions related to the qualification system and social contributions; the most important of these are collective negotiations and social security. The *salariat* is thus postulated to be a mode of the social recognition of work: it can be analysed contradictorily, depending on the meaning and the role assigned to the qualification system and social contributions.

*Qualification**

Wage and Welfare included the following explanatory note under the heading "Qualification and credentials":

> The word qualification exists in both English and French but with different meanings and in the continental countries conveys a notion that has no direct equivalent in the Anglo-Saxon countries. While in the latter the word, in its formal sense, relates to the accreditation of training, in the continental countries it expresses the articulation between credential (certificate, diploma or degree), job and wage. This articulation, which exists to varying degrees, is linked in particular to the existence of classification grids (*grilles de classifications*) which are societal realities essential to the functioning of the labour market in these countries. In order to avoid any confusion, for readers from the continental countries and English speakers alike, the term credential has been used as a synonym to replace the English qualification, and qualification system to convey the continental notion.

The term "qualification system" was used at the time to highlight the fact that the continental notion of *qualification* includes a fundamental reference to aspects resulting from the collective bargaining process. In the present volume, our analysis of this notion has been developed further, since we consider it to be crucial to understanding the continental model and the perspectives the latter opens up. Indeed, *qualification* cannot be naturalised as it is closely linked to institutions that produce or reproduce social hierarchies and are at the core of power relations.

In our first volume, the notion was essentially used to refer to the qualification linked to employment, since it is within the framework of employment that wage grids are negotiated in the private sector. In the

* In the chapters that follow, these words will be italicized in order to indicate that they are not being used in the accepted English sense, but with the specific meanings defined here.

present work, a distinction will be made between *qualification attached to a work post* in an employment framework, and *qualification attached to the person*.

In common usage, when the term "qualification" is applied to the person, it refers to whatever attests to the individual's practical and intellectual knowledge, including that derived from experience. From our viewpoint, if there is no collectively negotiated monetary recognition in the form of a wage, we call this certification, not *qualification*. For indeed, the latter is indissociable from a wage level, and the wage grid is linked to a qualification grid.

Qualification is thus either employment-based, if the wage is linked to the work post as in the private sector; or attached to the person, if the wage is linked to a grade as in the civil service (that is, for career civil servants, as opposed to public sector employees).

Social Contributions (cotisation)

In *Wage and Welfare*, we explained our approach to the use of the term *social contributions* to translate *cotisations sociales* as follows:

> Modes of financing social protection systems are historical constructions that are expressed by how they are named. Thus cotisations sociales in France and social insurance contributions in the UK, for instance, refer to very different societal systems. For want of a better way of expressing these realities, we have adopted social contributions as a generic term, but we are fully aware that this tends to mask what we consider to be fundamental differences between modes of sourcing. [...] It should be noted, moreover, that social contributions is also the term used by Eurostat (The EU statistical Office) to present harmonized data. Although the different forms of wage-based contributions and deductions levied on the wage are frequently lumped together under the heading "tax on wages", this is an expression we obviously contest, given that our approach postulates a differentiation of social rights on the basis of the source of financing.

Although our initial emphasis on historically constructed societal differences remains pertinent, we have expanded on this definition in the present work: social contributions are analysed here as a savings-free mode of financing social protection that is contradictory in that it is applied either to a deferred income or to a continued wage. The deferred income is based on the amount and the duration of past contributions, whereas the continued wage is based on a wage replacement rate. These two modalities stem from different conceptions of the *salariat*, and confer a different status on the wage-earner.

III. The Interpenetration of the European and the National Levels in the Development of Employment and Wage Policies

It was within the programme entitled "Employees' resources and social rights in Europe" (RESORE) that the resource regime analytical framework was developed. This theoretical proposal is broad in scope, and the authors of this volume have chosen to focus on different aspects, such as transformations in the origin and flow of resources, how these are measured, workers' social status, their representative organisations, or the institutions of what is conventionally called the "labour market". The developments observed with respect to the process of European integration and national policies on employment and social protection constitute the main field of analysis, while the approach adopted in the various chapters reflects the different disciplines within the group: political science, sociology, socio-economics or economics. The resource regime framework has enabled us to bring to light an ever more convergent reality dominated by European policies that tend to impose a considerable regression, in particular for the continental countries. This regression is accompanied by an attempt to disqualify the work force and to naturalise subordination and domination (in particular, that of the market). But, as will be seen, alternative paths and the possibility of opening up new perspectives do exist.

Let us now turn to the contents of the book. It comprises three main sections: the first presents and contextualises the problematic; the second analyses the Europeanisation of wage and employment policies; and the third explores the implementation of reforms at national level.

A. Employment, the Wage and Social Protection

This section focuses on the relationships between employment, the wage and social protection and their evolution since the 1980s, these being the decades of reform. Tracing research trends over this period, Andreana Khristova, Nathalie Moncel and Bernard Friot show that employment and social protection were traditionally approached as two separate fields until the growing preoccupation with economic efficiency led researchers to focus on the costs of labour, social protection and social assistance with a view to developing cost/benefit models. The idea that reducing the cost of labour would favour job creation gained ground despite studies revealing the absence of a simple correlation between the two. With European integration, the EU deployed the concept of flexicurity in order to promote an "employment friendly" model of social protection and the idea that the goals of social cohesion should serve to further economic goals. Based on their examination of the literature, the authors conclude that it is necessary to go beyond an analysis of the transformations of the capitalist system (by observing changes affecting labour markets or examining public employment policies). They argue that a more dialectical approach is needed in order to take account of the inherent contradictions of the wage; the presentation of the resource regime approach that ends the chapter precisely offers the possibility of addressing the transformations of capital and the wage together.

Bernard Friot then analyses the changing relations between employment and the wage in the light of the reforms introduced over the past 30 years and the overall aim to achieve a "full market" model. He takes a fresh look at a range of categories that serve to analyse capitalism but have been widely naturalised, such as the employer/employee duo, the market, labour value, labour time and labour power. Redefining these categories on the basis of their relationship to transformations in the social status of the worker, he offers a reading of the recent evolution of resource regimes. The chapter pinpoints the dual logic of employment: as an instrument of the subordination of labour, it generates a process of victimisation based on the notion of "employability"; but it has also been the matrix of the socialised wage mediated by a qualification system. Friot shows that the reforms have produced a change in the meaning of employment, as will be illustrated by a number of examples throughout the book. He then highlights the potentialities of the socialised wage, and draws on these to propose the outlines for a new, emancipatory wage society, founded not on the fetishism of the market, but on a system of personal qualification.

B. The Europeanisation of Wage and Employment Policies

The four chapters in this section examine the impact of the process of European construction on resource regimes. Each of the fields explored serves to illustrate how the language deployed in EU texts reinforces the power wielded by Community institutions. Indeed, Community law – which has primacy over national law – draws on a case law that only enforces competition rules without the necessary checks and balances to safeguard wage-earners' rights, since the wage and social rights remain within the competence of the Member States. In addition, the fact that tax expenditures on employment policies are not included in the Eurostat database reflects the failure to take full account of the transformation of wage-earners' resources produced by these policies. It then becomes easier to understand the difficulties encountered by European trade unions in influencing wage trends.

The first two chapters focus on the field of pension reforms. Corinne Gobin has based her study of Community rhetoric and pension reforms on the findings of the RESORE team she directed. This group conducted a lexicometric study of the French language corpus of the Broad Economic Policy Guidelines spanning the period 1993-2003, in order to draw out the political logics underpinning the reforms. An analysis of the discourse deployed has become crucial because, as the chapter shows, our national political systems have undergone a profound transformation: indeed, the linking of national institutions to those of the EU has given rise to a new political regime. Community norms now shape our social policies. Gobin's study brings to light the particular semantic system constructed by European policy, its aims and consequences. The discourse analysis also reveals the general argument expressed by the reform rhetoric, which can be summed up as follows: insufficient wealth is being created, the economy needs to be reorganised around the creation of jobs by enterprises, and social policies must become tools for achieving this employment growth. Raising the employment rate has become the main aim, while benefits such as pensions and health care are viewed as expenditures rather than as rights. Social protection, it is claimed, must be reformed with a view to reducing labour costs and public expenditures in order to transform the labour market.

Bernard Friot and Gaël Coron then propose an interpretation of pension reforms which will enable the reader to better understand the implications of the resource regime framework. This interpretation is based on an analysis of the instruments used by the EU to extend its interventions in the field of pensions: European Court of Justice case law, the Directive on Institutions for Occupational Retirement Provision (IORPs), the open method of coordination (OMC), and the 2005 reform of the Stability and Growth Pact – reinforced since 2007 by the provisions for EU control over Member State budgetary deficits. EU intervention in this particular branch of social protection may seem surprising given that pensions do not fall within Community competence, but is more easily understandable in the light of the considerable financial interests at stake and the strong emancipatory potential of the retirement pension. The analysis shows how tenaciously the European Commission has been pursuing its goals, and how the overall aim of these instruments is to exert pressure on the Member States to reform their national systems by adopting a two- or three-pillar model designed to boost financial accumulation: the objective, in short, is to reduce the socialised wage and public service resource regimes in favour of the deferred wage, tutelary allowance and wage-earner savings.

In the next chapter, Anne Dufresne focuses on the relations between trade unions and the European institutions, and the issue of wage bargaining at European level. She shows how the process of European construction with its convergence criteria based on wage restraint, the obsession with competitiveness, and the emphasis on austerity measures

– all of which have been reinforced in recent years – also threatens the autonomy of national wage bargaining processes. However, she highlights the ground the trade unions have already been able to cover in their efforts to organise European-level wage coordination, despite this difficult context and the sometimes problematic domination of the German model. She ends with a discussion of alternative paths for action which would enable the unions to overcome current boundaries.

The last chapter in this section presents a critical appraisal the Eurostat Labour Market Policy database and the categories used to record public expenditures on employment policies. Economists Ana Paula Ribeiro and Margarida Ruivo challenge the narrow scope of the database, pointing out that fiscal policies and reductions in social contributions – which represent a significant share of public spending on employment – are not taken into account. They argue that the absence of data on such measures, given their relevance in terms of expenditure and the number of participants involved, introduces a bias in the results, and that the database thus fails to provide a full account of the transformations underway.

C. Employment versus the Wage: Implementation of National Policies (back into the Labour Market!)

As has become clear from the previous chapters, the new political regime created by the EU has produced a unified cognitive framework which serves to orient national employment and wage policies so that they comply with the economic and monetary goals set at European level. The chapters in this section bring to light the logics underpinning these national policies.

Roland Atzmüller examines recent employment policy trends in Austria, tracing the evolution of the unemployment insurance system and the expansion of "active labour market policies" since the 1980s. The measures introduced – which have led to a multiplication of the institutions and governance mechanisms regulating the unemployed and the creation of a reintegration "market" – reflect the dominance of neoliberal thinking. The emergence of an ideological opposition between employment and social protection has changed the perception of the unemployed: rather than being treated as wage-earners, they are considered to be individually responsible for their situation, or even as parasites living off the social protection system, and the unemployment insurance system has accordingly been made more restrictive and disciplinary. This stigmatisation of the unemployed is not based on racial or cultural criteria, but on the individual's level of employability, with far-reaching consequences. Atzmüller's chapter offers more than a national monography, since the case of Austria clearly illustrates how the neo-liberal orientations underpinning employment policies are consistent with EU prescriptions, even though not subordinated to them.

The following chapter introduces the notion of subsidised employment. Marti López Andreu, Andreu Lope Peña and Joan Miquel Verd examine the so-called "active" employment policies introduced in Spain in the late 1990s and early 2000s, and provide examples of similar measures in Portugal, Italy and France to broaden the scope of their analysis. They show how such policies have fostered the development of employment forms that are characterised by a regression of the total wage and an emphasis on employability. Introduced on the pretext of increasing the volume of employment, these employment forms are based on a combination of various elements: reduced employer contributions, social assistance benefits to top up the wage, reduced social rights and a reduced direct wage, or even, in Italy, merely a bare wage.

The workfarist policies introduced in the UK during the years of New Labour rule are the subject of the next chapter. Roland Atzmüller shows why they failed to meet worker expectations. In contrast to the government's stated goals, the underlying aim of these policies appears to have been to push unemployed people into subordinated employment. Key measures such as the much-awaited minimum wage, the in-work tax credits or the New Deal programmes failed to attain the goal of securing the social inclusion of the lowest-income segments of the population. Doubtless because these policies were geared to making the unemployed "employable" rather than to providing them with qualifications and social protection, or addressing the question of redistribution.

In conclusion to this section, Joan Miquel Verd examines four "activation" measures introduced in three different countries, and compares them with the "passive" measures they were intended to activate. Looking beyond the arguments used to justify the measures and the deployment of the employability discourse, he shows how the use of tax resources to finance employment changes the status of the workers concerned, creating a category of benefit-recipient wage-earners that would previously have been unthinkable in the continental countries, and exerting a downwards pressure on social protection overall.

The four chapters in this section demonstrate the convergence between the policies implemented at national level and the prescriptions deployed by the EU institutions. Several complementary and convergent trends can be observed regarding the origin of workers' resources: firstly, entitlements to social assistance benefits previously intended to tackle poverty are now linked to employment; secondly, shrinking unemployment benefits – a component of the wage – push workers onto social assistance; and finally, the tax-financing of low-wage employment – whether through direct subsidies or reductions in social contributions – serves to define workers on the basis of their individual level of employability and proximity to poverty. Clearly, the past 30 years of reform have brought about a considerable change in the meaning of employment.

It was during the Enlightenment, thanks to the drive to separate reason from belief, that the individual's autonomy of thought and the obligation for science to be critical were asserted as universal principles (Todorov, 2006). In the concluding chapter to this volume, Corinne Gobin revisits the changes that have taken place in the fields of employment and the wage in Western Europe since World War II, and examines their political meaning, that is, their emancipatory potential (or the reverse). She shows how the recent banking crisis has served to reinforce "economic governance" policies oriented towards reducing the space of the wage and its actors, putting the nation-state under outside control and consequently, reducing popular sovereignty. But let there be no mistake, alternatives do exist, and one of the avenues proposed in this book is to extend the scope of social contributions and the qualification system. Several of the participants in the research programme that provided the framework for the present volume are currently pursuing this proposal within the European Institute on the *Salariat.*[5]

[5] For those interested, more information can be found on the Institute's web site: http://www.ies-salariat.org/.

PART I

EMPLOYMENT, THE WAGE AND SOCIAL PROTECTION

Reconsidering the Linkage between Employment and Social Protection

The Resource Regime Framework

Andreana KHRISTOVA

Associate researcher, Laboratoire Lorrain de Sciences Sociales, Université de Lorraine, Nancy

Nathalie MONCEL

Researcher, Centre d'études et de recherches sur les qualifications (Céreq), Marseille

Bernard FRIOT

Emeritus Professor, University of Paris Ouest Nanterre; member of the Institut Européen du Salariat

The past 20 years have seen an acceleration of employment and social protection reforms in all the European countries. The changes introduced by these reforms have rightly raised a number of questions for researchers and citizens alike regarding their effective impact, their explicit and implicit goals, and their underlying logic. And these are indeed understandable questions, inasmuch as it can be considered that employment, and more generally, work, still constitute the dominant mode of social integration, and that social protection reveals the degree of integration in a network of social and political rights. Employment and social protection are societal constructions that are historically rooted in and determined at the national level. Various typologies and comparative studies have revealed the key role played by national traditions and specificities (Esping-Andersen, 1990; Hall, Soskice, 2001; Amable, 2005; Coriat, Petit, Schméder, 2006, amongst others). Today, however, domestic policies are influenced, framed or co-determined at European level; national actors and policy makers determine their positions with regard to those of their counterparts in the other Member States, which they may draw on, adapt to or diverge from. It can thus be assumed that European orientations, although not yet hard-set but rooted in a process of integration that is still underway, prefigure the contours of the articulation between employment and social protection in a globalised context.

Using this angle of approach, we will seek to analyse the evolution of the linkages between employment and social protection on the basis of the comparative literature, on the one hand, and European integration, on the other. Comparisons today have a strong heuristic potential, for they no longer merely constitute a methodology, but have become a tool for political intervention used by supra-national institutions. And European integration raises crucial issues concerning the restructuring of the links between employment and social protection and the construction of a "European social model".

Our aim here is to propose an original analytical framework for interpreting the transformations generated by employment and social policies and their impact on national configurations. This approach is centred not only on the wage in the strict sense, but, more generally, on workers' (monetary) resources.

I. From Separation to Instrumentalisation

Until fairly recently, there was a notable separation between research on employment and labour market transformations, on the one hand, and on social protection reforms, on the other. Salais and Whiteside (1998) attribute this to an historical separation between social protection and the regulation of employment corresponding to a central opposition between the state and the market, a characteristic of the Anglo-Saxon perspective which also dominates the research at international level. Yet although this opposition between market and state is widely accepted, it is in contradiction with the historical, joint construction of employment and social protection that forged the dominant model of waged employment in Europe (Deakin, 2002).

The major labour market developments in Europe have been well documented: declining employment rates; the rise of selective and persistent unemployment; the switch from industrial to tertiary employment and the ensuing occupational mutations; changes in work organisation and the introduction of new technologies; flexible employment conditions and working time; and increasing wage inequality and the emergence of the working poor. The extent of these trends has also been contrasted between the various countries.[1] However, few of these studies investigate the role played by social protection in the division and

[1] Notably in the DG Employment and Social Affairs of the European Commission and MISEP publications, and Eurostat reports on employment in Europe.

organisation of social labour and the functioning of labour markets.[2] Instead, labour market research tends to adopt an instrumental approach to social policy, viewing it either as a means to remedy social problems stemming from transformations in employment, or as one of the causes of labour market dysfunction because of its effects on labour supply and demand.

Changes in national social protection systems have also been analysed extensively. Numerous studies have addressed the question of the future of "welfare states", in terms of their decline, redefinition or renewal, as well as the variety of identifiable ideal-types (Kuhnle, 2000; Pierson, 2001). The majority, largely conducted by political scientists, have focused on social protection policies, and tended to consider labour market and employment developments as stemming from exogenous economic determinants.

More recently, another approach has emerged which falls in between these two categories. This literature seeks to compare employment policies as well as social policies in different European states, drawing both on diagnoses and formalisations of labour market transformations and on typologies of social protection systems. The two policy areas are seen as forming part of a whole, underpinned by diverse national logics which can then be characterized from different angles: level and type of expenditures (distinguishing between active and passive expenditure); type of measures and their modes of implementation (notably by public services *vs.* the private sector); or the specific institutional frameworks and political contexts in which they are embedded (role of the social representatives; political orientations of the various governments; and constitutional provisions). This kind of research forms the basis of the typologies developed following on the works of Esping Andersen (1990, 1999) and is part of a broader current whose perspective, at a more overall level, is to analyse the diversity of capitalist systems (Hall and Soskice, 2001). The approach adopted consists in establishing a relationship between the variety of modes of organising economic activity and the variety of public policies. Social policies overall, regardless of the specific field concerned (employment, unemployment, education and training, family, health, etc.) are seen as contributing to the organisation of capitalism.

There are thus two traditional fields of research – labour markets and employment on the one hand, social protection systems and social policy on the other – which each draw on the contributions of the other but maintain a separation between their research topics. The relationship

[2] The issue is nonetheless addressed in studies on gender relations, see Lewis (1992) for an overview of the literature.

between employment and social protection will sometimes be reduced to a simple accounting linkage. This is the case in economically-oriented or econometric studies that examine the influence of social protection systems on growth and employment outcomes in different countries (Atkinson, 1995; Scharpf, 2000; Arjona, Ladaique, Pearson, 2002). This approach, which is strongly represented in OECD publications, is framed by the overall goal to reform social protection systems in order to render them "sustainable" and "employment friendly". The classical method used is to investigate the correlations between level and type of public social protection revenues and expenditures[3] on the one hand, and indicators relating to employment and the functioning of the labour market on the other (activity, employment and unemployment rates for different categories of populations; labour productivity; effects in terms of inactivity traps, etc.). Here, interpretations are based on causal relationships which are mostly derived from neoclassical labour market theories. A term-by-term comparison of national situations is used to set benchmarks for assessing the outcomes in different countries in order to single out exemplary cases and best practices.

This type of analysis limits the links between social protection and employment to the sole factor of "cost", which makes the question of their financing an essential one, and places cost-benefit analyses at the heart of the reforms. In Italy, for example, the macro-economic constraints imposed by the Maastricht criteria played a decisive role in accelerating employment and social protection reforms; at the end of the 1980s, the high level of public spending[4] and the will to join economic and monetary union were levers for introducing budgetary restrictions and a focus on the "cost" of social protection (Fargion, 2001). In a large number of European countries, public debt constraints have served as leverage for a series of reforms to the financing of social protection systems; these have included raising the legal retirement age (as in France, Spain, Italy, or Germany), and tightening up the duration, amounts, and conditions of entitlement to unemployment benefits (Lefresne, 2008; Lefresne and Sauviat, 2011). The persistence of a high rate of structural unemployment has constantly been used as an argument to justify the introduction of so-called social policy measures expressly geared to promoting employment. Slogans such as "from welfare to work" or "making work pay" clearly express the tensions

---

3 It is interesting to note that the data mainly concern public resource flows, and leave aside private flows (mandatory and optional) and accounting data on tax exemptions, both of which are essential components of certain social protection systems.

4 According to Fargion (2001), the public debt rose from 54% to 104% of GDP and the annual budgetary deficit to 11% during the 1980s.

created between employment and social protection (Higelé, Khristova, 2007).

However, the direct causal relationship established between employment, social protection and wage costs is both theoretically and empirically questionable, and particularly so within a comparative framework. The reasoning is premised on the existence of a mechanical quantitative adjustment as postulated in the dominant theories: the assumption is that a hike in wage costs will translate into a drop in employment, increased unemployment and higher social protection costs. But the hypothesis underpinning this relationship is problematic to say the least, and contrasts appear depending on national experiences.[5] Countries where wages are relatively high and "equal" do not necessarily perform poorly in terms of social protection and unemployment, as is the case for Denmark, Norway, Switzerland and Austria (Sarfati and Bonoli, 2002). Conversely, high unemployment rates have been the lot of countries with a low level of social protection (Italy and Spain). Thus, a high employment rate associated with low unemployment can be achieved through a variety of combinations: a high degree of flexibility combined with a high level of social security, as in the case of Denmark, Finland or Switzerland; limited flexibility combined with a high level of social security (Sweden, the Netherlands), or high flexibility with a low level of security (the UK) (Keune and Pochet, 2009). The British Low Pay Commission, in its 2007 Report, made recommendations along these lines to the government. It considered that the introduction of a minimum wage did not impact negatively on either employment or inflation. Weak social protection and a downward pressure on wages do not always have a positive effect on employment, which suggests that structural changes in employment cannot be limited to the question of an arbitration between employment and social protection or between wages and employment.

Not only is this analysis challenged by empirical data, its very basis is shaky. Despite Keynes' warning that low nominal wages were not necessarily an effective remedy for unemployment, the idea that wage restraint is essential for job creation has gained ground and continues to shape current reforms. But its necessary and rarely mentioned condition

5 In a comparative study, the OECD (1998) assessed the impact of minimum wages on employment and found that minimum wage rises had a negative effect on teenage employment. Although the conclusions were presented as significant, clear reservations were also expressed: "there is also little evidence that negative employment effects are larger in relatively high minimum-wage countries as compared with relatively low minimum-wage countries" (OECD, 1998, p. 47). In short, the marked discrepancies in employment and unemployment rates across countries can, at best, only be marginally attributed to differences in minimum wage trends.

is that the share of profit remains constant. However, there is no assurance that this will hold true in practice, and the economic dynamic has, in fact, been characterised by the redistribution of productivity gains to capital. The result is a historically unprecedented configuration exhibiting concomitant trends towards an increase in profit margins, the share of non-invested profit, and unemployment, on the one hand, and a drop in the investment rate and the share of wages in value added, on the other (Ramaux, 2012; Husson, 2010; Héritier and Maurice, 2010). It should be noted that the financial crisis sparked off in 2008 momentarily slowed down this process, but did not bring it to a halt.

Formalising the linkage between employment and social protection exclusively in terms of costs and financing tends to sideline an analysis of the complexity of these links, and notably of their temporal and spatial embeddedness in economic relations. While a quantitative adjustment is mathematically possible, it rests on the hypothesis of a universal conceptual construction of employment and social protection, a hypothesis that has been increasingly called into question by comparative studies. This premise of universality can, in part, be attributed to the temporality of the initial studies, which were carried out at a time when economic relations were predominantly forged at the national level.

II. The Conceptual Frameworks Deployed at European Level

The diagnosis of the destabilisation of the modes of regulation that once linked labour markets and social protection systems has brought to the fore the question of how to reconcile an increasing flexibility in the spheres of production and employment with the need to provide individuals with adequate protection against growing social risks.

The work undertaken by the Foundation for the Improvement of Living and Working Conditions (Eurofound) has boosted the development of comparative studies examining the links between employment and social protection (for example, "Linking Welfare and Work", 1999; "Flexibility and Social Protection", 2003). In this line of research, the concept of "flexicurity" has been popularised by studies exploring the idea of providing social protection for wage-earners in flexible forms of employment. Flexicurity, a term used by the European Commission to cover a range of common principles (CE, 2007), is presented by Wilthagen and Tros (2004) as a political strategy that seeks the concomitant development of flexible labour markets, work organisation and employment relations, on one hand, with social security on the other, particularly for the most vulnerable groups inside and outside the labour market; it is intended to combine the different dimensions of flexible employment (numerical, functional and wage-related) with forms of security in terms of work, employment, social protection and work-life balance.

Advocates of the transitional labour market (TLM) approach (Schmid, 2002; Gazier, 2003, 2008) also participate actively in the debate on employment policy reforms, with proposals for improving the management of transitions in and outside labour markets. This approach is both descriptive and prescriptive, and takes as starting point the observation of workers' different transitions around employment in order to propose measures to make career paths more secure and achieve full employment.

The notions of flexicurity and TLMs claim to present a concomitant approach to employment and social protection. However, they are constructed on an instrumentalisation of social policy with a view to achieving the goal of raising employment rates. The perspective adopted thus reflects an economic interpretation of the social question which sees the proper functioning of the market as the exclusive precondition for social cohesion (Serrano Pascual, 2009) and disregards the socio-political links between wage relations and economic relations.

These frameworks have contributed to shaping the employment policy implemented at European level. Initially, there was a relative disconnection between macro-economic policies – in particular monetary policy – and employment, the latter being seen more as related to social issues and thus social policy. The European Employment Strategy (EES) was only adopted in 1997, and appears to have been developed as a counterpart of economic and monetary union. The Lisbon Strategy of 2000 marked a change in direction: an explicit link was established between employment policy and the Broad Economic Policy Guidelines (BEPGs),[6] without yet extending this link to social policy. Then, in 2005, the Integrated Guidelines for Growth and Jobs finalised the interconnection between employment policies and social policies. This meant that, since employment had already been linked to economic goals, social policies would, in turn, be tied to furthering macro-economic aims and competitiveness. The current flexicurity strategy, combining deregulation of the labour market and the activation of social protection, has been interpreted in different ways. For some, it serves the overall goal of economic efficiency but has not been accompanied by an economic mechanism for wage distribution or for a political compromise in favour of redistribution (Théret, 2010; Amable, Demmou and Ledezma, 2009). For others, it represents a necessary social invest-

6 This change took the explicit form of introducing numerous quantified goals. Intermediary targets were set: the overall employment rate was to reach 67% by 2005, and the rate for women 57%, while that for older workers was set to reach 50% by 2010 (Stockholm European Council, 2001).

ment, "reforming the welfare state to adapt it to the new economic context by reorienting its spending towards 'preparing' rather then 'repairing'" (Morel, Palier and Palme, 2009, p. 16) in a coherent overall approach encompassing a citizenship regime, social policies, employment policies, education and investment in human capital.

The instrumentalisation of employment and social policies, which became evident once employment was integrated into a logic of social cohesion with the Single European Act (1985) and the Protocol on Social Protection (1992), has led to a blurring of boundaries and a shift in the kinds of tools used. This is clearly visible in the numerous recommendations to develop active employment policies. In the original policies developed in Sweden, activation generally meant direct public intervention in the labour market to prevent or limit unemployment through measures focused on job placement, training and job creation. The OECD and the European Commission, however, have developed an entirely different approach which associates activation with the idea that labour costs are a disincentive to job creation. It should be noted in passing that the analytical frameworks used by these two institutions were not always developed at the same periods. Whereas the OECD continued to prioritize the promotion of flexibility during the 1990s, the European Commission had already introduced the notion of occupational security in its first Employment Guidelines; the OECD only came out in support of flexicurity fairly recently (OCDE, 2006; Freyssinet, 2009). While the interest shown by these institutions in both supply-side and demand-side aspects has led certain researchers to use the term "inclusive liberalism" (Jacobsson, 2009), it has, nevertheless, had little effect on their approach to activation. This not only contrasts with the Swedish approach in which activation and a high replacement income were not seen as antagonistic, but also introduces a dichotomy opposing active and passive expenditures. This latter distinction marked the departure from the sole logic of regulating employment, and led to social protection measures being incorporated into a job creation strategy.[7]

The approach to activation underpinning EU and OECD discourse has resulted in a "standardisation" of employment policies that overrides societal logics. It implies more than a mere semantic shift, and the European Union has played a particular role in spreading this language (Barbier, 2008), with the European institutions acting as the "promoters of ideological socialisation. Whilst it is true that the European Union did

7 This trend can also be seen with regard to civil society and its capacity to "innovate". Under the banner of "social innovation", the Commission now intends to "tap into the ingenuity of charities, associations and social entrepreneurs" in order to create new activities and jobs, some of which could be taken up by the market in a logic of competition and economic growth (EC, 2010).

not invent the activation-based discourse, it has nevertheless played a major role in its propagation and in establishing the terms used to address the problem of unemployment" (Crespo and Serrano Pascual, 2004, p. 14). A paradigm change can also be seen at the level of social policies (Surel, 2010; Amable, Gatti and Schumacher, 2006; Gatti, and Glyn, 2006). Several recent works have stressed the numerous pathways of dissemination deployed via the Open Method of Coordination (OMC), and their impact on national employment and social policy reforms. Heidenreich and Zeitlin (2009) have identified various influencing mechanisms, such as external pressure, financial support, socialization and discursive diffusion, mutual learning and creative appropriation by domestic actors, that are, in their broad lines, similar to those described by Serrano Pascual and Magnusson (2007). On the one hand, this interpretative and political interdependence contributes to reformulating the determinants of wage relations at national level. On the other, these studies also point to the intrinsic links between employment and social protection.

III. Employment and Social Protection

If we are to avoid the pitfalls of universalism or reductionist economism, it is important to set the links between employment and social protection within the context of an overall transformation of economic and wage relations.

Social protection systems were introduced in order to offset discontinuous periods of earned income due to exclusion from employment, and to ensure the reproduction of labour power. The strong ties between employment and social protection within the wage relation can be traced to the close temporal connection between the development of the norms governing these two fields (Freyssinet, 2002). They were established and generalised during a period of strong economic growth and the generalisation of waged employment.[8] The articulation between employment and social protection, as Simon Deakin (2002) recalls, was at the heart of the contractualisation of the employment relationship

> which had two central aspects: the placing of limits on the employer's legal powers of command, limits which were given a contractual form as either express or implied terms; and *the use of the employment relationship as a vehicle for channelling and redistributing social and economic risks,*

8 In Germany and the UK, with the early decline in the share of agricultural labour in total employment and rapid industrialisation, the rate of participation in waged employment rose considerably. Italy, and France to a lesser degree, joined this trend at a relatively late stage compared to the more developed industrial countries. By the second half of the 1990s, the rate of waged employment had stabilised at around 90% in Germany, France and the UK, and 75% in Italy (Eurostat).

through the imposition on employers of obligations of revenue collection and compensation for interruptions to earnings. (Our emphasis)

This reference to waged employment as the basis of social protection does not, however, appear as a central feature in typologies emphasising the institutional characteristics of national social security systems. Esping-Andersen (1990), for instance, proposes a typology of welfare regimes in which two distinct modes of articulation between employment and social protection are defined on the basis of the type and intensity of the linkage. On the one hand, the "conservative-corporatist" regime (deriving from the Bismarckian tradition) is characterised by a direct and visible link: companies are made to participate in the socialisation of the wage via the mutualisation of a significant portion of the wage in the form of social contributions; access to benefits is conditioned by the employment status, or more generally by the career path. On the other hand, social protection in the "liberal" and "social democratic" regimes (based on the Beveridgean model) is largely financed through taxation: in the first of these, access to benefits is selective because means-tested (and notably linked to poverty), while it is universal in the second, because tied to citizenship. In both, however, the legal dissociation between employment and access to benefits is often taken to suggest a discontinuity or relative independence of employment and social protection: the link is not as explicit as in the "conservative-corporatist" regime. This explains the various studies focussed on assessing the capacity of Bismarckian social protection systems to change and adapt in a context of structural unemployment (Palier, 2008).

However, when we look beyond this purely institutional analysis, the reference to employment remains as present as ever. "The reason for this is simple: benefits and social services have to be paid by the taxes and social security contributions from those in work" (Eichhorst, Hemerijck, 2008, p. 5). All the models invoked, including that of the welfare state, have proved to be "effective" because consistent with a particular configuration of waged employment as the dominant form, economic growth, and a relatively low unemployment rate; benefits were conceived, "explicitly or implicitly, in reference to the occupation or loss of waged employment, which constituted the standard mode of socialisation, if not for all the population, at least for the heads of household" (Freyssinet, 2002, p. 156).

One of the interesting contributions of the regulationist approach is the postulate that changes in wage relations[9] result from a concomitant

[9] We are referring here to the wage relation as defined by regulation theory: the set of conditions governing the relations between capital and labour, such as the organisa-

evolution of economic relations (Boyer, 2004). If it is accepted that productive labour power is socially determined, this implies that its dynamic stems from the effects of a two-fold transformation: of the conditions of the work process on one hand, and the conditions of existence of waged employment on the other. The reproduction of the wage relation and the reconfiguration of the linkage between employment and social protection are embedded in the overall dynamic of the evolution of the accumulation of capital, and there is an intrinsic interconnection between economic relations and wage relations. However, this interconnection is currently being challenged in two ways. Firstly, economic relations today are, on the whole, determined at European level (Boyer, 2003), and the mobility of capital has been internationalised (Coriat, Petit and Schméder, 2006; Aglietta and Berrebi, 2007), whereas the forms of regulating wage relations are still predominantly conceived and set at the national level. There is thus a relative disconnection between the levels at which capital, on the one hand, and the wage relation on the other, are determined. The question that remains is whether this is a transitory disconnection, or whether it is a constitutive component of the new regulation of capitalism (Khristova, 2012). Secondly, since the latter half of the 1970s, and as noted above, Europe has been seeing simultaneous trends towards the near-continuous growth of profit margins and the persistence and growth of unemployment. Consequently, it can be argued that while the wage relation is in "crisis", capital is not experiencing a "crisis" in the full sense of the term,[10] and this translates into a relative disconnection between financial returns (productivity gains) and income formation (wages).[11] In this context, understanding the transformations of the linkage between employment and social protection means taking account of three interrelated dimensions: firstly, the interactions between economic and wage relations, notably how changes in national wage relations tend to follow similar trends under the effects of globalised economic relations. Secondly, the fact that these transformations reach beyond the framework of the wage relation and reveal a redefinition of the relations between the state and the economy (Boyer, 2007). And thirdly, that they also involve a restructuration of the territorial frameworks within which social states develop (Ferrera, 2005; 2008; Théret, 2010).

---

tion of labour, wage and income formation, way of life, and rules on hiring and firing (Boyer, 2007).

10 The financial crisis revealed the internal contradiction of capital with the decoupling of productive/non-productive investments. Above all, it brought to light the need to rethink the redistribution of productivity gains.

11 The word "relative" is to be stressed here, because the disconnection is essentially observed at the macro-economic level; in contrast, at the micro-economic level, certain sectors are seeing the expansion of workers' participation in company profits.

The transformation of the reciprocal, intrinsic links between employment and social protection thus becomes a crucial issue in an historically unprecedented situation where waged employment, the principle vehicle for the development of capitalism, has practically reached the limits of its extension. As noted by Clasquin and Friot (2001), "the transformations of societal constructions of employment, beyond the trends towards flexible employment forms specific to each country, rest on changes in the modes of socialising resources and these changes impact on all the dimensions of the construction of employment".

IV. An Analysis in Terms of Resource Regimes

Social relations are formed in work relations, which owe much to the monetary recognition of labour. Money, far from being the passive expression of an "already-existing" value, is an institution that plays a central role in the attribution of value – a social convention – to the only "already existing" entities, that is people, their capacity for work, and the products of their labour. The distinction between activity, defined as the production of goods and services (wealth), and work, the part of that activity that is assigned a monetary value, is important here. Not all activity is assigned monetary value, and not all wealth is value. The relationship between activity and work is a decisive one both at the level of the individual and at that of society as a whole: the level and structure of the activity that is transformed into work play a decisive role in the definition of social relations. Control over the monetary recognition of work is thus crucial:

- at the macro-social level: what work is assigned value – that dedicated to the sovereign, the community, or to capital (to cite just these)? Is it recognised by money that supports or subverts the established order? And under what circumstances: a market exchange, individual biographical events such as birth, or economic planning?
- at the micro-social level: people's social personality is defined by that part of their labour that is assigned value, and by the type of money (a wage, unearned income, or an allowance) used to do this.

Thus, the recognition or the negation of our activity as work is at the basis of our social existence, and money is a key institution in our individuation. For instance, students' academic activity can be 1) denied recognition as work by a bursary granted on social criteria or by an *allocation d'autonomie universelle* (universal independence allowance); 2) recognised as able to generate a future job by a public system of student loans that are to be reimbursed on the expected increase in earnings linked to the degree, or 3) recognised as their present free (non-subordinated) work by a wage paid for the free work of studying. These three modes of resources determine very different kinds of student status. As for pensioners, it is one thing to receive an income that denies that their activity is work, as in the case of the minimum old-age pension which defines them as old people; the investment return on profit-making savings which defines them as inactive *rentiers*; or a state-guaranteed strictly contributory deferred income (as in the Swedish model) which defines them as former workers who have provided for their future. It is an entirely different thing for them to continue to receive a wage and be considered as wage-earners in the same way as active workers, because their current activity is considered to be free work deserving of monetary recognition. What these examples show is that the support provided through monetary resources[12] – whether in cash or kind – can have either an alienating or an emancipatory effect for the individuals concerned, depending on the circumstances: it will tend to be alienating if their work is either denied recognition as such or maintained in a situation of subordination to an employer, the state or a capitalist. On the other hand, these resources will tend to be emancipatory if they subvert the conditions of subordination by providing people with the basis for a liberated relationship to work. Liberated does not, of course, mean free of constraints, for even when the ends and means of work are decided by the workers themselves – this being the definition of free work – it still involves being part of a collective with its rules and its hierarchy, having to meet dead-lines and clients' expectations, and to make rational use of time and means. Clearly, a fine analysis of the alienating or emancipatory potential of monetary resources implies constructing a grammar of resources. And this is why the research programme to which this book contributes seeks to define "resource regimes" on the basis of two intersecting variables: the type of work to which these regimes assign value, and the money used to do this.

The type of work to which value is assigned constitutes an ongoing debate, and remains subject to constant redefinition. For instance, there is fierce opposition today between views that base the pension on pensioners' past work, on the present work of the employed, or on the current work of pensioners themselves. The fact that it is so difficult to define pensioners' activity as work, despite it being the object of large-scale monetary distribution, shows the extent to which the definition of work is eminently social and conflictual.

The second variable, money, has an inherent constraint because, as we have seen above, wealth and value are not necessarily superimposed.

12 The resources analysed here concern those related to public financing (and thus not stemming from the informal economy), whether monetary (as in the retirement pension) or assigned a monetary value (such as free health care provision).

There is no society in which monetary recognition of work is such that individuals are directly valorised for the wealth they create. Valorisation is mediated by power relations which ignore certain types of work that generate wealth, while monetising types of work that generate pollution. Monetary constraint is the expression of the distance between wealth and value. It varies according to the type of money, and the resource regime problematic thus seeks to define the different monetary constraints and the types of subordination of work they generate. Let us examine the capitalist form of monetary constraint, the dominant form today, which subordinates work by submitting it to the ends and means imposed by the owners of capital.

Capitalist societies are defined here not from the point of view of markets where the key issue would be a greater or lesser degree of state regulation, but as societies characterised by centres of capital accumulation whose goal is to transform people into labour power. The possibility of carrying out this transformation then becomes the central question. There is capitalist subordination of labour when workers' creative capacity is dedicated to the production of a surplus value: this value is then invested in financial portfolios which both organise and plunder productivity gains. Capitalist subordination involves a specific monetary constraint such that:

- only the products of labour dedicated to the accumulation of capital (commodities) are assigned monetary value.
- ownership of profit-earning savings permits owners to tap part of the value attributed to the products of this labour.
- people victimised by the negation of their creative capacity are granted the right to a minimum income.

These three conditions of the capitalist monetary constraint (strictly contributory benefits based on work dedicated to capital; constitutional profit-earning property rights; and minimum income guarantees for the working poor) compete with non-capitalist forms of monetary constraint linked to the corporatist logic developed primarily in specific sectors or the professions. Above all, they are in contradiction with the anti-capitalist forms arising out of the wage conflict and which give rise to forms of money that challenge all three of the above conditions.

The two principal questions determining the definition of a resource regime are thus:

- what *work* is assigned value? Is it free or subordinated, and in the latter case, for what kind of employer and what kind of enterprise? How is it *measured*: according to criteria that are more, or less, abstracted from concrete situations of work (product, project, qualification of the job, qualification of the worker), and more, or less, contributory?

- what *money* expresses this value? A wage, a tax (what kind), or savings (and what is their relation to financial accumulation)? Who defines it and administers the flows (collective agreements and the social representatives, company-level agreements, employers, the state – acting as a social state[13] or a tutelary state, local authorities, or the financial industry)? What is it allocated to (type of benefits)?

In this way, the type of *monetary constraint* corresponding to each resource regime can be defined: for example, the monetary constraint is capitalist if only the product of labour dedicated to capital is assigned monetary value, or if the money expressing the value assigned to free work contributes to the accumulation of capital. The type of *law* or *right* founding this resource regime can also be identified (labour law, employment rights or wage rights for instance), and the *ideal-type of the social group* defined.

The table below proposes a nomenclature of resource regimes based on the six characteristics we have just detailed. It should be noted that the definition of the type of workers concerned by each regime (first column), or of the ideal-type social group determined by the regime (last column), includes not only active workers (employed or unemployed) but pensioners as well, given the proximity of earned income and pensions. Similarly, it includes self-employed workers as well as wage-earners, since the distinction between the two is of little relevance from a resource regime perspective. In order to avoid any misunderstandings, it should be added that in the last column, the types of law or rights that are defined as the basis of the various resource regimes are theoretical notions: thus "labour law" for example does not refer to the legal discipline, but designates an analytical category opposed to "employment rights" or "wage rights", although, in concrete terms, all of these rights fall within that field of law called labour and social security law. Similarly, and still in the last column, "employees", "workers", "citizens" and "wage-earners" are ideal-type groups that do not refer to the groups customarily designated by these terms.

Thus, the tutelary allowance recognises, by means of a flat-rate sum financed by taxation, the work of target populations that the public authorities define on the basis of the denial of their *qualification*; whereas the corporatist wage provides the staff of a company, the employees in a given sector, or the members of a profession, a direct wage and occupational social protection schemes that are linked to a hierarchy of

[13] As defined by Christophe Ramaux (2012).

qualifications defined by the social representatives. The socialised wage surpasses both these regimes: here, social benefits – whether linked to the qualification system (pension, unemployment) or not (health, family, housing) – are partially disconnected from employment, and attributed to the person, by a large-scale pooling of the wage implemented according to national rules, without recourse to savings. Roughly speaking, resource regimes are divided between those based on non-capitalist forms of subordination of labour and monetary constraint; capitalist regimes that develop the three dimensions of the capitalist form of monetary constraint; and regimes that subvert the latter – and are thus anti-capitalist – and develop new forms of monetary constraint. These are not to be regarded as hard-set categories given the interpenetration and the contradictory dynamics of these regimes.

Proposal for a nomenclature of resource regimes

	Valorised labour (economically active + retirees)	Measure of labour	Form of money	Monetary constraint (1)	Rights to resources *Social group (ideal-type)*
Corporatist wage	Civil servants; professionals; employees in sectors such as banking, public transport, energy	Qualification, wage classification, Nomenclature of professional acts	Social contributions (specific schemes), corporatist tax, Sectoral or company collective agreements, Joint management	Community-dependent	Employment rights *Employees*
Pre-financed wage	"	"	Funded defined-benefit schemes Pension industry; sectoral or company collective agreements; joint management by the social representatives	Community-dependent Capitalist monetary constraint (B)	Employment rights + profit-making property rights *Rentier employees*
Deferred wage	Employees of capitalist firms; self-employed without capital	Strictly contributory (task, project, competencies); actuarial neutrality	Individualised wage, social contributions (virtual savings) Collective bargaining possible	Capitalist monetary constraint (A)	Labour law *Workers*
Bare wage	Dependent "self-employed"	Product, project, piece	Product price project contract reduced social contributions, or none at all	Capitalist monetary constraint (A)	Commercial law *Labour power*

Wage-earner savings	High-wage employees in capitalist firms; self-employed with capital	Project, competencies, company results or profits	Defined-contribution schemes, tax incentives, investment returns Pension industry	Capitalist monetary constraint (B)	Profit-making property rights *Rentiers*
Tutelary allowance	Victimised low-paid workers; positive discrimination	Flat-rate: percentage of reference income	Tutelary tax, subsidised wage or reduced contributions Local management, tutelary state	Capitalist monetary constraint (A), (C)	National solidarity rights *Benefit-recipients*
Public service	Universal scheme	None (or possibly, duration of residence)	Universal direct tax, free public service, flat-rate benefits Welfare state	Loosens CMC MC: citizen-related needs	Citizen-based rights *Citizens*
Socialised wage	Universal scheme	Qualification (of worker or post), politically negotiated	Cross-sectoral social contributions Managed by State and social representatives	Loosens CMC MC: level and structure of qualification	Wage rights *Wage-earners (salariat)*

(1) Three conditions of the capitalist monetary constraint (CMC): (A) only work dedicated to capital is valorised, (B) profit-making property rights, (C) guaranteed minimum income for the invalidated working poor

Conclusion

The particular contribution of the resource regime approach is to consider the wage as a distinctive dimension of employment and as pivotal to the circulation of resources serving the overall reproduction of the labour force (Clasquin *et al.*, 2004). Here, institutional forms of resource flows are differentiated according to the type of financing, the nature of the benefits provided, the conditions of entitlement and the modes of managing the resources linked to employment and social protection. This conceptual framework analyses employment policies as one of the vehicles for the transformation of these institutional forms – and therefore of employment – through their impact on the modes of financing and entitlements to social rights, as well as through the derogating forms they develop with regard to the recognition of job qualifications and wage determination (Moncel, Ruivo, 2002).

The interest of this approach is multiple: to begin with, it seeks to address the transformations taking place within the fields of capital and the wage relation together. Mutations in employment and social protection systems are examined in conjunction with the resultant labour force differentiations and changes in the mode of financing the total wage (direct and indirect).

Then, in its most recent developments (Friot, 2010, 2012), this approach rests on a reasoning that takes into account socio-economic and anthropological aspects, by bringing the human subject to the fore: the analysis of changes in the linkage between employment and social protection and of the mediation of resources (money) reveals various statuses of the worker and their transformations (subordination versus emancipation). This reading based on a re-interpretation of the Bismarckian model enables us to identify the *salariat* as the essential component of social and economic construction.

One of the questions that remains open at this stage is how to take account of the European level, that is, of the articulation between the societal logics underpinning wage relations and the process of European integration. While there are plentiful political science or legal studies on the topic, sociological or economic research attempting to address this articulation remains rare. The current debate appears to be confined to an opposition between the persistence of national differences versus an overall convergence towards a similar model. However, as Barbier (2001) notes in his analysis of the different logics underpinning the activation of so-called passive expenditures, the two are not necessarily incompatible. The discrepancy between the initial objectives of activation measures and their actual outcomes suggests that the implicit goals also need to be examined. Unravelling the combination of explicit and implicit goals could then contribute to a fuller understanding of what appear to be contradictory phenomena. Thus, from an analytic point of view, the explicit goals of employment and social protection policy measures (forms, devices, criteria, target populations, etc.) may diverge (or be diverse) while at the same time, the implicit goals may converge. It can be argued, for instance, that the measures geared to activating passive expenditures, or any other measure aimed at "promoting employment", have the same implicit aim to dismantle waged employment norms. In this case, we would be seeing a convergence of the general normative orientations being followed in Europe today (Lefresne, 2005).

Employment and the Wage

Relationships on the Move

Bernard FRIOT

Emeritus Professor, University of Paris Ouest Nanterre; member of the Institut Européen du Salariat

Employment is such a central reality of how work is conceived today that "job" and "work" tend to be treated as synonyms in everyday language. Yet employment is a recent construction, since it largely emerged after World War II. And a fragile one at that, for on reaching its high point in the mid-1970s, it would immediately become a target for reform. This is because employment is a contradictory institution: it is an institution of capital, because it is the instrument of the submission of work to labour value; but it has also been the matrix of the socialisation of the wage with the development of a *qualification* system and social contributions. It is thus both the expression of subordination and a vehicle for emancipation, a dual logic which culminated in the 1960s and 1970s, and has been challenged by reformers ever since. Because it has created a space for wage-based institutions that subvert the institutions of capital, this contradictory dynamic can thus lead to two antagonistic forms of the relationship to work: employability, on the one hand, and, on the other, what will be designated here by the term "personal *qualification*", that is, the transfer from the post to the individual of a transversal system of job classification based essentially on levels of skill and responsibility.[1]

The first form constitutes a key element in the counter-offensive launched by the European ruling classes with their reforms promoting the free movement of capital, goods and persons, the competitiveness of companies and the modernisation of the labour market. Since the late 1990s it has been embodied in the EU policy of flexicurity, which reasserts an employment logic more suited to financialised capitalism and promotes the figure of what will be defined here as "provident

1 See the Introduction for a definition of the term "qualification" as used in this volume.

employable workers", in that their future is provided for by means of a deferred income.

The second, in contradiction with the logic of these reforms, is the dynamic of a wage for life linked to a *qualification* attached to the person. It is based on the wage rights gained within the employment dynamic, namely: the *qualification* attached to the post and transferred to the retired person with the pension as the lifelong continuation of the wage; the marginalisation of the labour market; and the promotion of non-market production financed by social contributions.

Parts I and II of this chapter will present the two poles of the contradiction inherent in employment, and Parts III and IV the two possible paths for the resolution of this contradiction.

I. Employment as the Locus of Submission to Labour Value

Employment presupposes a distinction between "employer" and "employee". This is not a "natural" distinction, but one that was gradually constructed over the past two centuries. It lies at the heart of the capitalist form of work relations, and is based on the expropriation by a minority claiming to be the sole economic actor – the employers – of the capacity to produce wealth[2] of the majority – confined to the status of employee. Let there be no confusion here between the term "employer" and the necessary functions of running a company or managing staff: "employer" designates an entity that forms a system with "labour market" and "labour value". The labour market defines people as "job-seeking" units of labour power, and this labour power can only be put to use by employers who buy it on the market and utilise it according to the logic of labour value.

To avoid any possible misinterpretations, it must be stressed that labour value has nothing to do with work as a value: it designates the core of capitalism. Capitalism is that specific form of the organisation of production in which a product is assigned a value on the basis of the socially necessary labour time required to produce it. Labour has no value: in its abstract form, present in all production, it is a measure of value. Capitalism is the only mode of production that functions in this way. Some societies do not even have a generic term equivalent to "work" to designate the activities that are described by this abstract term; they do not separate such activities from family relations, religious rites or the exercise of political power. In the course of history, different societies have measured the value of production according to such

2 Wealth is constituted by the whole range of useful goods and services produced by human activity.

criteria as the social status of the producer, the prestige it bestows on the state in the symbolic competition with others, the taxes it allows sovereigns or the clergy to levy, and numerous others.

Only capitalism uses labour as a measure of production, because it has been constructed on social relations of a new kind, abstracted from any consideration of family relationships, honour or social rank, allegiance to a deity or sovereign (and in this sense, it plays an emancipatory role), and also from any consideration of the specific good produced or its use. This founding relationship is an exchange relation between the sellers and buyers of "labour power", between "employees" and "employers". And this labour power will produce goods and services, permitting its buyers to extract profit from the sale of such products, while the private accumulation of this profit is legitimated by a founding, profit-making property right, that is, the right to draw income from capital. In order for there to be profit, it is necessary for everything – workers and products – to be transformed into commodities, and therefore that the common denominator of these commodities, the abstract labour time required for their production, become the measure of all things. Hence the emphasis capitalism places on abstract "labour" measured in terms of time, and the dictatorship of labour time that inter-capitalist competition introduces. We can see here that a commodity is not an item produced for sale, as claimed by a commonplace definition that confuses it with a monetary transaction: farmers selling their tomatoes at the local market are not selling commodities, any more than is a French doctor in private practice who charges the social security rate for a consultation. Challenging the production of commodities does not mean denying the usefulness of monetary transactions. A commodity is an object produced under the dictatorship of abstract labour time in order to valorise capital.

The organisation of production based on this kind of abstraction is marked by an essential contradiction: it is liberated from the traditional modes of labour – and this is the source of an infinite dynamic of commodity production – and at the same time it deepens the effects of both the exploitation of producers dispossessed of their creative abilities, and their alienation, since they are condemned to producing commodities over which they have no control. In Part III we will see the level that this contradiction has reached today, but for the time being, let us first take a closer look at the disqualification that lies at the root of employment.

The employer-employee duo goes hand in hand with another pair, the shareholder-victim duo, and particular attention should be paid to the way in which the discourse on victimisation is being constructed today. While it is a traditional discourse in capitalism, our belief in "the Markets" gives it a particular twist. Tune into any radio station catering for a general audience, at any hour of the day: the moment will inevitably arrive for the live reports coming direct from the "Market" – with the latest stock quotes that you couldn't care less about – followed by an economist's editorial sermon. The two go together. The journalist-reporting-live-from-the-Market ushers you into the place of prayer, so that, even if you are not particularly devout, you can enter into communion with the editorialist's religion, and participate in an endlessly repeated ritual designed to keep your faith alive. His sermon will invariably express the following discourse: only the shareholders and the "highly talented person" they have placed at the head of the company have the legitimacy to decide – depending on the topic of the day – to close the plant, merge with another group, or change their products and manufacturing procedures. The shareholders and their highly-talented-person are the only legitimate actors in the economy, while wage-earners are social minors reduced to the status of victim, victims of the inevitable job cuts and just as inevitable delocalisations, of being insufficiently trained, of the crisis, of China. All of these victims are entitled to national solidarity, which of course is the responsibility of the public authorities. The shareholder-victim couple is thus constantly reactivated and naturalised, because it is essential to the preservation of capital's institutions. Profit-making property rights and the tyranny of labour value – capital's central institutions – could not exist without the denial of *qualification* rights, a denial that precisely defines the victim. Capital cannot exist without the disqualification of the working population, and the victimisation of the latter is a central element of the capitalist logic and the political philosophy that accompanies it.

Employment, therefore, because it rests on the disqualification of human beings reduced to labour power dedicated to the production of commodities, is the locus of the submission of work to labour value, in other words, of the subordination of labour. But it is also its opposite.

II. Employment as a Vehicle for the Socialised Wage

In practice, employment has also served as a vehicle for the emancipation of labour for two reasons, one external and the other internal.

The external reason is that the expropriation constitutive of employment had to and still must conquer a space for itself in social formations that are not capitalist and are thus not subjected to labour value.

Historically, the construction of employment in the private sector was concomitant with the construction of the civil service. The latter is radically antagonistic to the former and has exerted a strong attraction on private sector workers. Let us take the example of France. A founding principle of the civil service is that wage rights are not tied to the post but to a person's grade, that is to his or her personal *qualification* as recognised by a competitive examination. This means that civil servants are not subjected to a labour market logic because their rights are not determined by the post they occupy. The head of their department, to whom they are answerable, has no control over their wage rights (wage level, promotion, conditions of mobility, social protection coverage), since these depend on their grade and not on their job. Employment and employer are marginal realities. This is also why there are no unemployed civil servants. And their pension is a continuation of their wage, since it is calculated on the basis of their last (and thus best) wage: civil servants who are no longer employed retain their grade and thus the right to the wage linked to it. Attracted by this civil service status, organised private sector workers have also sought to disconnect their rights from their post and make them personal rights – and they have partly succeeded in doing this, as will be seen later.

Furthermore, the figure of the white-collar "employee" was initially constructed to differentiate it from that of the blue-collar worker[3] in workplaces which were sheltered internally from the labour market logic by a paternalistic or a corporatist dynamic, depending on the sector (such as the steel industry in the former case, or banking and public enterprises, in the latter). Thanks to collectively negotiated sectoral agreements, an employee status carrying wage rights attached to the post was constructed – while the "employers", as regards the permanent staff at least, were not simply managers of labour power but also functioned within a logic of attributing certain wage rights to the post. Collective agreement provisions established a hierarchy of job qualifications, usually linked to occupational categories, together with the corresponding wage grids, which the employers applied. Supplementary schemes at sectoral level directly financed by the employers, with or without social contributions, acknowledged time "out-of-work" (sickness, incapacity, retirement) because these were strongly correlated with employment. The employment dynamic thus marginalised the labour market by creating internal markets within large companies or sectors. And here again, this regulation by means of collective agreements setting pay scales and rules governing mobility, working conditions, hiring and firing, functioned as a force of attraction for private sector workers overall.

The internal reason for the construction of an employment situation transcending its dimension of exploitation and alienation stems from the very consequences of reducing persons to labour power in non-

[3] The classical distinction within the enterprise between white collar "employees" and blue-collar workers was that the former were paid monthly whereas the latter were paid by the hour.

corporatist capitalist sectors. Workers are denied recognition as producers endowed with a capacity to produce: defined as labour power, they possess only a capacity to earn, that is, to function as a form of capital that is the source of their income (what economists call human capital). Remuneration for work thus becomes the central focus of the conflict between employers and employees. And this conflict has produced two major innovations: the wage linked to a qualification grid, and social contributions. Thanks to these two elements, pay ceases to be equated with an income from capital and becomes, potentially at least, the opposite: a wage linked to a personal *qualification*. Here we have the crucial point, and this is what needs to be fully understood.

The wage linked to a qualification grid came into its own when collective agreements were standardised across the private sector in the 1970s, and, at the same time, qualification grids were defined to cut across work posts rather than being based on a rewording of occupational categories. True, in the private sector, given the logic of labour power and labour value, the qualification system is not as rich as in the civil service – in particular because it is linked to the job and only indirectly to the jobholder. But the qualification linked to the post is also, through the wage, partly linked to the wage-earner, since the qualification of a previous post can be used to negotiate a wage level when changing jobs, and in some countries, the courts can rule in their favour if they refuse to be deskilled by a downgrading of their post.

Employment was also the matrix of social contributions. The considerable expansion of this other dimension of the wage was often the result of an employer response to the demand for higher direct wages. In France, for instance, the strikes of 1936 prompted employers to increase their contributions to a family benefit fund, limited to the head of the household, in order to avoid a general pay rise; similarly, supplementary pension schemes in the metals industry experienced strong growth in the 1950s to avoid a sector-level pay hike. But this pragmatic development would have unforeseen effects, because social contributions correspond to a pooling of the wage which originates within the employment relation but extends beyond it. A wage-earner, whether employed or not, has the right to health coverage, family benefits, unemployment benefits, and a pension, and all of these are elements of the wage. In other words, the scope of the wage is far broader than that of a job.

Social contributions – the indirect portion of the socialised wage – are an exciting innovation because they pool the wage based on the qualification system and thus recognise non-employment situations on the same basis. They are strictly proportional to the gross wage, and the only factor taken into account for calculating their rate is the job qualification to which the gross wage is linked. They thus reinforce recognition of the *qualification* both of the contributors and of those on the receiving end – such as pensioners, carers, parents, or the unemployed. By financing pensions on the sole basis of the wage, social contributions extend the reference to *qualification* to the non-employment time of retirement. The *qualification* attributed to the post giving rise to pension contributions, becomes, in the pension benefit financed by these contributions, a personal attribute of the retiree, who is thereby guaranteed the irrevocable status of a *qualified* person even though s/he is no longer in employment. This is where the logic of the socialised wage is totally opposed to employment, even if arising out of it and constitutive of it. The socialised wage reaches beyond employment, it signifies the recognition of people's capacity to produce, and this is the polar opposite of the capacity to earn underpinning employment.

I would like to stress what an exceptional innovation it is to finance retirement by a wage continued in the form of a pension. This is traditionally the case for civil servants, but once private sector retirees claim their pensions, they are assigned the qualification attached to their best jobs for the rest of their lives, and thus enjoy the same wage-earner status as civil service retirees, with a wage for life and a recognized capacity, in short, a personal *qualification*. In our everyday lives, new retirees are more often than not seen off with envious congratulations – rather than with speeches of sympathy for the unhappiness that lies ahead. They can now enjoy the happiness of a lifelong wage and the freedom to engage in activities liberated from subordination. For, if they are in good health, and the difference between their pension and their last wage is not too great, and they are part of a motivated social network, they are active. It is the retirees themselves who say so: they have "never worked so much", and have "never enjoyed it so much". Of course, this only applies to a minority, but given the tens of millions of pensioners, that minority means a lot of people. It means children seeing that work is a pleasure for their grandparents, while their parents' experience is often a mixture of bitterness, anguish and rage. The dictatorship of labour value is subverted by the widespread happiness of those paid to work outside of its hold. The fact that non-subordinated, non-commodity-producing work can receive a wage subverts the whole capitalist form of the relationship to work. Better yet, this wage is irrevocable: from age 60 until they die, pensioners can work without being subjected to the labour market or exploited by an employer. And social contributions, it should be added, marginalise profit-making property. They are the demonstration that such a long-term, massive commitment as pension provision (representing over 10% of GDP today) can be met without any recourse to savings, interest rates, financial accumulation or credit. In short, without any of the institutions linked to profit-making property. Social contributions, that is, the attribution to the wage of a part of the flow of value that will immediately be transformed into social benefits, are an anti-capitalist technology that demonstrates the uselessness of profit-making property.

The socialised wage opens up extraordinary possibilities for emancipation by subverting the labour market, the dictatorship of labour value and profit-making property. Hence the vast counter-offensive launched by the European ruling classes since the late 1970s, after a brief interlude during which they had been destabilised and even prepared to make concessions, as will be seen in Corinne Gobin's concluding chapter.[4] The foundations of this counter-offensive were laid by the Cassis de Dijon judgment of 1979[5] and the Single European Act of 1985, and then endorsed in the Maastricht protocol of 1991. Indeed, the principle of subsidiarity which leaves wages, social security, and labour law (including the right to strike) within the exclusive competence of each Member State, does not rest on the will to jealously preserve national control over wage rights, as argued by those who claim that Europe's "democratic deficit" stems from the overly cautious behaviour of the Member States. Subsidiarity rests on the firm determination of the national elites to prevent recognition of wage rights at European level, for fear that such rights, which have begun to subvert the capitalist form of the relationship to work at national level, could challenge the dogma of fundamental freedoms that is the cornerstone of the EU. Maintaining these rights within a national framework is a prerequisite for their possible defeat: given the primacy of Community law, limiting Community competence to the sole sphere of competition means that reforms can be imposed in the name of competition to quash wage rights in each Member State. Hence the strategic importance of restricting EU competences to the field of competition, as formalised in the Single European Act and as endorsed by the European Trade Union Confederation (ETUC) in the Maastricht social protocol – which excludes the wage and the right to strike from Community competence.[6]

---

4 The concluding chapter also shows that the trend analysed here in the shift from the affirmation of employment as the basis of wage rights towards the utilisation of employment to reduce these same rights, is reflected in the evolution of EU discourse on employment policy.

5 The Cassis de Dijon judgment confirmed the principle of the country of origin as the basis for the free movement of goods, thereby opening up a breach for the revival of a Community dynamic that had momentarily been interrupted by the Commission's timid attempts to introduce EU-level social and economic legislation during the 1970s.

6 See the chapter by Anne Dufresne Part II.

III. Moving towards Employability?[7]

The 1970s thus saw both the affirmation of the logic of employment under construction since the 1920s, and the first moves to challenge it. Employment in the private sector had by then become a highly unstable compromise because it was the vehicle both for the radical disqualification of people reduced to labour power, and for a socialised wage liberating them from the burden of the labour market and labour value. For the past 30 years or so, what the ruling classes call "reform" has been the attempt to reduce employment's emancipatory thrust by restoring it to its sole dimensions of exploitation and alienation. The primary targets have been the civil service (because it does not function within a logic of employment), and in the private sector, all means of attaching *qualification* to the person: this has meant attacking the wage based on the *qualification* grid in the name of individualising pay; attacking the pension as a continuation of the wage by turning it into a deferred income (as in the Swedish model of the *inkomstpension*); and challenging the right to a wage during unemployment, a wage that the reforms define as a "passive" resource to be "activated". This reform undertaking is summed up in the EU policy of flexicurity, which aims to replace the right to *qualification* by a right to employability.

By pillaging the wage under the more socially acceptable banner of "wage moderation", the reforms have been a direct cause of the financial crisis. But, at the same time, in seeking to resolve the contradiction of the 1970s to the benefit of the institutions of capital by attacking wage institutions, they have brought this contradiction to such an explosive level that it would now be possible for a sufficiently determined worker movement, aware of the enormous stakes, to successfully challenge the labour market, employment, labour value, commodification, profit-making property and financial accumulation, by asserting a universal right to personal *qualification*. But that will be the topic of the concluding section. For now, let us continue our examination of its polar opposite, employability.

Employability is at the heart of the transformation of employment that the reformers are attempting to bring about. They went along with health, family benefit and pension rights based on the wage and attributed to the person – until they realised that the pension today allows healthy young retirees to continue to receive a good proportion of their wage to perform emancipated work, and thereby to subvert the monopoly of subordinated labour as the only form of work that is assigned monetary value. Worse still, they saw that a longer life expectancy

7 For national examples of the developments presented here, see Part III of the present volume.

enhances retirees' prospects of embarking on a second career which is both free and remunerated. This attribution of a personal right that challenges their control over the relationship to work sent employers into a panic. They thus sought the help of politicians and experts, who came to their rescue by inventing the demographic peril and launching pension reforms that can be summed up as the attempt to reduce the scope of the continuation of the wage to the benefit of a deferred income. As a result, those 60-year-olds who until now enjoyed the status of retired wage-earners, are to be transformed: 1) into subordinated workers (by raising the retirement age, and by allowing simultaneous collection of a pension and a wage); or 2) into pension fund *rentiers*; or 3) into recipients of an extended minimum old age benefit, or above all, 4) into former workers receiving the exact equivalent of their past contributions. These four main avenues of the reforms[8] agreed upon at EU level all have the same goal: to put an end to the prospects of attaching *qualification* to the person and of the lifelong continuation of the wage, and to redefine people in employment as units of labour power.

Let us take the example of the two contradictory forms of pay-as-you-go (PAYG) pension schemes: one is wage-based and the other, a provident scheme. In the first, the pension as a *continuation of the wage* rests either on maintaining the personal *qualification* of the civil servant, or on the attribution to a private sector retiree of the average *qualification* of his or her best jobs: it posits people as wage-earners endowed with a capacity to produce. In contrast, the pension as *deferred income* (provident scheme) rests on entitlements that are proportional to the individual contributions record with a guaranteed level of purchasing power: it posits people as employable individuals endowed with a capacity to earn.

The core goal of current pension reforms concerning PAYG schemes is to move from the first to the second form. The three levers used to do this are: freezing the contribution rate; indexing the pension on prices; and increasing the contributory dimension, which is what is meant by "individual actuarial neutrality" (the total pension must be equal to the total contributions paid during the person's working career). And a PAYG pension becomes a deferred income when it is 1) based on a contribution rate that has been stabilised over the long term, 2) calculated on a strictly contributory basis, and 3) its purchasing power is secured by consumer price indexation. But those promoting this deferred income are well aware that, since it is based on an individual calculation excluding periods during which contributions were not paid and including the low-pay periods in the working career, it will leave with insuffi-

8 See Bernard Friot (2008) and the chapter by Coron and Friot, Part II.

cient resources all those (and particularly women) who have not been able to build up an adequate contributions account. This is why the promotion of actuarial neutrality is always coupled with the call for a broad programme of national solidarity to finance a guaranteed "contributory minimum pension" together with "non-contributory benefits" (such as an old-age minimum income, or a bonus for having children). The reform discourse thus claims to combine two virtues: the justice of strictly contributory benefits, and solidarity with the "poor". But these "virtues" constitute a considerable regression when compared to the justice and solidarity of the continued wage.

A regression in terms of justice, first of all. A pension that is provided in return for contributions paid in the past, and thus for past subordinated labour, instead of for an individual's present *qualification* (and thus for emancipated work), presupposes and reinforces the labour market, employment, commodification, subordination and profit-making property. Here, the "provident employable worker" is denied recognition as producer, but maintained in a position of economic minor permanently at the mercy of the employer. A capacity to provide for the future is what remains when wage-earners have been stripped of that essential attribute – their *qualification*. The multiplication of notional accounts then becomes necessary to ensure workers' security and their capacity to adapt given that, even within their firm, they are subjected to the labour market and to the constant suspicion that they are not up to the job they hold or are applying for.

The wage-based scheme, on the other hand, bears the promise of attributing a *qualification* to each person without exception, with the indefinite continuation of the wage. Here, people's contribution to their resources does not rest on their capacity to save a part of their earnings as units of labour power, but on their capacity to participate in the definition of the work they will perform liberated from commodification and labour value. Their relationship to the future is based on maintaining their *qualification*, and not on a capital intended to produce an income to replace their earnings: the distinction between employment and non-employment is transcended in the continuum of *qualification*. Here, whole new continents for the expression of the human personality are waiting to be discovered. In contrast, the provident scheme locks us into the capitalist past.

A *regression in terms of solidarity*, in the second place. Promoting solidarity with the victimised is without doubt one of the most perverse dimensions of the reforms. Positing people as "poor" and as "victims" entitled to solidarity serves to naturalise the disqualification inherent in capitalism. Capitalism posits shareholders and the "highly talented person" they have put at the head of the firm as the only actors in the production process. Wage-earners are maintained in a position of social minors and reduced to the status of victims if they are unable to remain employable. In contrast, wage-based solidarity rests on promoting *qualification* for all, and is the basis for solidarity between equals. This is not the solidarity of the provident towards those they will define as poor, but that embodied in the political decision to attribute a *qualification* to each and every one and to ensure that this right will effectively be exercised.

Promoting the figure of the "provident employable worker" over qualification for life: we can see here how pension reforms are consistent with the overarching reforms that are being deployed in the name of employability and flexicurity. The aim is to extend the labour market by attacking the internal markets existing at company and sectoral level. Under stress from their increasingly traumatic transitions on the labour market, many wage-earners no longer dare leave their jobs. Alternatively, they try to seek refuge in the internal markets of large organisations, the liberal professions, or the civil service. But the reformers want to put an end to these corporatist forms in order to achieve a "true" labour market. Criticizing employment forms that secure wage rights for workers as creating inequalities and discriminating between "insiders" and "outsiders", they are challenging these rights via the promotion of employability over the *qualification* linked to the post. The focus is thus no longer on the post, its *qualification* and corresponding rights, that is, on job quality and security. Instead, the goal now is to "protect" mobility, through what is hypocritically called "career path security" – the dominant flexicurity theme in France today – which allows employers to cut back wage rights.

Flexicurity requires substantial public intervention: for wage-earners to readily accept repeated transitions on the market, it is claimed, they need a secure replacement income, the support of an efficient public employment service, to be ensured of the right to a new placement, able to transfer certain entitlements such as training or supplementary health care benefits to the new job, and so forth. The reformers insist that the labour market requires efficient intermediaries. Thus, they advocate improving the financing of public employment services (PES), now under obligation to produce results, via a "polluter pays" type of tax levied on companies that downsize. The service will profile the unemployed, that is, assess their employability, and then direct them to placement agencies whose obligation to produce results is materialised in the way they are paid: they will, for instance, receive one-third of their fee when the unemployed person comes to them, the second third when that person is effectively placed and the last third six months later, if s/he is still in employment. This obligation to produce results is always coupled with the workers' obligation to take up what are called "valid", "reasonable", or "suitable" job offers: there is no lack of adjectives to designate the disqualification these may entail. This central feature of the PES is accompanied by a right to lifelong training which, together with the other rights securing improved employability, will no longer be linked to the post, but to the person. In the reform agenda, the right to a new placement, access to PES services, and the right to training will no longer be linked to the type of job, the size or sector of the company, or the type of employment contract, but be universal, transportable rights with an obligation for the new employer to honour them at the previously acquired level.

The acquisition of these rights ties into a logic that is altogether different to the wage-based logic, because promoting employability opens the way for the massive marginalisation of the wage that accompanies its stagnation. It is, moreover, significant that the term "wage" is now largely absent from the public debate, but has been replaced by "purchasing power". On the one hand, by challenging the *qualification* of the post and job security (to the benefit of employability and protected mobility), the reformers are challenging the wage based on *qualification*, application of collectively negotiated wage grids, sectoral collective bargaining, and the hierarchy of norms governing the employment contract. With the considerable help of the EU, furthermore, as illustrated by several recent judgments of the European Court of Justice:[9] by asserting that the labour law of the country of origin is to be applied to workers posted to another Member State, subject to compliance with the minimum provisions of the national legislation of the host country, these rulings entirely destroy the principle of favourability to the worker underpinned by the hierarchy of norms. On the other hand, the socialised wage is being called into question, and in particular its indirect component, social contributions and their anti-capitalist thrust. Social contributions that generate a PAYG benefit based on the wage are denounced as a "tax on labour", and under the guise of "saving" low-skill jobs, are being replaced either by a (real) tax or a "pillar" arrangement: a first pillar of a state-guaranteed deferred income based on the Swedish or Italian models, and a second pillar of wage-earner savings. The wage has disappeared, and we now have a logic of "providing for the future" in which pension rights – just like rights to training, paid leave, complementary health coverage, and unemployment benefits – can accumulate in individual accounts. Notional savings can be applied to almost anything, and although they do not generate financial accumulation, they function within a logic of savings and thus replace the wage

[9] Laval, Viking, Rüffert, and Luxembourg cases.

and serve to re-legitimize the very profit-making property and financial accumulation that social contributions had succeeded in challenging.

If this dynamic were to prevail, we would no longer have job holders, but *provident employable workers*. Employability would replace *qualification*, while provident schemes linked to subordinated labour and secured in savings accounts would replace the part of the wage constituted by social contributions. The socialised wage would give way to a deferred income or financial accumulation.[10] Only subordinated labour would generate rights, and in forms adapted to the labour market and profit-making property. In a context dominated by reactionary monetarist policies and financial markets, all this would add up to putting the institutions of capital firmly back in the saddle, and signal the defeat of the wage institutions that were beginning to develop out of the employment dynamic.

But it's a far way from cup to lip – for the reforms exacerbate the contradiction they claim to lift. Whereas employment was constructed by attributing wage rights to work posts, the goal of employability is a move in the opposite direction: making wage rights "employment friendly". This strips employment of its emancipatory content, leaving it only with its role of subordinating labour power bought on the market. Likewise, the "employer" of the previous phase, who conceded to wage rights attached to the post, becomes a mere buyer of labour power. This change in direction represents the central thrust of the European Employment Strategy, and has become omnipresent since the 1990s. "*Jobs, jobs, jobs*" – such was the emblematic title of a report delivered to the Commission by former Netherlands prime minister Wim Kok (2003), a one-time union leader who initiated a national pact on "wage moderation" in 1982 that was cited at the time as a model by the EU authorities. Indeed, employment has been the excuse for all the attacks launched on the wage, with the result that the wage share in value added has dropped to 60% compared to 70% before the reforms. Those ten points have gone to profit, not to invest in production, but to feed speculative bubbles that the population is being made to pay for today – with their jobs and their wages. What is being touted as "wage moderation" is in reality a pillaging of the wage that has proved disastrous for both employment and work. Today our countries are far richer than they were 40 years ago[11] – but we are having a far harder time at work, that crucial dimension of our lives. Being able to consume more does not offset the uncertainty, lack of interest, fatigue and disrespect experienced at work, nor

[10] This trend is analysed in the chapter by Coron and Friot, Part II.

[11] At an annual growth rate of 1.6% the GDP doubles in 40 years.

our growing doubts about consuming products whose evermore commercial nature has altered their quality and purpose.

In short, it is becoming patent that the capitalist form of the relationship to work, that is, a highly inventive commodity production which mutilates humans and deflects products from their purpose, is a dead end. All the more so since financial globalisation not only exacerbates inter-capitalist competition but – by accelerating the turnover of capital invested in production and separating the centres of accumulation of profit from the necessarily concrete places generating that profit[12] – manipulates commodities with tools that evolve in a permanent abstraction. Thus, food prices are set on stock markets thousands of miles from where the crops are grown, in ignorance of the producers, and using abstract procedures that can be applied to any kind of commodity. The evermore abstract forms of the dictatorship of labour time open the way to establishing a globalised equivalence between units of labour power all over the world. While this may well, in the long term, construct the basis for solidarity between workers worldwide – in the short and medium term, it exerts an extraordinary downward pressure on their rights in developed countries. The use of abstract labour time as a measure of the value of production has already caused considerable damage to labour, to workers' status and to products.

To *labour*, first of all. True, the concrete dimension of labour remains present, since useful things are being produced, but it is increasingly trapped in the vice of abstract labour. What looks like a tomato on the supermarket shelves is in fact a commodity produced off-soil, under carefully controlled greenhouse conditions, and by interchangeable units of labour power following strictly identical procedures all over the planet. Telephone operations have been "outsourced", that is removed from the enterprise where they made sense, in order to be handled in the abstraction of call centres where the time spent is constantly monitored in terms of results, and the conversation so turned into a commodity. The sale of a piece of clothing or a cubic metre of wood is caught up in the snare of a franchise or any other kind of system permitting a very small number of profit centres to benefit from the time gained through the world-wide use of identical commercial procedures which have themselves been transformed into commodities. The dexterity (a particularly skilful way of producing or selling) that was once the prerogative of workers has been extorted from them by bringing in consulting firms to analyse their skills, which are then modelised according to precise rules of time, and universalised. Engineers and doctors have seen their most complex acts transposed into codified procedures that managers

[12] We are all familiar with financiers' dreams of "manufacturers without factories".

transform into commodities which are then sold to clients (often other departments within the group) or to the social security system. Workplace stress today highlights how impossible it is to "do one's job well" when what is being produced is transformed into a commodity. This was less visible before because shareholders had fewer means at their disposal to accomplish this transformation. It has become particularly evident with the privatisation of public enterprises where the personnel had previously been able to conduct their activities without being subjected to the constraint of labour value.

Damaging to *workers' status*, in the second place. Activities become "labour" in capitalism when they are performed by so-called "free workers" who have been detached from everything so that they can be attached solely to capital's time, in other words, as pure "units of labour power". This reduction of persons to labour power, although present before, remained relative until financial capitalism could bring the dictatorship of labour time to the heights and level of contradiction we are seeing today. Now, the reforms are here, with discourses and measures that are intent on eliminating the spaces of workers' professional autonomy. Financial capitalism not only has the means to reduce this autonomy, it is impelled to do so, because of inter-capitalist competition and, more crucially, the continuous drop in profit rates due to the enormous productivity gains engendered by the dictatorship of labour time. Of course, because usable goods and services still need to be produced, workers' professional skills must be mobilised to a certain extent; but it is essential that they lose all control over their expertise so that it can be entirely dedicated to producing the commodities that will provide profits for the shareholder. Personal *qualification* – that is, a person's control over his or her professional skills – and even the *qualification* of the post constitute obstacles that the reformers are intent on eliminating. Clearly, the use of abstract labour time to measure the value of production causes significant damage to workers' status.

Finally, we come to the *products*. I will not linger here on the too-familiar mediocre quality of production, its polluting methods and polluted products. Suffice it to go back to my earlier example of the bunch tomato: it looks and may even smell enticingly like a tomato when on the supermarket shelves, but what a huge disappointment is in store for anyone who cares about taste. I would like instead to draw attention here to a trend that can best be illustrated by the quotas that are being imposed on the police. Ticketing drivers has shifted from being a task performed on specific occasions, as determined by a civil servant whose activity is rooted in public service ethics, to a standardised task executed according to universal procedures and calculated in terms of "productivity goals". It is ripe for becoming a commodity produced by units of labour power. I have intentionally chosen this example of the disastrous transformation of the products of labour into commodities within an essential state function that is supposedly shielded from privatisation, to show that this claim is illusory indeed.

In short, the reformers have attempted to restore the capitalist form of the relationship to work, but at the – potentially high – political price of it losing all credibility among workers in the developed countries as they see their wage rights and working conditions continue to deteriorate. No doubt the increasingly insistent discourse warning them against the perils of "the return of the religious" has served to divert their attention from that very religion that already has them in its hold and has been crippling them since the reforms were launched in the 1980s: the belief in "the Markets". Even as they suffer from the disastrous effects of "the Markets", workers turn to them desperately, afraid of causing displeasure, and ready to sacrifice mountains of money that they know will have to be paid back by enduring grim austerity. For the more they are trampled underfoot by the markets, the more they depend on them for their salvation, or at least that is what, in their numbed state, they still firmly believe. Still, but not necessarily forever. The contradiction between that belief and the insolent spectacle of markets thriving off the crisis they have produced is becoming clearer day by day. As is the fact that they are proving to be obstacles to the general interest. This is why the alternative path remains open: employment can give way to personal *qualification* instead of employability.

IV. The Alternative: Moving towards Personal *Qualification*

If we stop at this point, and look no further than the staggering effects of the crisis engendered by the reforms, we risk losing sight of the contradictory and polemical nature of the reform dynamic. For indeed, the dynamic of employability is antinomic to that of the wage linked to personal *qualification*, for which the groundwork has already been laid by such powerful precedents as the wage linked to a qualification grid, social security, collective agreements, and the civil service.

Let us come back to the happiness of retirees at work. It stems, precisely, from the fact that, assured of a wage for life, they can work freely, liberated from the yoke of labour value. Yet this widespread experience is rarely voiced in public, for many pensioners often feel uncomfortable when they compare what they see as their privileged situation with the unhappiness that is the lot of so many "active" workers. This private happiness needs to be made public, by showing that the enjoyment pensioners derive from work can become the standard experience for all.

The continued wage rests on personal *qualification.* Those pensioners who are working in ways and in fields they have chosen themselves usually have three assets to draw on: a pension that is not too far from their best wage; recognised cross-cutting capacities that they will be able to apply to their new activity (such as a former small company manager who will become a commercial court judge, or in the case of an accounting teacher, the treasurer of an amateur sports club); and a personal peer network that they generally developed before retiring, or have been able to build up in the first years of retirement. These are the three essential ingredients of personal *qualification*, which is attached to the person and not the job, and can indeed be deployed in freedom: without all three, it becomes more difficult for a retiree to develop a "second career". Armed with their personal *qualification*, retirees are able to work outside of the constraint of labour value: they have no need to be on a labour market, submit to an employer, or transform their production into a commodity.

The perspectives opened up by pensioners can be extended to all the economically active. In the flexicurity model, only the strict minimum of rights are transferred from the job to the person because these are rights that are linked solely to making worker mobility somewhat more secure (savings accounts for training, pensions, and health coverage; and the right to a new job placement). In contrast, the wage for life linked to personal *qualification* rests on the transfer of the major rights linked to the job today: *qualification*, the wage, and participation in representative labour institutions. If *qualification* becomes a personal attribute, one which cannot be called into question and revised downwards for those who change posts or whose jobs are cut back, this means that the wage itself, which is linked to the *qualification* grid, cannot be called into question either. What we have here then is a situation of a lifelong wage and thus of a wage for all.[13]

This wage-for-life therefore means that the pension is the continuation of the wage (and that there is no reason for *qualification* to stop at retirement), and that there is a continuation of the wage between jobs. The ongoing improvement of personal *qualification* will generate smooth wage progression and free mobility, secured and financed in part by a personal *qualifications* body administered by workers' representatives. From this it can be seen that making the pension the continuation of the wage is far more than a mere method of calculation, for it constitutes the beginnings of the metamorphosis of the "employee" with a job into a "wage-earner" with a *qualification*.

---

[13] It is to be remembered that the wage-for-life is tied to qualification and not status: it can be applied to the self-employed, and allows for far easier changes in status than are possible today.

In this model, doing away with the labour market presupposes attributing a recognised capacity and the corresponding wage to each person from the beginning of their career. This recognised capacity and the wage tied to it are attributes of the person, they cannot be withdrawn or reduced, but can only progress over the life course.

Personal *qualification* provides a new basis for rights that are currently rooted in employment. As defined here, it will be a collective right (just as the pension is a collective right, although its amount is personal), attributed to every person – from the end of their schooling for instance – and will progress without interruptions or cutbacks until that person dies. It will have four indissociable components:

- a certificate attesting mastery of a range of capacities cutting across several occupations belonging, for instance, to the fields covered by six or seven major cross-sectoral collective agreements (communications, education and culture, energy, transportation, etc.) in order to avoid fragmentation;
- a wage level corresponding to the recognised level of capacities; for example, in a qualification hierarchy ranging from 1 to 4, the monthly net wage would start at 2,000 euros for the first level, 3,500 euros for the second level, 5,000 for the third and 6,500 for the fourth, with a wage hierarchy ranging from 2,000 to 8,000 euros net;
- a peer network to maintain ongoing socialisation in the person's field of *qualification*; for example, a professional association, a network of local actors, or an international network of specialists that can provide a framework for exchanges, services, training, establishing rules for the exercise of the activity and monitoring these, pooling tools, and valorising the individual activities of their members;
- the right to a representative institution in order to claim the entitlements afferent to the person's *qualification* and its progression.

We can see how far this proposal goes in creating equality: it eliminates the labour market and thus job-seekers' subordination to employers; it provides every one with access to the same status (as the holder of a *qualification*) and the corresponding wage. It unifies in an upward direction the demands of retirees, students, civil servants, the unemployed, private-sector wage-earners (including those working in very small structures or deprived of trade-union representation), and the self-employed. It strengthens the civil service with the demand that the distinction between grade and post be extended to all wage-earners, which means that all will benefit from a recognised *qualification*, the absence of unemployment, and an individualised control over their mobility. For, indeed, all goods and services should be produced by wage-earners liberated from employment and commodification!

Conclusion: Moving towards the *Salariat*

The wage-based personal qualification needs to be backed up by a wage-based transformation of the two key institutions that operate on a capitalist logic today: monetary creation and investment.

A monetary flow passes from job-holders to pensioners via pension contributions. But this is not a transfer of value: it is the retirees who produce the wealth to which the value corresponding to their *qualification* is assigned. Pensions demonstrate the immense potential of a monetary creation that would anticipate the product of work by assigning value to a personal *qualification* instead of to commodities. Monetary creation is always a question of anticipating what will be produced. Instead of creating money in anticipation of the product of labour or, even worse, only its commercial product (as has been the case ever since the reactionary monetarism of the 1980s took hold),[14] why not base this anticipation on the capacity of individuals to create wealth as measured by *qualification*? The restoring force of monetary creation would then be used for deploying personal *qualifications*, and thus for emancipated work.

The reformers defend profit-making property in the name of investment which, they say, requires investors. But investors "contribute" nothing other than profit-making property titles that give them the right to tap the value of current production for the funds necessary to supply mains services, purchase a building or machinery and so forth, and therefore to expropriate the producers of this value. This entitles them to transform the latter into labour power: the expropriated producers are thus obliged to produce the commodities the investors have decided to produce, in short, to labour under the yolk of labour value. In one operation an investor robs us and alienates us. In contrast, our successful experience with pension contributions shows that we already have a large-scale example of the benefits of investing without investors. Since it is possible to finance pensions without any savings or loans – and this to the great advantage of pension schemes and pensioners – it would also be possible to finance investments in the same way by allocating an economic contribution to the wage, levied on value added like social contributions or the direct wage. This contribution would be collected

---

[14] According to which the central bank is prohibited from financing public expenditures, with the disastrous consequences that we are paying so heavily for today.

by investment bodies[15] that would provide interest-free financing since there would be no private accumulation of capital. Institutions such as financial accumulation, bank credits, loans with interest, or stock markets can clearly all be replaced by transposing the experience of social contributions to the financing of investment, since all investments are financed on current production. The social contribution has rid our individual daily lives of usurers, and the economic contribution will rid our collective daily lives of the stock market and bankers.

We see here how liberating it is to dissociate work from employment. Work has no "essence": what is designated as "work" is contingent and differs widely between societies and over time. It is an ongoing subject of public debate. According to the employment logic, work that is not measured in terms of time is not really work and does not warrant being paid for. But because employment, which reduces people to labour power subjected to labour value, has also historically been a vehicle for the socialisation of the wage through social contributions and the *qualification* attributed to the post, the definition of work today is torn between employment and the socialised wage. Is "work" that part of our activity devoted to producing commodities in order to feed capital (employment), or that part which deploys our *qualification* (socialised wage). The recent integration into ***employment*** of a whole range of personal assistance services has transformed them into work, and in the worst way for the last wave of these – household services – given their weak link with the socialised wage. Contradictorily, when the pension is seen as a continued *wage*, this opens the way for considering the activities that pensioners perform outside of any form of employment as work. We can then take full measure of the implications of the change in meaning of the word "work" when applied to activities that are liberated from the labour market and labour value. And we can use the experience of retirees to create a new basis for the social recognition of work, which would no longer be employment, but the *qualification* attached to the person

The pension as a continued wage is a wage institution. It demonstrates that we can produce freely, without the labour market and employers and thus without employment, commodities and labour value; that we can invest without investors, the stock market and bankers; and that we can free monetary creation from the yoke of commodification and base it on the *qualification* of persons. The only way to end the crisis, since its origins lie in the pillaging of wages carried out over the past several decades, is to replace the institutions of capital by wage

15 Administered by workers' representatives, as in the case of the personal qualifications bodies.

institutions. And it is precisely the affirmation of the full range of wage institutions, insofar as they succeed in replacing those of capital, that will constitute the *salariat*, instead of that addition of wage-earners a common and somewhat pedestrian definition would have it be. With the *salariat*, we thus place ourselves in an entirely different perspective to that of full employment. Full employment means a society full of employers. But *qualification* and thus the wage should no longer depend on decisions made by employers on a labour market. The reforms cannot be defeated by returning to "true" full employment with a "true" labour market, but by replacing these with full *qualification.*

The goal, here, transcends obtaining secure conditions for workers. The security discourse has internalised the fact that in capitalism, workers are social minors who are denied recognition as producers and thus have no right to be actors in the economy; all they have a right to is the security of an income and a job. The crisis has demonstrated that the owners of capital are incapable of playing a socially responsible role or serving the general interest. The issue today is precisely to be able to move beyond the demand for a secure income and secure employment and to promote a new figure of the worker, one that will be able to nourish our common aspiration to participate in directing the economy in order to put an end to the economism of labour value. That means wage-earners entitled to a qualification-based wage for life, and who benefit from institutional supports permitting them to uninterruptedly exercise their qualification because their capacities are fully recognised, their wage secured, their integration into a peer network sustained, and their recourse to representative institutions ensured.

Qualification is thus a political attribute that enriches citizenship, just like the right to vote. Just as universal suffrage made it possible for everyone to attain a political majority and thereby founded the first stage of citizenship, universal *qualification* will allow all to attain their wage majority and provide the basis for a qualitative extension of citizenship.

Part II

The Europeanisation of Employment and Wage Policies

European Pension Reforms

The Development of a Reform Rhetoric: 1993-2003

Corinne GOBIN

Senior Research Associate, Fonds National de la Recherche Scientifique, Université Libre de Bruxelles, Belgium

The European Community has been empowered to intervene in the field of retirement pensions since its very beginnings. Its initial role, in compliance with Article 15 of the Treaty of Rome, was to coordinate the social security regimes of the Member States and to organise the "portability" of social security entitlements in order to facilitate the free movement of workers within the Common Market. But the implementation of the Internal Market (White Paper "Completing the Internal Market", June 1985) opened the way for the European Commission to progressively develop a specific policy on pensions in keeping with the overall aim to liberalise the Member States' economies. The policy on the free movement of capital, enforced by Directive 88/361/EEC adopted by the Council on 24 June 1988, provided an avenue for the Commission to attempt to develop a capital market in the field of supplementary pensions; it drafted several directive proposals to this end in the 1990s, but came up against stiff opposition from France and Spain (Coron, 2003). It was not until June 2003 that it finally succeeded in getting a directive adopted to promote the development of funded occupational pension institutions (Directive 2003/41/EC). And, despite the financial crisis that hit Europe in October 2008, the promotion of private pension schemes remains a preferred option for the Commission. This is attested by its publication in 2010 of a booklet entitled "Private pension schemes – Their role in adequate and sustainable pensions", in which it associates the notion of "adequate" pensions with the development of private schemes.

We thus considered it important to revisit the ten-year period during which the Commission met with a succession of failures, in order to see how it developed an argumentation for reform that would then serve as a common discursive framework for the Member State governments.

This chapter is based on the results of an in-depth lexicological study of a French language corpus of the Broad Economic Policy Guidelines (BEPGs) conducted within the framework of the RESORE research project.[1] The methodology is presented in Section 1. Section 2 examines the most frequently occurring words in the corpus, and Section 3 focuses on a selection of 16 key words related to pension reforms. The conclusion summarises the political logics underpinning the reforms revealed by the lexicological analysis.

I. Hypothesis and Methodology

The general hypothesis I will develop here, drawing on over 20 years of observing how the Community political system operates, is that the process of European construction has led to a profound transformation of our national political systems, and that this has been achieved through an intense, continuous production of public policies since the introduction of the Single European Act. The national institutions of the Member States today have been linked up with EU institutions in such a way as to constitute a new political system governed by a transnational college[2] of policy-makers operating within a framework that gives primacy to European legal norms over all national sources of law. While European legal norms (such as the convergence criteria defined in the Growth and Stability Pacts) do not have the same binding nature, they nonetheless carry sufficient weight to generate tense transnational debates when a Member State strays from the set policies. This merging of national and EU systems has been noted in a particularly pertinent analysis by Wessels (1997). The idea of a "soft hegemony" exercised by a transnational system of European and national policy-makers over national systems, rather than by the Brussels Commission over the Member States, has begun to feature in some policy studies (see in particular Balme *et al.*, 2002, pp. 44-45). When Community policy-makers declare, "Economic and Monetary Union has been accompanied by a major regime change that can only succeed if all the principle economic policy actors take on new responsibilities" (BEPGs, 2001),[3] this corresponds to a statement of

1 The original RESORE report, Deliverable 33: "European discourses glossary on pension reform and employment reform", was a collective endeavour directed by C. Gobin, with N. Castel, R. Cusso, J.-C. Deroubaix, M. Robert, and M. Schirmann.

2 Based on a complex articulation between the European Commission, the Ministers convened for the Council, the Heads of State and Government meeting for the European Council, and the Executive Board of the European Central Bank. The European parliament can currently only play a relatively marginal role, and thus far has made extremely parsimonious use of its legislative veto.

3 Council Recommendation of 21 June 2002 on the broad guidelines of the economic policies of the Member States and the Community [Official Journal L 182 of 11.07.2002].

fact and not just a declaration of intent. An analysis of the discourse of this new political regime, whose central dynamic is monetary and economic (EMU), thus provides a particularly pertinent entry point to assessing the transformation of social policies. Our study shows that one of the major consequences of the far-reaching reforms undertaken by this new political system has been the deligitimation of the numerous trade union and public policy tools that previously contributed to furthering socio-political equality by creating institutions which were strongly protective of workers. The current political situation, where regulations on economic governance will allow national and European leaders to radically reduce the economic sovereignty of nation-states, is thus the outcome of an earlier, deep-seated transformation of state systems of public and social policy.

An analysis of the discourse of this new political regime, whose central dynamic is monetary and economic (EMU), thus provides a particularly pertinent entry point to assessing the transformation of social policies. Our study shows that one of the major consequences of the far-reaching reforms undertaken by this new political system has been the deligitimation of the numerous trade union and public policy tools that previously contributed to furthering socio-political equality by creating institutions which were strongly protective of workers.

For our study, we chose a corpus of the Broad Economic Policy Guidelines (BEPGs) for the period 1993 to 2003.[4] These texts, which are a direct outcome of the Maastricht Treaty, are highly representative of the collegial process used by the various European decision-making institutions in their efforts to give substance to Economic and Monetary Union (EMU). With the 1997 Treaty of Amsterdam, an explicit link subordinating social policy to the BEPGs was established, and this link was then reinforced in 2003 through the process aimed at "streamlining open coordination in the field of social protection".[5] It thus becomes difficult to study social policy without studying the content of these texts.

The research method adopted comprised an initial, overall analysis of the corpus using a lexicometric software programme.[6] Our hypothesis was that in recurrent institutional policy discourses (produced on an annual basis, for example), the frequency with which a word is repeated

4 The European Commission first expressed its desire to overhaul social protection in 1995 (COM (95) 466 final), and the June 2001 Council initiated the process of pension reform in Europe via the "OMC on pensions". The period examined permitted us to capture this particular time in the construction of the demand for reform.

5 See COM (2003) 261 final.

6 Lexico3, developed by SYLED-CLA2T, Université Paris 3; www.tal.univ-paris3.fr/lexico/lexico3htm.

takes on a particular symbolism when the aim is to define the main lines of a multiannual programme. The identification of the most frequently used words and the systematic, exhaustive study of their usage[7] thus makes it possible to draw out the major political logics that run through the texts. On the basis of this general context, we then singled out 16 keywords for in-depth study. Here, the choice of words was not based on frequency, but other criteria came into play: the selected words were either obvious, given the focus of the group research on the transformation of wage-based rights, and in particular, pension rights (*retraite*, *retraites*, *réforme*, *réformes*, *droits*, *droit*, *salaires*, *salaire*)[*]; or they carried a political and historical emotive power deriving from recurrent conflicts between executive powers and socio-professional organisations (*vieillissement*, *cotisation*, *cotisations*, *coûts*, *coût*, *répartition*, *capitalisation*, *prestations*). The method adopted was to study the variety of usages of each term (at the lexical, semantic and chronological levels) by analysing the close lexical context (sentences or syntagmas in which the term does or does not appear, verbs or nouns "attracted" by the term, etc.) and its broad semantic context (analysis of the content of the paragraph(s) in which the term occurs, and of the place where it appears in the text in relation to the overall logic of the statement). Given the total number of occurrences of these 16 words, 1,324 immediate and broader contexts were analysed,[8] we thus feel justified in considering that the bulk of European discourse on pension reform contained in the BEPGs was captured.

II. A General Approach to the BEPGs

Our corpus of 11 texts comprised 6,441 lexical forms[9] and 160,464 occurrences (see annex). The texts were of unequal length: the first BEPGs were very short, but the rise in the number of occurrences was

---

7 One of the most robust scientific aspects of this type of method is that it enables the researcher to establish an exhaustive list of the contexts in which high-frequency words or words chosen for the purposes of research are used. In this way, the full range of meaning of a word can be studied. It should be stressed, for those who are not familiar with lexicometric analysis, that reading a text through the systematic examination of lists of words breaks down the usual linear approach, and thus makes it possible to perceive linguistic phenomena that would otherwise rarely be spotted.

* Translations of the terms appearing in French in the text are provided at the end of the chapter.

8 It took three people from the GRAID research team at the Université Libre de Bruxelles (Roser Cusso, Corinne Gobin and Michaël Robert) six months to complete this task.

9 A lexical form corresponds to the graphic form. This means that the plural or feminine form of an adjective, for instance, generates a separate form to be counted (*petit*, *petite*, *petits*, *petites* = four lexical forms).

almost constant, with a striking upsurge starting in 1999. This corresponds to the year when the Treaty of Amsterdam came into force, and when the European System of Central Banks was launched with the introduction of a fixed parity in 11 countries marking the beginning of the passage to the single currency. From that year on, the documents included a systematic country-by-country evaluation of Member State policies. An examination of the 40 most frequent forms[10] provided a surprising result on two counts: the approach to programming the European economy was found to be essentially focused on *emploi* and *travail*; and the socio-political actors tended to be eclipsed in this type of economic discourse. Let us now look at this in more detail.

A. A Corpus Centred on Employment, Work, the Market and Growth

Because these texts grew directly out of the economic programme adopted at Maastricht, we expected to find the vocabulary linked to the problematic of "stabilising public finances" among the most frequent forms. It was indeed present, but not at the levels expected: *budgétaire*[11] (8th on the list), *publiques* (10th) *dépenses* (17th), *stabilité* (23rd), *finances* (36th) (see annex). On the other hand, at the top of the list, we found *emploi* (816 occurrences), *travail* (749 occurrences), *marché* (740 occurrences), *croissance* (720 occurrences). These four forms represented close to 2% of the vocabulary of the entire corpus! The most frequently mentioned line of economic reform thus concerned employment and work. Systematic examination of the usage of these four forms showed that they largely functioned in pairs: *emploi* was most frequently associated with *croissance* and *travail* with *marché*.

Emploi, the leading form in the corpus, was used extensively in expressions and sentences aiming at pushing the Member States to increase their employment rates (*taux d'emploi* = 141 occurrences). In addition, the forms *emploi* and *emplois* were very frequently found in connection with the notion of growth. Growth, it is said, will lead to job creation, and the employment rate will make growth possible. A circular lexical ballet is thus used to set the stage for implementing this virtuous circle, and under the effects of repetition, it becomes difficult to tell in

---

10 The number 40 was an arbitrary choice. In the present case, these 40 forms (see annex) represented 10% of all the words (nouns, articles, conjunctions, verbs, etc.) used in the corpus. In order to elicit the maximum amount of information on the semantic content of the corpus, only the "full" forms were retained for study, that is, after articles, prepositions, conjunctions and auxiliary verbs had been eliminated.

11 For the 474 occurrences, the segment *assainissement budgétaire* (budgetary stabilisation) was found 102 times, *discipline budgétaire* 23 times, *excédent budgétaire* (surplus) 11 times, *position budgétaire* 11 times, *ajustement budgétaire* 11 times…

the end what the actual goal is: growth for employment, or employment for growth?

The form *travail* most frequently attracted the notion of *marché*[12] (*marché du travail* = 373 occurrences, that is, slightly more than half the times *marché* appeared). *Emploi* strengthened the theme but was rarely used together with *marché* (*marché de l'emploi*, 16 occurrences). Generally speaking, the idea was to introduce measures to reform the "labour market" in order to increase employment rates and to respond to employers' demands for reforming this "market".[13]

An earlier lexicometric study of another EU text corpus – the presentations of each new European Commission's work programme to the European Parliament (1958-1999) – had revealed that a strong association between *travail* and *marché* first made its appearance in 1985 (starting with Jacques Delors' first speech, marking the launching of the single market programme), whereas the corpus contained no examples of *travail* associated with *marché* before 1985.[14] This signalled the opening up of a field of public action that would lead to a radical reform of the wage relation. With labour being reduced to a market subjected to reforms based on expert analyses, work has ceased to be described as a key sphere for the expression of social and political conflict, the formation of law, and collective negotiations and deliberations. Moreover, the hegemony of the expression *marché du travail* has become such that it seems justified to raise the question of the effect of its lexical circulation in the mass media. Is the word *travail* (work/labour) not being progressively emptied of all the political rallying power it acquired during the long history of union struggles? Can one fight for a better *labour market*? And how can a post-capitalist agenda's actors and prorammes be defined when the primary reference is a market? In traditional trade union discourse, it was easy to move from *work* to *workers*, that collective entity, that *world of work* united to obtain better *working conditions, labour law, and collective labour agreements* (Hetzel *et al.*, 1998). Today, it is the word *emploi* that seems to have taken on a positive connotation by virtue of its association with economic growth.

But can collective solidarity be constructed lexically through social demands that focus on jobs and employment? Ever since the end of the

---

12 Then, in order of frequency: *marché intérieur* (internal market) (108 occurrences), *marché unique* (single market) (46 occurrences), *marché du capital* (44 occurrences).

13 If we add the 40 occurrences of *marchés du travail*, it can be seen that for over 56% of its usage, *travail* is made to go with *marché* and *marchés*. The next most important syntagmas are *productivité du travail* (38 occurrences) and *offre de travail* (labour supply) (35 occurrences).

14 See Gobin, 2002. For a study of technocracy as the nature of the process of European construction since the EEC, see Gobin, 1997.

1970s, with the imposing of wage restraint and the steep rise in unemployment, union claims have concentrated on the need for job creation at the expense of fighting for a more equal redistribution of wealth (via a reduction in working time without wage loss, for instance). This shift in focus can be attributed to the rise to prevalence of the idea that industrial societies are facing a problem of declining resources ("growth is no longer strong enough…"). In line with the other international economic organisations, the EU has taken advantage of the social demand for jobs to deregulate working conditions and reduce both the direct and indirect components of the wage. Union demands for a more social Europe for more jobs have thus paradoxically accompanied the adoption of government policies that serve to reduce the wage share in GDP and heighten competition between workers. The focus on *emploi(s)* has also facilitated the ascendancy of a more individually-oriented reading of the world of work (through individualised career paths and target populations).

B. Eclipsing the Socio-political Actors

Those familiar with the lexicometric analysis of political discourse know that the particular terms belonging to the vocabulary used to identify socio-political actors generally feature among the most frequent forms. It is usually in the speakers' interest to repeatedly identify themselves as the source of the statements, and to indicate the precise group of interlocutors they are addressing. Surprisingly, then, the list of the 40 most frequent forms in the corpus leaves us in the dark as to who is formulating the economic guidelines addressed to the Member States. Who is speaking? No institutional name appears in the forms that top the list. On the other hand, the weight carried by the verb "should" (*devrait*, 5th place) is striking: the use of this modal auxiliary in the singular is reinforced by its plural (*devraient*, 29th place), so that the two taken together head the frequency list (879 occurrences). The examination of the usage of this verb shows that the overall style is that of a disguised command (softened by the conditional) or a false economic forecast (where the desired goal is presented as an existing trend). The way these verbs are used helps side-step the question of the political actor: either the Member State designated in the discourse is invited to follow a precise direction or, more frequently, the subject of the verb is a disembodied economic orientation.[15]

While political institutions are indeed designated, they rank fairly far down on the list, with the exception of *États* (12th place, 399 occurrenc-

[15] For example: "*…deficit public devrait tomber progressivement à zero d'ici 2004*" (public deficit should gradually drop to zero by 2004).

es).[16] In order of frequency, we find *UE* (56th place, 191 occurrences), *Union* (103rd, 141 occurrences), *Conseil* (107th, 130 occurrences), *Communauté* (119th, 124 occurrences), *gouvernement* (134th, 114 occurrences), *administrations* (154th, 105 occurrences), *autorités* (251st, 69 occurrences), and *Commission* (311th, 59 occurrences). Only *Commission* and *Conseil* (Council) are used in a way that treats them as the deciders of this programme, but their frequency is extremely low relative to the political weight they carry in the process of developing and executing the BEPGs. All the other forms are inserted in enunciative strategies (overuse of the passive voice and the verbal style of obligation; grammatical specialisation of these forms as complements of abstract nouns) which turn them into the passive subjects or objects of the policies to be implemented. Is it because the EU is equated to a market in these texts that the political actors appear so evanescent? The general impression created contributes to making the economic programme seem a natural and unproblematic procedure, one which apparently requires little debate but just needs to be applied.

In a context marked by an evanescent political actor, one might expect that a discourse focusing so insistently on the sphere of employment and work would use words designating the traditional actors of socio-economic life: employers' organisations, trade unions, and wage-earners. In our search for these designators, we were only able to find nine significant terms: *enterprises* (25th place, 299 occurrences), *travailleurs* (73rd, 168 occurrences), *main-d'œuvre* (92nd, 160 occurrences), *population* (93rd, 150 occurrences), *femmes* (187th, 92 occurrences), *partenaires* (218th, 80 occurrences), *personnes* (246th, 71 occurrences), *chômeurs* (375th, 50 occurrences), *jeunes* (392nd, 48 occurrences).[17] In examining their usage, we found no indication that the suggested orientations should be debated or negotiated with any of the groups concerned.

The analysis of the most frequently used term – *enterprises* – shows that European policies are designed to improve the environment in which companies operate. The idea conveyed is that businesses are victims of a rigid context and will only be able to become full actors after all the programmed reforms have been implemented.

The use of *travailleurs* corresponds to what was observed above with regard to *travail*. This form is caught up in an administrative logic of market management and loses its political value: it no longer signifies a

[16] The lexical form *membres* (Member) comes 14th on the list, and goes with *États* (States) (12th place).

[17] This list was obtained by the systematic examination of all terms that might designate an actor (institutions or groups of persons). We set a cut-off point at 45 occurrences, in order to avoid frequencies that were too low.

collective of wage-earners at work, capable of mobilising and asserting itself as an actor. Of the 168 occurrences of the word, 139 described categories of problematic target populations: 91 concerned workers between 55 and 65 years of age (*travailleurs âgés*, *travailleurs les plus âgés*, *travailleurs plus âgés*) and in the vast majority of cases, the focus was on increasing their employment rate by 2010; 12 concerned *travailleurs peu qualifiés*; and 11 described a series of problematic categories consisting of *femmes* and other workers. At lower frequencies, we found *travailleurs bénéficiant de contrats à durée indéterminée* (4 occurrences), *certaines catégories de travailleurs* (4 occurrences), *travailleurs frontaliers* (3 occurrences), *travailleurs faiblement rémunérés* (3 occurrences), *travailleurs non qualifiés* (3 occurrences), *travailleurs atypiques* (2 occurrences), *travailleurs à temps partiel* (2 occurrences), *travailleurs qualifiés* (2 occurrences), and *jeunes travailleurs* (2 occurrences). All these problematic categories seem to come in infinite variety, for they are also used in all the possible combinations with *jeunes*, *personnes*, *chômeurs*, *femmes*, *main d'œuvre.*[18] The impression created corresponds to the situation generally described in the sociology of work: the wage-earner status that had been achieved in the past through the open-ended employment contract has undergone a major fragmentation in the last 20-some years.

The overuse of categories of classification – or rather declassification – is a lexical strategy that serves to make the increasing diversity of precarious statuses appear even more marked: the various categories are presented as clear-cut and compartmentalized, whereas in reality, they often overlap (a person can be a young unemployed woman, or an older skilled female worker, etc.). This strategy of categorizing large numbers of target populations creates the impression that there are masses of people needing to be reintegrated into the labour market (which corresponds to the strategy to increase the employment rate), and that these people are not normal workers; this, in turn, given the need to integrate a problematic workforce, legitimates the various policies designed to reduce "labour costs" (reduced social contributions; wage restraint in collective negotiations; or part-time and temporary agency jobs).

The lexical form *partenaires* is essentially linked to the syntagma *partenaires sociaux* (in 72 out of 80 occurrences). Here too, as in the case of the form *États* and other institutions, labour and employer

[18] It may be noted that the form "*population*" is primarily caught up in three syntagmas: *le vieillissement de la population* (ageing of the population), *la population active* (active population) and *la population en âge de travailler* (working-age population). The latter two reflect the change in paradigm resulting from the focus on increasing the employment rate, with "working-age population" becoming the standard to the detriment of "active population".

organisations are invited to play a part in disseminating and applying the recommendations developed in the BEPGs, and more particularly, given the long-time role they have played in wage bargaining, to implement wage restraint. Once again, these are "constrained actors", with one of them being more so than the other, since the discourses make companies the beneficiaries of the programme, while the workers and their wage-earner status are the target of change.

III. Pension Reform Vocabulary

The lexical environment of the 16 forms selected – that is, the sentence within which they appeared and the preceding and following sentences – was explored systematically. Rather than using a word-by-word approach here, the results have been synthesised in order to examine in turn the arguments for reform, what is to be reformed, and the logic of reform.

A. Arguments for Reform: Ageing as a Problem

The reform arguments are essentially based on the "ageing" of the population. Examination of the form *vieillissement* (159 occurrences) shows that 93% of its usage was gathered around two syntagmas: *vieillissement de la population* and *vieillissement démographique*. Its frequency rose from a single occurrence in 1998, to 75 occurrences in 2003. This word was the only representative of the lexical family *vieillesse* (old age). The question of age was also used in the corpus to introduce the theme of mobilising the "working-age population", mainly via putting "older workers" back to work. Ageing is presented as a problem: it is argued that there are too many non-workers relative to the number of active workers. Thus, 75 occurrences of *vieillissement* were used to describe the problems induced by this social phenomenon. In 64 cases, the EU identified ageing as a budgetary problem. It is of interest to note that ageing is presented as a factor creating an overall imbalance of public finances; only 4 occurrences related it specifically to the financial imbalance of the social protection system. At a far lower frequency (8 occurrences), we find the question of a decrease in the size of the active population. Three further problems supposedly provoked by ageing were only touched on, each one indicated by a single occurrence: weaker economic growth; the effects on the level of aggregate savings; and hindering an increase in employment rates.

An overall examination of the contexts of the form *vieillissement* shows that these essentially serve to propose solutions to the "problem". The solutions are then presented as the key challenges facing the Member States. By playing on the three terms – problem, solution and challenge – the EU blurs the temporal perception of ageing, presenting it both as an immediate problem and as a major challenge for the future. The proposed solution hinges on transforming four major fields: the state budget, pension and health systems, the labour market, and the economy at the macro-economic level. This is indeed a programme for large-scale change.

1. Transforming Public Budgets (92 References)[19]

We have seen that the BEPGs primarily define ageing in terms of its negative impact on public finances. It is thus not surprising that the main remedy advocated is to transform public budgets. The bulk of the recommendations concern the need "to ensure the long-term sustainability of public finances in the face of population ageing". This sentence even becomes a subtitle in the 2003 BEPGs, and is repeated throughout the country-specific recommendations to the Member States. The call for stabilizing national public finances began with the Treaty of Maastricht and was presented at the time as a condition for entry into the single currency. However, after the introduction of the euro, it became necessary to set a new horizon to justify the call for pursuing these "efforts" to achieve "stabilisation". Demographic ageing then made its timely appearance. The lexical context of the form *vieillissement* that introduces the theme of the sound management (*gestion saine*) of public finances frequently refers to the guidelines set in the 1997 Stability and Growth Pact and updated in the annual reports on monetary stability. Little explanation is given on what exactly is meant by "sustainable public finances", since the Member States already know what the expression covers. However, the main line of argument can be reproduced here on the basis of the contexts that recall the key points: it is important to reduce public spending not only because an ageing population will lead to increased expenditure on pensions and health care, but also because the Member States must comply with the general requirement to reduce taxation. The EU thus encourages the Member States to reduce their public debt and achieve a budgetary surplus in order to offset the loss in revenue stemming from reduced taxation. This surplus may also be directed towards creating reserve funds for pensions. The emphasis is on the need to manage the public budget differently, and for a different relationship between the state and money, and between the state and collective resources, but the simple fact of bringing in new revenues to cope with rising expenditures on pensions is never mentioned. While reform is the issue, what is essentially being presented here is a reform

[19] The total number of references to the solutions listed exceeds the 159 occurrences of *vieillissement*; the sentence containing this word, as well as the following and preceding sentences were examined each time, and the solutions were also often intermingled in these sentences.

of the political philosophy of the state. And this kind of reform is as much a goal as it is a solution.

2. *Transforming pension and Social Protection Systems (54 References)*

The issue of ageing is essentially linked to pension reforms, but some occurrences indicate that the EU was also beginning to show an interest in public health care systems (3 occurrences) and to open the door to transforming the social protection system as a whole (4 occurrences). The contexts show that not only have pension reforms in Europe been underway for some years, but that most importantly, they are to be pursued. The immediate lexical context contained few instructions to the Member States as to the direction these reforms should take, but the objectives are of course influenced by the massive presence of the question of the sustainability of public finances along the lines outlined above. Thus, pension and health care systems are expected, above all, to be financially sustainable over the long term. And this theme of financial sustainability leads *de facto* to the idea of reducing expenditure. The suggestion to reduce pension levels was found in close proximity to the statements on pension reform. Social benefits, not only for pensions but more generally for the other social protection branches as well (health care, unemployment benefits) need to be reduced (15 references). The call for increasing the employment rate was also latched on to the theme of reducing social provisions. The conjunction of these three orientations – monitoring public budgets, monitoring social protection budgets, and promoting a higher employment rate – leads almost automatically to the general recommendation to raise the age of retirement (11 references). Two of these references opened the door to extending waged activity beyond the legal retirement age, although this was not stated in explicit terms (but by using expressions such as "active ageing").

3. *Increasing Employment Rates and Promoting Employment Incentives (40 References)*

The theme of labour market reforms is closely interconnected with that of pension reforms. Putting more people to work is the advocated solution both for coping with rising social protection expenditures and for limiting them (workers will access their pension benefits later and thus for less time). The idea is to provide incentives for the economically inactive to become active,[20] and under cover of the slogan "making work pay", to encourage them to choose a "less taxed" job over a situation of poorly remunerated "inactivity".

---

[20] The most targeted populations are housewives and older workers who are unemployed or have (been) retired early.

4. Economic Recovery (10 References)

The final theme introduced with the form *vieillissement* is the goal of macro-economic recovery. The focus here is largely on increasing productivity in order to maintain standards of living despite the increased expenditure generated by ageing populations. But this increased productivity is never considered as being enough in itself to be able to secure the financing of social protection schemes.

B. The Object of the Reforms

What we have seen emerging here is the call for wide-reaching reform of state public apparatuses, confirmed by the strong usage in the corpus of the words *réformes* (292 occurrences) and *réforme* (175 occurrences). The depth and extent of these reforms are clearly indicated by the expression *réformes structurelles*, used 75 times.

An examination of the context of *réforme(s)* reveals that the primary loci of reform are the systems permitting the constitution of public resources: taxation (*fiscalité*, 52 references) and social security (32 references), that is deductions and benefits (*prélèvements* and *prestations*, 36 references), with a pronounced stress on pensions (*retraite*, 44 references) and the labour market (*marché du travail*, 25 references), and to a lesser extent, the public sector in general (10 references). It is of interest to note that the notion of deductions (*prélèvements*, 41 references) is preferred to that of social contributions (*cotisations sociales*, 26 references). *Prélèvements* was most often accompanied by *prestations* and almost always in the phrase *systèmes de prélèvements et de prestations* (34 occurrences). The technical tone of this expression seems to be used to depoliticise the debate, while at the same time introducing a confusion between levying a tax and transferring a right to resources. We thus find that the lexical forms *salaire(s)*, *coût(s)* and *cotisation(s)*[21] are set in a similar semantic system: they represent a burden on enterprises and public finances and need to be reduced. Three major themes illustrate the topic of costs (113 references): the dominant theme was reducing labour costs (*réduction du coût du travail*, 56 occurrences), whether by reducing wages or what are called "non-wage" costs (*coûts non-salariaux*).[22] Then came the theme of reducing the costs weighing on public finances (18 occurrences), notably the *coût du vieillissement*; the third concerned the costs – seen as a burden weighing on enterprises –

---

21 For the purposes of brevity, the singular and plural forms have been grouped together here, but each form was processed separately in the study.

22 Thus 45 of the 81 occurrences of *coûts* focus on the need to reduce labour costs, and the syntagma *coûts salariaux* (wage costs) is found 24 times.

of implementing laws and administrative procedures (8 occurrences).[23] Note that the syntagma *coûts non salariaux* is used to designate social contributions, and thus presents these as a cost rather than a source of rights, and treats them as distinct from the wage whereas they constitute a crucial part of the socialised wage.

Examination of the contexts of *retraite(s)* (202 occurrences) confirms the structural nature of the reforms that are called for, since over half the occurrences (111) are attached to *système [*or *régime] de retraites* (pension system or scheme). The next most frequently occurring theme related to retirement, seen as constituting a problem and therefore necessitating reforms, is that of the premature withdrawal of workers from productive activity because of early retirement (28 references) or a retirement age that is considered too low (24 references).

C. Reform Logics

Two logics of pension reform run through the argumentation, following a binary good *vs.* bad code. The first is revealed by the examination of the contexts of the forms *droit(s)* (48 occurrences). According to this logic, there are "good" rights that should be strengthened and extended, and bad ones that need to be limited or reformed. Property rights and Community rights are to be strengthened and extended relative to national rights (positive reform). But national rights in general and social rights in particular – both of which are considered to be ill-adapted – must be limited and/or reformed (negative reform). The second logic is based on the opposition between types of pension systems, that is between funded and pay-as-you-go (PAYG) schemes. Examination of the contexts reveals that PAYG systems (*répartition*, 4 occurrences) are considered as fragile and requiring a complementary source of financing based on a different logic. In contrast, funding (*capitalisation*, 9 occurrences) is presented as a means of improving the "sustainability" of pension systems.

Conclusion: The General Reform Rhetoric

A more overall analysis of the main lines of BEPG rhetoric was undertaken by reconnecting all the contexts examined in the two preceding phases, and enlarging the focus beyond the neighbouring sentences to encompass the entire paragraph.

The heart of the general argument rests on the question of the production of collective resources. The postulate is that economic growth in Europe is too weak to meet the needs of development or to cope with

---

23 The remaining usages were scattered in numerous other topics, but none of these emerged as recurrent themes.

increasing social expenditures, notably pension rights which are considered as poorly adapted to the "ageing" of the population. The institutions ensuring the distribution of collective resources, it is argued, no longer satisfy the needs of companies, the State and wage-earners alike. This means that the EU must introduce a "new deal" in order to ensure that all possible resources will be directed at improving the competitiveness of companies, since the latter are capable of ensuring the best allocation of wealth. For, while work produces wealth, it is the entrepreneurs who are the most capable of increasing the value of this wealth, and it is they who must be at the centre of job creation. In short, insufficient wealth is being created, the economy needs to be reorganised around the creation of jobs by enterprises, and social policies must become tools for achieving this employment growth.

The examination of the forms *salaires*, *cotisations*, *coûts non salariaux*, and *prélèvements* shows that these terms are presented as factors impacting negatively on the distribution of resources because their "costs" put a strain on businesses' natural propensity to create jobs. "Moderating" these costs would make it possible to stimulate job creation, and limiting unemployment benefits would be an incentive for their recipients to seek employment. The goal of raising the employment rate, which is considered to be a key element in stimulating growth, calls for employment policy reforms directed at "activating" target groups (the long-term unemployed, women, young people, low-skilled workers). The idea being to improve their employability by: providing training programmes tailored to meet the "needs" of the market; reducing social contributions for newly hired employees (especially in the case of unskilled or low-paid workers); greater variations in wage levels based on productivity, individual qualifications and disparities in regional development; and a more flexible work organisation (notably more part-time jobs). The policy of monetary stability, which sets absolute priority on maintaining an extremely low level of inflation and thus affects the progression of wages, is another element contributing to this reorganisation of resources to the benefit of enterprises. The perception of wage-based rights as a cost makes it possible to present income taxation as being so high that it puts unbearable strains on companies' and people's capacity to take initiative. Consequently, social contributions (*cotisations*), which are called non-wage costs or designated by the preferred accounting term "deductions" (*prélèvements*) and are thus treated like a tax, need to be reduced for the benefit of all. The systematic lexical association of deductions and benefits plays into the same leitmotif of the need to reduce what are seen as a burden (*poids*), and this underpins the call for reducing contributions when unemployed and low-skill workers are hired.

Examination of the entry *vieillissement* (ageing) reveals the theatrical overtones of the discourse on the constraints facing the national state, that is, the political actor that has been at the heart of democratic control over resources since 1945. Retirement pensions and health care are treated as expenditures that will reach such high levels due to demographic ageing as to destabilise not only social protection systems but public finances as a whole. This opens the way for linking up this argument on the need to transform public finances, pensions, and social security in general, with the argument on the need to transform the labour market.

More specifically, these new demands regarding public finances and employment rates translate into: the call for reducing public pension, unemployment and health benefits; pressure to reduce early retirement opportunities; the call for introducing a stronger link between benefits and contributions paid; opening the way for the idea of extending waged employment beyond the legal retirement age or for increasing the latter; distrust of pay-as-you-go systems and encouraging reforms promoting funded schemes by creating a second pillar for pensions; demands for reforming educational structures so that they become vocational training providers responsive to the demands of the "market".

To use the words of Gilbert Rist (2002), the BEPGs come close to representing an ideal-type of the "formulaic style" used by large international organisations. Highly impersonalised (one does not know who is talking), they use a performative style, and employ highly repetitive, euphemised, stereotyped expressions where an accounting logic prevails. The tone is one of economic expertise (Cussó and Gobin, 2008): all trace of political debate has been evacuated and replaced by a call to implement what is presented as the only possible approach, in texts forming a political programme that is extremely stable but whose political actors are absent. The call for pension reforms made its first appearance in 1997. This coincides with the European Commission's second communication in the field, "*Modernising and improving social protection in the European Union*",[24] which presents its key idea that social protection must be seen as a productive factor and be more closely linked to employment policy. The call for limiting early retirement schemes appeared for the first time in 1999, and recommendations for monitoring and limiting health care expenditures in 2000. Then, to an increasing extent each year due to the Lisbon strategy, these themes

[24] COM (97) 102 final.

were to become incorporated into European policy via the open method of coordination.[25]

The requirement that public finances be stabilised in order to facilitate the massive transfer of collective resources to private sector enterprises (in reality to their shareholders), led national governments to adopt a vision of social relations close to employer positions – where rights are seen as costs. The expression "non-wage costs" thus serves to transform the earlier notions of "social contributions" and "benefits" and marks a shift from the right to remuneration and wage rights, to a constricting vision of a tax burden that weighs so heavily on businesses and workers alike that it needs to be reduced. But reducing taxation on income also reduces the autonomy of national governments to intervene in the economic and social fields. The rising power of the EU as the locus of control over monetary sovereignty and thus of sovereignty over the allocation of resources overall, translates concretely into the separation of rights into two spheres (as seen above with respect to pension rights). The result is a clear divide in public policy: developing binding laws at EU level that strengthen profit-making property rights is viewed positively, whereas national social rights instituted before EMU are stigmatised and earmarked for reform.

This brings us to what now clearly stands out as the key word in the corpus: *réforme*. Each entry word leads directly to a demand for the far-reaching reform of one of the elements structuring the production, capture, political control or redistribution of collectively produced resources. When linked together, these multiple demands add up to a vast programme to bring about a change in political regime through an administrative process (via the open method of coordination) applied by the Member States: reforming public finances, reforming transfer systems, reforming wage formation systems, reforming labour markets, reforming social protection systems, and reforming educational structures.

The explicit interaction between all these demands for reforming the public sphere means that we are not dealing with timely, short-term policies but with a full political agenda to substantially modify the Member States' former modes of operation. Under the guise of "govern-

[25] The Lisbon Summit (2000) set an agenda for the reforms to be introduced in the Member States via the open method of coordination (OMC), a strategy used for planning the national reforms to be included in government programmes for the major social fields (employment, social inclusion, pensions, health care, environment) to make the EU the world's most competitive economy and to organise full employment in the EU. The 2005 revised version of this strategy heightened the subordination of all the social domains to the BEPGs and grouped these calls for reform in a single tool: the National Reform Programmes (NRPs).

ance" – or adapting governmental and administrative structures to meet the goal of efficient management (i.e. reducing expenditures) – national political systems are being transformed in the absence of a democratic political debate. What is being called into question is not only the legitimacy of social rights, and their future extension, but the legitimacy of a public authority to redistribute resources more equitably. In light of this, the concept of "resource regimes" as an angle of approach to analysing the current transformation of public action becomes all the more pertinent.

We have seen here that the years 1993-2003 were central to the production of a discourse aimed at shaping the economies of the Member States and to the honing of the reform argumentation. This look back in time reveals how carefully the terrain was prepared for the current "economic governance". Today's "new governance" is not simply a pragmatic response to the financial crisis. On the contrary, the latter has merely provided a window of opportunity for increasing the technocratic control over national public finances that, as illustrated by the argument on the sustainability of pension expenditures, was already well underway.

Annexes

Table 1. Distribution of lexical forms in the corpus sections (French corpus)

Section	*Number of occurrences*	*Number of forms*
GOPE 1993	2541	765
GOPE 1994	2827	797
GOPE 1995	3890	975
GOPE 1996	3519	952
GOPE 1997	5401	1205
GOPE 1998	8417	1614
GOPE 1999	16142	2259
GOPE 2000	22394	2750
GOPE 2001	32230	3213
GOPE 2002	30892	3127
GOPE 2003	32211	3162

GOPE: Grandes Orientations de Politique Économique – the French-language Broad Economic Policy Guidelines (BEPGs)

Table 2. The 40 most frequent forms in the French-language BEPG corpus (1993-2003)

Frequency	*Form*	*Rank*
816 times	emploi	1
749	travail	2
740	marché	3
728	croissance	4
597	devrait	5
586	taux	6
508	mesures	7
474	budgétaire	8
462	oeuvre	9
434	publiques	10
424	marches	11
399	états	12
399	politiques	13
391	membres	14
378	chômage	15
376	niveau	16
373	dépenses	17
373	PIB	18
358	économique	19
344	concurrence	20
344	politique	21
331	améliorer	22
313	stabilité	23
305	terme	24
299	entreprises	25
295	notamment	26
293	économie	27
292	réformes	28
282	devraient	29
279	compte	30
266	particulier	31
263	années	32
262	efforts	33
255	encore	34
250	salaires	35
247	finances	36
242	investissement	37
242	prix	38
237	renforcer	39
236	économiques	40

Table 3. Frequency of lexical forms related to pension reform

Lexical Forms	Number of occurrences in the corpus
réforme(s)	467
salaire(s)	257
retraite(s)	212
vieillissement	159
coût(s)	113
droit(s)	48
prestations	41
cotisation(s)	27
capitalisation	9
répartition	4

French-English vocabulary list (for terms not translated in the text)

autorités	authorities
budgétaire	budgetary
capitalisation	funding
certaines catégories de travailleurs	certain categories of workers
chômeurs	the unemployed
communauté	community
conseil	council
cotisation(s)	social contribution(s)
coût(s)	cost(s)
croissance	growth
dépenses	expenditure(s)
droit(s)	right(s)
emploi	job, employment
états	states
femmes	women
jeunes	young people
jeunes travailleurs	young workers
main-d'œuvre	workforce
marché	market
partenaires sociaux	social partners
prestations	benefits
publiques	public
réforme(s)	reform(s)
répartition	pay-as-you-go
retraite(s)	pension(s)
salaire(s)	wage(s)
stabilité	stability
travail	work, labour
travailleurs	workers
travailleurs âgés	older workers
travailleurs les plus âgés	the oldest workers

travailleurs plus âgés	older workers
travailleurs peu qualifiés	low-skill workers
travailleurs bénéficiant de contrats à durée indéterminée	workers with open-ended contracts
travailleurs frontaliers	cross-border workers
travailleurs faiblement rémunérés	low paid workers
travailleurs non qualifiés	unskilled workers
travailleurs atypiques	atypical workers
travailleurs à temps partiel	part-time workers
travailleurs qualifiés	skilled workers
UE	EU
vieillissement	ageing
vieillissement démographique	demographic ageing
vieillissement de la population	ageing of the population

How Community Interventions Converge to Bring about a Shift in Resource Regimes

The Example of Pension Reforms

Gaël CORON

Associate researcher, Laboratoire Lorrain de Sciences Sociales, Université de Lorraine; member of the Institut Européen du Salariat

Bernard FRIOT

Emeritus Professor, University of Paris Ouest Nanterre; member of the Institut Européen du Salariat

What are pensioners? Pensioners are people who receive money while working freely – "freely" in the sense that they define the means and ends of their work. This simple observation instantly reveals the considerable social stakes that pensions represent: paying a free (non-subordinated) worker clearly subverts an organisation of labour that is overwhelmingly based on subordination. It is an invitation to read the current pension reforms appearing throughout the European Union in terms of a political conflict, whereas the very way the EU functions not only tends to depoliticise the issue, but also to treat it in terms of a self-evident "demographic problem".

However, nothing is less self-evident than this "demographic problem", since its existence depends how pensioners' free work is defined. Is this work simply useful work that only produces use values? Or does it also produce economic value? In the latter case, the question of a demographic problem does not arise, because pensioners produce the economic value that corresponds to the pensions distributed. But this central point is never the subject of debate: for the reformers and those whose ideas they follow, it is "obvious" that retirees are useful, but not productive people, just like women. They will only be productive if they are put back into employment.

Let us take the example of the introduction to the Joint Report on Pensions of November 2010,[1] which looks back on "a decade of pension reform in the EU":

> The projected increase in public spending due to population ageing poses an important challenge to EU Member States. [...] Recognizing the progress, the challenge of adapting the pension systems in some of the EU Member States to expected demographic changes is still very real. Additional reforms of pension policy will be needed in several countries. Furthermore, there are signs that ongoing reforms might bear considerable risks in terms of both adequacy and sustainability. As changes in pension systems will tend to make benefits more contingent on developments in labour and financial markets, important risks relate to employment rates not increasing enough or capital markets not delivering as expected. Budgetary consolidation, which is more urgent after the economic crisis, is essential in order to reduce public debt and to contribute to financing the future increase in public pension expenditure.

This reference to "population ageing", as we see, functions as a *fatum* which dictates the need for pension schemes to be evermore closely tied to the labour market (by increasing the employment rate) and the capital market (by increasing retirement savings); and these markets, far from providing a solution, are described by their promoters as bearing greater risks of inefficiency, which in turn can only be solved by administering more of the same toxic remedy. Then, 2007 miraculously added a second *fatum*: the economic crisis, a miracle produced by that "essential" budgetary consolidation, makes it even more urgent to deal with population ageing by further pursuing the growth of the employment rate and retirement savings, and thus by exposing pension schemes to even greater risks, which can only be dealt with by more of the same treatment ... If bleeding fails to kill the patient, it means the disease is more serious than was thought, and "additional reforms of pension policy will be needed". Because "lower growth prospects and increasing deficit and debt affect sustainability. Regarding adequacy, today's pensioners have generally been well-protected against the crisis, but pensions may be affected by unemployment periods and lower contributions and poorer returns in financial markets." In case the message has not come through clearly enough, it is immediately spelled out again: "This implies that there will be an unprecedented need for coordinated fiscal consolidation." Which will once again increase labour and capital market risks, and thus heighten the urgency of tying pension schemes even more tightly to these markets. This is reiterated in the opening

---

[1] European Commission, Directorate-General for Economic and Financial Affairs, *Progress and key challenges in the delivery of adequate and sustainable pensions in Europe*, Occasional Paper 71, November 2010, pp. 5-7.

sentences of the 2012 White Paper, An agenda for adequate, safe and sustainable pensions:[2] "An ageing population presents a major challenge to pension systems in all Member States. Unless women and men, as they live longer, also stay longer in employment and save more for their retirement".

Note that in this forging ahead down the same path – which turns out to be the core of the "agenda" – the idea of "safety" has been added to the notions of adequacy and sustainability, the two declared ambitions of the reforms until then.[3] Labour and capital market risks are so obvious today that linking pensions even more tightly to these markets will make them more secure: suffice it to believe in the *urgency* of applying the policy recommended in the White Paper, which "reflects these common concerns [...] by creating the conditions for a high level of labour force participation of women and men throughout their lives and enhancing the opportunities to build up safe complementary retirement savings."

For, indeed, these reforms are an attempt to restore the capitalist convention of labour: here, the only activities which have economic value are those dedicated to producing commodities and performed by the supply of labour power on the labour market in order to valorise capital; all other activities are merely useful, and the possibility of their social recognition would weigh on labour market actors and the accumulation of capital. The incessant repetition that there is no salvation outside of these two key institutions of capital – the labour market and financial accumulation – describes *a contrario* what reformers are actually attacking by invoking the *fatum* of the demographic problem and public debt: namely, pension schemes which subvert these institutions by paying a life-time wage to pensioners who thus no longer need the mediation of the labour market to produce economic value; and which, by financing it exclusively through the socialisation of the wage in social contributions, prove the uselessness of financial accumulation.

In order to understand this conflict between two conventions of economic value (and thus of labour), it is necessary to analyse both the forms of money involved (the expression of the value attributed to work) and the types of work entitled to a pension. A pension that provides a lifelong return on financial savings (form of money) to a retiree who, at the age of 67 and after a long career of subordinated work, has earned the right to leisure (type of work), does not subvert the institutions of capital, unlike a pension that is the continuation, from the age of 60, of the final wage (form of money) of a retiree who is accepted, if not

[2] COM (2012) 55 final; Introduction (p. 2-3).

[3] See the title of the first Joint Report, 2003: *Adequate and Sustainable Pensions.*

defined, as a free worker (type of work). The former reinforces financial accumulation while establishing subordinated labour as the only form of work entitled to remuneration, whereas the latter disconnects the wage from subordinated labour while resisting the financial sphere. Between these two extremes, we find a range of pension forms that run the gamut from the subordination to the emancipation of labour, and from sustaining to challenging the accumulation of capital. This chapter will analyse these modes of retirement pension using the "resource regimes" framework presented in Chapter 1, and paying particular attention to the articulation between the variables of "forms of money" and "type of work".

The pension reforms introduced in Europe since the 1990s will be interpreted here in terms of shifts in resource regimes. To this end, we will examine the instruments used by the European Union (EU) that serve to define the cognitive and institutional framework shaping these reforms. In the last decades, the EU has extended its interventions in the field of pensions well beyond its traditional policy of coordinating migrant workers' pension schemes. These instruments include European Court of Justice case law; the Directive on Institutions for Occupational Retirement Provision (IORP) that was under discussion from 1990 to 2003; the open method of coordination (OMC) applied to pensions since 2001; and the 2005 reform of the Stability and Growth Pact, reinforced since 2007 by the provisions for EU control over Member State budgetary deficits. The use of this wide range of tools stems from the fact that, since pensions do not fall within EU competence, Community intervention is exercised via other fields that do, such as the internal market, monetary policy, or employment. The EU also uses a non-binding approach, by promoting "best practices" based on reference systems that are unremittingly constructed in consensual processes. We will show that in resource regime terms, all these instruments pursue the common objective of reducing the socialised wage and public service regimes in favour of the deferred wage, tutelary allowance or wage-earner savings.

I. Setting up a Single Market for Occupational Pensions

The first interventions undertaken by the European institutions were aimed at establishing a European market for pension funds, based on the application of the economic freedoms written into the treaties. Since they had no power to intervene directly on Member States' pension schemes, the Community authorities proceeded to develop a conceptual framework which enabled them to define these schemes as constituting a public "first pillar" to be completed by a "second pillar" of funded occupational schemes. Since funded schemes fall under the single capital market and thus within Community competence, this would then make it possible to exert pressure on national schemes.

From the beginning, the idea was to achieve this aim by means of a binding Community document permitting the creation of pan-European pension funds (that is, pension funds operating at EU level within a specific legal framework). The first attempt to draw up a proposal, however, met with reservations on the part of the Member States and made such slow progress that the initial ambitions had to be toned down and the scope of the text reduced. Incentives for funded schemes re-appeared in other fields of EU intervention (such as the Stability and Growth Pact, as will be seen below).

A. The Restrictive Conceptual Framework of the "Three Pillars"

In 1990, the Directorate General for the Internal Market (DG MARKT) of the European Commission clearly expressed its intention to obtain approval for a directive on pension funds that would be based on both the free movement of capital and the freedom to provide services. The "three pillars" approach, which is also used by the World Bank, appears in a working paper on the directive proposal drafted that year. This intellectual construction is essential because it provides a common cognitive framework for all the EU actors despite its ambiguous status. Is it a description of national realities, or a performative project acknowledged as such? The first hypothesis is not tenable. For it must be noted that, as a political project, the three-pillar theory raises two essential issues: firstly, with regard to accumulation (what is the role of financial markets in social protection?) and secondly, with regard to the regulatory actor (how to apportion power between the EU and the Member States?)

In order to explain this framework, the DG MARKT document began by dividing pension systems into three categories:

- social security systems;
- occupational or employment-linked supplementary systems;
- private systems for optional individual retirement provision.

Although the Commission acknowledged that this division was difficult to apply, it asserted that it was valid throughout Europe and that it would be used to define the scope of the proposal ("The present document will deal with the second pillar and in particular, financial institutions other than insurance firms which provide private employment-linked retirement benefits to individuals or groups". European Commission, 1990, p. 2). Moreover, in the rest of the paper, as in subsequent documents, the Commission presented advanced funding as one of the defining features of the second pillar. This shift is particularly noticeable in connection with the French AGIRC and ARRCO schemes ("Recourse to this system (i.e. PAYG) for private pensions is essentially limited to France […] In fact, these schemes will be considered more as an extension of the social security system than as a component of the second pillar." European Commission, 1990, p. 6). The importance of the definition of the second pillar is also linked to the issue of the legal competence of EU institutions. Social security and social protection fall within Member State competence (and the final text took the precaution of re-asserting this principle, together with the freedom for Member States to choose between PAYG or funded schemes). The European Commission, on the other hand, has competence to ensure compliance with the economic freedoms guaranteed in the Treaties establishing the European Union. The division into "pillars" introduced by DG MARKT and the definition given to the second pillar were designed to bring private pensions into its field of competence.

Beyond this, the terms of the debate (State or Community competence; choice of financial manager; or the prudential level required for the safeguard of pensions) tend to disqualify and exclude the actors traditionally responsible for managing pension systems in most countries (mainly trade unions and employers' associations). They also imply that the choice to develop funded schemes has already been made, while claiming that Community initiatives remain neutral with regard to this preliminary, key question.

B. Initial opposition from Member States and Financial Institutions

In a speech delivered in 1990, European Commissioner Leon Brittan noted that British pension funds held one-third of the London Stock Exchange, and stressed that the single financial market could not be completed without integrating supplementary pensions. However, this ambitious plan was to meet with considerable opposition from Member States and certain financial players.

Four issues served to crystallise Member State opposition:

- The development of pan-European pension funds would mean intervening in fiscal policy – an area that requires unanimous Council approval – to create a harmonised context favourable to the development of these funds;
- National administrations wished to safeguard certain prudential rules that the Commission viewed as infringements of competition law;[4]

[4] In other words, an incentive to acquiring national stocks.

- Some Member States wished to safeguard mechanisms for compulsory membership of supplementary schemes (often written into collective agreements). Countries with an extensive insurance sector and limited pension fund industry were concerned that their insurance industry would risk facing unfair competition (see below);
- If European pension funds were to be allowed, Member States wanted to obtain a mechanism for the prior authorisation of institutions seeking to operate in their territories.

Within the financial services sector, the Commission's proposal was also seen as clashing with certain interests:

- Insurance companies were initially concerned about possible competition between individual and group products. This position was largely attributable to the fact that the Commission proposed more flexible prudential rules for occupational pensions than those existing for life insurance companies, which were already coordinated at EU level (non-life, life Directives);
- Some pension funds were opposed to a purely market regulation of occupational pensions. Particularly those operating defined-benefit schemes that had often been set up via collective agreements and were co-managed by trade unions and employers' associations (usually at sectoral rather than enterprise level).

C. Failure of the First Attempt and Success of the Second Attempt

A first phase, which lasted from 1990 to 1997, ended in the proposal being rejected.

The Commission had sought to anticipate Member State opposition, and the proposal could thus appear as falling short of Leon Brittan's initial ambitions. Above all, it was presented as aiming solely to apply the treaties. The main points were thus linked to the economic freedoms that form the basic framework of the single market:

- The freedom to provide services should also apply to the employer/pension fund relationship. Employers paying contributions for their employees' pensions should thus be able to choose a pension fund anywhere in the EU.
- The freedom to provide services should benefit pension fund managers. Pension funds must be free to choose asset managers anywhere in the Union;
- The free movement of capital should apply to pension-related assets. The Commission wanted to prevent Member States from maintaining restrictions on the choice of assets that were not

strictly proportional to prudential goals (for instance, compulsory investment in government bonds, and currency matching requirements).

Although the proposal presented in 1995 only included the first two freedoms, it was rejected by the Council, where the discussion crystallised around the question of currency matching requirements. France, in particular, sought to protect its insurance industry and demanded alignment with Insurance Directive rules (an 80% currency matching requirement). The Commission felt that this would completely change the nature of its proposal, and preferred to withdraw it. However, it then presented a virtually identical text in the form of a Communication. The French and Spanish governments referred the matter to the Court, which ruled in their favour, considering that the Commission had overstepped its sphere of competence.[5]

Shortly after this failure, the Commission launched a new cycle with a view to adopting a directive. In order to obtain the agreement of the Member States, it had to make two major concessions:

- The insurance companies were able to obtain the possibility of entering the market without having to set up specific subsidiaries.[6] The only requirement was that they establish a separate balance sheet for their occupational pension activities. They thus ceased to oppose the proposal;
- Taxation was removed from the scope of the Directive and dealt with in a separate Communication. As will be seen later, the question of taxation would be reintroduced via amendments to the Stability and Growth Pact.

The process was finalised in May 2003, after Member States gained increased control over the IORPs. The key principles obtained by the new proposal were as follows:

- For the first time, the division into pillars was explicitly integrated into Community law;
- The directive defined IORPs, and established the distinction between an IORP and the sponsoring enterprise that pays contributions for its employees (the two are established separately);

5 A Communication, as an incentive instrument, theoretically has no legal value. However, the text included mandatory targets with precise figures which created obligations from Member States. The Commission's argument was that the text did not create a law, it only provided an interpretation of the treaties. What the Court censured in its ruling was not the policy guidelines or the extensive nature of the interpretation, but the fact that its monopoly on interpreting the treaties was being challenged.

6 However, in the final text, this was left as an option for host Member States.

- All European IORPs are subject to a set of rules and the obligation to obtain authorisation from their home Member State, or be monitored by the latter. They are obliged to communicate certain information to their members. Above all, they are subject to asset investment rules. The approach adopted is said to be qualitative since, the document claims, it has proven its ability to obtain better returns in the countries where it has been implemented. IORPs are thus required to invest in accordance with the "prudent person" rule;
- An additional set of rules applies to cross-border activities. Before engaging in cross-border activity, the IORP must obtain prior authorisation from its home State.[7] The host State must inform the competent authorities in the home State of the requirements of social and labour law relevant to the field of occupational pensions under which the pension scheme must be operated. Then, if there is a breach of social legislation, and no action is taken to redress the situation, "the competent authorities of the host Member State may, after informing the competent authorities of the home Member State, take appropriate measures to prevent or penalise further irregularities, including, insofar as is strictly necessary, preventing the institution from operating in the host Member State for the sponsoring undertaking" (Article 20).

Transposing the Directive was not an easy matter, and several Member States, including France, failed to meet the deadline of 23 September 2005. Given the situation, in October of that year the French senate authorised the government to act by ordinance. However, this did not prevent the Commission from delivering a reasoned Opinion[8] against France on 19 April 2006 for non-transposal of the IORP Directive. More generally speaking, although this directive does not appear to have had a massive direct effect thus far, it illustrates the Commission's determination to promote legal instruments for a funded transnational scheme; these instruments, which it controls in the name of the primacy of Community competition law, are used to exert pressure on public systems and for the patient construction of an alternative framework to

[7] The terms "home" and "host" Member State are defined in Article 6 as follows:
'home Member State' means the Member State in which the institution has its registered office and its main administration or, if it does not have a registered office, its main administration;
'host Member State' means the Member State in whose social and labour law relevant to the field of occupational pension schemes is applicable to the relationship between the sponsoring undertaking and members.

[8] Second step towards referral to the ECJ to initiate proceedings for failure to fulfil obligations.

national PAYG schemes whose stagnation is programmed in the name of the "sustainability" of pension benefits. For example, the 2010 Joint report (page 23) declares, "Presently funded schemes only play a significant role in a few Member States. But as newly introduced schemes mature they are set to play a major role in the incomes of futures pensioners in many countries across the Union"; it then produces a figure predicting that by 2048 most countries will see the share of funded schemes in total gross replacement rates reach proportions ranging from 20 to 50%. Even if these predictions correspond to a form of self-persuasion, it is extremely significant that the documents produced at EU level since 2007 – such as the 2010 Green Paper[9] or the 2012 White Paper – focus much of their discussion on legal devices for "developing complementary private pension savings", despite the fact that they have to admit to the vulnerability of funded pension schemes.

Key dates for the IORP Directive

1990: Speech by Leon Brittan (European Commissioner for the Internal Market); Working Document

1991: The Commission drafts a Directive Proposal on the activities of Institutions for Occupational Retirement Provision (IORPs)

1993: Opinion of the European Parliament

1994: The Council rejects the Directive Proposal; Adoption of the Communication

1995: Complaint lodged by France and Spain

1997: The ECJ annuls the Communication; Green Paper on supplementary pensions in the single market, and summary of the responses

2000: The Commission draws up a new Directive Proposal on the activities of Institutions for Occupational Retirement Provision (IORPs)

2001: Discussion in the European Parliament

2002: The Council adopts a policy position

2003: Second reading by the European Parliament; Final adoption by the Council

However, the insurance industry has continued to demand that the "distortion of competition" in favour of pension funds come to an end. The revision of the IORP Directive, postponed until 2013 after the phase of public consultations launched in 2012, will be the scene of a new showdown. For, in terms of the institutional agenda, this revision will

9 Green Paper towards adequate, sustainable and safe European pension systems COM(2010) 365 final 07 2010.

coincide with the application (notably to the insurance industry) of the Solvency II rules.[10] These significantly raise the prudential obligations laid down in the Insurance directives. The suggestion put forward by the European Insurance Committee (EIA) – which the Commission appears to have accepted – is thus to subject IORPs to the same constraints as those included in Solvency II.

To conclude: the extension of the second pillar cannot rest solely on a scaled-down IORP directive. The Commission's plans have come up against disagreements between market actors, and opposition from Member States seeking to defend their national financial industry. However, an invaluable "window of opportunity" has been provided by the legal constraints included in the 2005 Stability and Growth Pact and reinforced since 2007, notably with the new EU budgetary deficit rules that followed in the wake of the action taken to save bank shareholders, as will be seen in Part III. We have, here, the political strategy described in the introduction to this chapter. The very failure of capitalism is being used to strengthen its positions. The following passage from the 2012 White Paper (p. 14) can be cited – among so many others! – to attest to the headlong rush down the same path that has been at the core of Community policy since 2007:

> The crisis has highlighted the vulnerability of funded pension schemes to financial crises and economic downturns. It has also emphasised the need to review the regulatory framework and scheme design to improve the safety of private pensions. The EU has legislative competences in this area [...]. The Green Paper consultation has confirmed that the Single Market is a key instrument to support pension adequacy and fiscal sustainability. There is untapped potential to realise further efficiency gains through scale economies, risk diversification and innovation. [...] This is why the IORP Directive will be reviewed with the aims of further facilitating the cross-border activity for IORPs and modernising their supervision.

These amounts to saying: over the past 20 years, we have constructed a single market for pension funds and created a legal framework for large-scale cost cutting, diversifying risks, innovation, cross-border activities and modern supervision. The crisis has shown that all this is vulnerable, and that the design and regulatory framework of these funds needs to be revised. We will thus speed up the pace of large-scale cost cutting, risk diversification, innovation, cross-border activities and modernising supervision.

---

[10] Directive 2009/138/EC, that codifies and harmonises EU insurance regulation, scheduled to come into effect on 1 January 2014.

II. The Open Method of Coordination on Pensions: an Attempt to Preclude the Emancipation of Work

Initiated at the time of the Lisbon "social turning point", the open method of coordination (OMC) was launched with two goals at the institutional level:

- To construct a common vision for European institutions, in situations where the fragmentation of competences sometimes resulted in contradictory interventions (construction of an internal market for pension funds, reduction of pension expenditures, or defence of a social model);
- To produce common observations and tools for comparison in order to direct the Member States towards the most suitable reforms. From this point of view, rather than being a self-realising prophecy, the OMC looks very much like an incentive to do what has already been done – in other words, to continue and even intensify reforms based on policies that have been implemented at national level. This makes it very difficult to assess the effectiveness of the process itself, but it has undeniably provided support for national reformers thanks to the construction of an international argumentation and the statistical tools to back it up; in the course of incessant meetings and exchanges between national experts and politicians, these mutually reinforcing arguments and statistical instruments are progressively established as the exclusive frame of reference.

In 2001, the OMC was extended to pensions (henceforth referred to as the pensions OMC) as part of the OMC on social protection and social inclusion, or the "social OMC". The pension reforms promoted by the pensions OMC pursue two goals (2003 Joint Report): increasing the employment rate of the population over 60 years of age (in particular by raising the retirement age), and increasing complementary retirement savings. To quote the two opening sentences of the 2012 White Paper: "An ageing population presents a major challenge to pension systems in all Member States. Unless women and men, as they live longer, also stay longer in employment and save more for their retirement, the adequacy of pensions cannot be guaranteed as the required increase in expenditure would be unsustainable."

We have here, in a nutshell, all the key words of the pensions OMC: ageing as a threat; employment rate; retirement savings; adequate pensions; unsustainable expenditures if future pension benefits are not made adequate and *vice versa*. The term "adequate" warrants clarification: it implies a change in the meaning of pensions, since their aim is no longer to replace the wage, but to ensure a decent income for retirees.

The central issue here is to replace subversive pension forms, and in particular the Bismarckian model of the pension as the continuation of the wage based on the socialisation of the latter in social contributions, with forms that comply with the valorisation of capital, that is, a contributory deferred wage, a minimum benefit based on national solidarity, and retirement savings We will examine the following five key OMC proposals, and analyse the shift in resource regimes that they engender:

- Increasing employment rates for the over 55 and raising the retirement age;
- Reducing the role of first pillar PAYG public pension schemes;
- Making pensions more contributory;
- Increasing the role of funded occupational pensions (in order to maintain pensioners' buying power that the two preceding proposals serve to erode);
- Strengthening the redistributive role of the first pillar in order to make it an effective tool for combating poverty.

A. *Increasing Employment Rates for the over 55 and Raising the Retirement Age*

The pensions OMC justifies this proposal in the name of the long-term sustainability of pension schemes, using an endlessly repeated demographic argument which only has meaning if pensioners' activity, albeit useful, is seen as not producing economic value. This is the case in the capitalist convention of value, where only profit-generating activities produce value because they are executed by labour power recruited on a labour market and used by company owners. In this convention, pensioners do not work (nor, for that matter, do civil servants): the use-values they produce are not coupled with economic value. But this convention is challenged by another, which we describe as wage-based,[11] and where the main institutions are the *qualification system* (applied to the post in private sector "employment", or to the person in the civil service "grade"), and social contributions. Qualification marginalises the labour market, and social contributions show that financial accumulation is not needed to finance such long-term commitments as pension benefits. It would be possible to generalise the qualification of persons in a life-long qualification-based wage for all from 18 years of age. And to transpose the model of social contributions to an economic contribution to finance investments by pooling value-added, without going through the unnecessary step of profit and credit.

[11] For an analysis of the conflict between these capitalist and wage-based conventions see Bernard Friot, 2012.

The Bismarckian tradition, by constructing pensions as a continued wage pooled in social contributions, attributes a qualification to retiring wage-earners (that is, to the person and no longer to their post). By virtue of their life-long wage, they are defined not simply as producers of use-values but as producers of economic value. In short, in this system, pensioners reinforce the wage-based convention of labour.

Century-long struggles over wages in our countries have resulted in the non-market monetary recognition of products of labour that were not previously assigned value. This is overwhelmingly the case for pensioners' work, which has always existed but which has only been assigned value since the wide-spread provision of pensions at levels approaching those of wages. In other words, if the share of pensions in GDP has increased from 5 to 12%, it is not because the subordinated labour of the "economically active" has produced an increasing value from which it has been possible to tap the wherewithal to pay the "inactive", but because the recognition of the already-existing work of pensioners has been raised to a 12% share of GDP thanks to conflicts over wages and taxes. And in our societies that enjoy a long life expectancy, is it not perfectly natural that pensioners' increasing share of the products of labour be translated into an increasing share of pensions in GDP? Pensions are not levied on the value produced by the "working population", as in a naturalised perception of capitalist value – they are based on the product of the work performed by pensioners themselves.

This immediately does away with the demographic argument that pollutes any thinking about the future of pensions. And opens the way for extending the happiness of being paid for emancipated work to the whole of society. Why indeed should emancipated work not be paid before age 60?

The ruling class finds this large-scale social experience of the recognition of free work alarming indeed, and either strives to define retirement as a time of leisure, or attempts to turn it into a new time for subordinated labour by raising the retirement age.

In 2003, the first Joint Report of the Commission and the Council in response to the initial national plans of action for pension reform stressed that retirement is a time of leisure that comes as a reward after a long life of work: as retirees, pensioners are and must remain "inactive"! Any form of emancipated relation to work that retirees may invent is considered null and void – they must be satisfied with their assigned role of leisure-time "actives" who are "inactive" when it comes to work!

But the reactionary reforms are even bolder: the promise of a long life means that these active leisure-timers must be put back to (subordinated) work. The Commission's 2005 Green Paper on demographic change[12] takes the Pensions OMC guidelines a step further: it not only stresses the need to increase the employment rates of the over 55, but attempts to spread a new nomenclature for age groups – "older workers" for the 55-64 year-olds, and "elderly people" for the 65-79 age group. The latter, the Commission notes with surprise, have a mediocre employment rate in the EU compared to the USA – where it already exceeds 10%.

And, as illustrated by the 2010 Joint Report and the 2012 White Paper, the EU authorities continue to consistently define the core reforms as: raising the retirement age, lengthening the period of presence on the labour market, and increasing the employment rate for the over-1960s. Thus, the national reforms undertaken in the EU since the 1990s have introduced mechanisms to adjust the length of the working life to increasing life expectancy, either automatically (as in Sweden, Denmark and Italy) or through collective agreements (Finland and France). They also include a progressive increase in the statutory retirement age (Bulgaria, Czech Republic, Denmark, Greece, Spain, France, Hungary, Ireland, Lithuania, Latvia, Malta, the Netherlands, Poland, Romania), and in particular for women in countries where it was below that applying to men (Portugal, Belgium, Austria, UK). Generally speaking, all these reforms multiply measures to increase the age at which pensions can be drawn (including cutting back or abolishing early retirement measures) and to make it possible to combine declining pension levels with part-time employment. The overall plan is thus clearly to transform pensioners' free work into subordinated labour.

B. Reducing the Role of First Pillar PAYG Public Pensions: Freezing the Socialised Wage and Public Service Resource Regimes

It is not possible to understand this second OMC-pension proposal, or those that follow, without taking into account the impact of the Community doctrine on the social protection "pillars" presented in the first part of this chapter. The emergence of this doctrine owes much to the case law constructions of the European Court of Justice.[13] In the name of the application of the Treaties organising the Common Market, the Court has asserted that competition between financial service pro-

---

12 Commission of the European Communities, Green Paper "Confronting demographic change: a new solidarity between the generations", Brussels, March 2005.

13 The Court itself is influenced by the Member States, and by the Commission. The latter has, since the 1991 legal proceeding leading up to the Poucet and Pistre judgment, presented European pension systems in terms of pillars. The Commission's legal service uses the categories defined by the Internal Market Directorate General.

viders is the norm, and that only solidarity and being subject to state regulations justify special derogation for public monopolies. Without actually using the word "pillars", the Court laid the foundations for a theoretical framework distinguishing between a public first pillar providing national solidarity benefits, and a second pillar tailored for the main pension industry players on the European market. Once again, the scope for legitimate state action is confined to its tutelary functions. This "three pillars" doctrine – based on the equation state = solidarity = basic scheme – serves to singularly reduce the role of the state. It performs the amazing feat of both defining a system that is essentially based on social contributions and is thus private, as a "state" system, and of calling "first pillar" a range of schemes that in France for instance account for 97% of pension expenditures. According to this doctrine, a social security system that is emancipated from financial accumulation cannot be implemented at the European level, for the market alone is European. In other words, a social security system that is defined by a political process is reduced to providing national solidarity – which is the opposite of wage-based or citizen-based solidarity. Whereas in the latter case, equal citizens pay general taxes to finance general public services, and wage-based solidarity is produced by equal wage-earners pooling 40% of the wage to finance general social benefits, national solidarity does the exact opposite: it establishes a hierarchy between rich and poor, with the former financing targeted benefits for a large part of the disqualified active population.

Thus, national reforms to general schemes categorised as "public pensions" (although unjustifiably so), provide for introducing ceilings on social contributions (Germany, Italy, Sweden, the Netherlands) and reductions in replacement rates (Germany, France, Austria, Portugal, Italy, Sweden, Belgium, with considerable reductions in Poland, Sweden, Latvia, Estonia). As "public" schemes, these general schemes must become "basic", and thus call for "supplementary" schemes. What could be more natural?

C. Making Pension Schemes More Contributory: Extending the Scope of the Deferred Wage

The transformation of public or socialised wage pensions into deferred wage pensions can be radical, as in the Italian and Swedish reforms. Here, individual annual pensions, strictly based on individual contributions, correspond to the notional capital constituted by the sum of contributions paid during a person's working life divided by the average life expectancy of each retirement-age cohort. This kind of "actuarial neutrality" pushes workers to postpone their retirement as their life expectancy increases in order to maintain the same pension level. It thus contributes – systemically, without requiring further recourse to politically sensitive revisions of calculation parameters – to restraining the progression of the period of free time and thus of free work. The deferred wage, by treating the pension as simply a deferment of unconsumed earnings, convinces both workers and retirees that pensions are paid in exchange for past subordinated work. In this sense, although it does not generate savings, it is based on the same fiction as savings, which is why the individual contributions account is described as "notional". It convinces them that non-subordinated work cannot be paid, and that only strictly measured subordinated work is entitled to monetary recognition.

The other measures linked to the deferred wage logic are:

- Lengthening the period of earnings taken into account to calculate the reference wage (from the ten best to the 25 best years in France, with similar trends in Spain, Austria, Finland, Bulgaria, Czech Republic, Ireland, Greece and Portugal);
- The distinction between contributory and non-contributory benefits, the latter being financed by income tax (Spain; and in France, the CSG for the *Fonds de solidarité vieillesse* – Old Age Solidarity Found);
- Indexing pensions on prices instead of on wages, as if pension rights were financed by pensioners' past work and not by current productivity (Italy, France, Spain, Belgium, Latvia, Austria, UK).

Thus the prime aim of pension reforms is to promote the deferred wage resource regime, that is, to activate the first condition of the capitalist monetary constraint: only work dedicated to capital can be assigned value.

D. Increasing the Share of Funded Occupational Schemes: Promoting Wage-earner Savings in the "Second" and "Third" Pillars

A serious difficulty facing the 2003 Joint Report on Pensions was that pension systems in which savings play only a minor role, if any, provide more favourable results for pensioners overall. Using what can only be called an auto-suggestive approach, the Report endlessly repeats the following strange syllogism: funded private schemes are unfair, risky and poorly adapted to increasingly chequered working careers, and since we want fair, secure pensions adapted to worker mobility, the role of funded private schemes must be increased. This, it may be added, is why the Report advocates reform methods that involve the trade unions in defining, and even managing, funded occupational schemes, and stresses the need to address the portability and vesting problems that contribute to making these schemes so poorly "adequate".

And indeed, national reform programmes introduce defined-contribution schemes in countries where they did not exist before (i.e. the majority, especially those following the Bismarckian tradition), and extend them in the others (Sweden, Denmark, UK, Netherlands) in particular in Ireland where the public pension is very low. Defined-benefit schemes that are co-managed with the trade unions continue to survive in countries or sectors where they are firmly established (the Netherlands, the British public sector). To top it all, the reforms create reserve funds for PAYG schemes.

These reforms, which are presented as the necessary response to the relative scarcity of employment in the coming decades, can be expected to strengthen the conviction that savings represent an inter-temporal transfer of value, as if value could be put in the freezer during our working lives and taken back out when we draw our pensions. This absurd conception of savings feeds the propaganda that funding introduces "intergenerational fairness", with each generation "financing its own retirement". Whereas, in reality, this promotion of wage-earner savings means promoting profit-making property rights, the second condition of the capitalist form of monetary constraint.

E. Strengthening the Redistributive Role of the First Pillar to Provide an Effective Instrument for Combating Poverty: Promoting the Tutelary Allowance

It is important to note that, at the time of its launching, the pensions OMC placed such emphasis on preventing poverty in old age that this goal tops the list of the common objectives summarized in the five key proposals examined here. As seen in Chapter 1, a minimum income guarantee for the invalidated working poor is the third condition of the capitalist monetary constraint. Reducing the share of public service and socialised wage pensions and extending the scope of the deferred wage and wage-earner savings will turn many wage-earners whose pension entitlements had been based on a positive affirmation of citizenship or qualification, into recipients of a tutelary allowance whose entitlements are defined negatively on the basis of what they "lack". The "social" sphere, far from compensating for the "economic" sphere, is subordinated to it – as witnessed, for example, by all the measures intended to make social protection "employment-friendly". This devaluation affects half of the active population in some countries, such as France, where low-wage jobs are exempted from employer contributions.

Thus, all the national reform programs introduce or extend minimum pension guarantees. The most spectacular example of this trend is found in the UK, where supplementary public pensions target low-wage jobs, and a means-tested pension credit that is 30% higher than the public pension will progressively concern half of retired households.

As can be seen, the reaffirmation of the capitalist convention of labour in the pensions OMC, over the wage-based convention under construction in the Bismarckian countries, cannot be reduced to simply promoting funded over PAYG schemes. Another key component is the change in meaning of PAYG, with the shift towards benefits that are increasingly contributory, a deferred wage, and a guaranteed minimum: these are all, together with funding, the characteristics of a capitalist pension reform.

III. Using the Stability and Growth Pact to Develop the Second Pillar and to Change the Meaning of PAYG

As we have seen, two elements that were essential for developing funded systems could not be included in the scope of the IORP Directive:

- The freedom to become a member of an IORP. This did not receive the unconditional recognition that Leon Brittan had suggested, which, in its broadest sense, would have implied competition with PAYG systems;
- Taxation, which is linked to the above. The Communication added little in this area. It merely encouraged Member States to bring their methods of taxation closer by basing them on the EET model (Exempt contributions, Exempt investment income and capital gains of the pension institution, Taxed benefits), and to abstain from using fiscal policy to provide a competitive edge to national institutions managing retirement provision. However, if the European institutions truly wish to envisage competition between funded and PAYG systems, large-scale tax exemptions are indispensable, despite the fact that this is persistently denied in Community documents dealing with the subject. Moreover, such a measure would come into conflict with supposed Member State autonomy and even with the budgetary constraints imposed by the Stability and Growth Pact, for the cost of such measures would weigh heavily on state budgets.

An important step was taken in 2005 with the reform of the Stability and Growth Pact. After strong criticism from the French and German governments in particular, the Commission launched a debate on the method of calculating public deficits. Although the stated goal was to exclude certain investment expenditures (such as research expenditures), it provided the opportunity to put tax incentives for funded schemes on the agenda. The Conclusions of the European Council held in Barcelona on 22 and 23 March 2005 state the following:

> The Council is mindful that the respect of the budgetary targets of the Stability and Growth Pact should not hamper structural reforms that unequivocally improve the long-term sustainability of public finances. The Council acknowledges that special attention must be paid to pension reforms introducing a multi-pillar system that includes a mandatory, fully funded pillar. Although these reforms entail a short-term deterioration of public finances during the implementation period, the long-term sustainability of public finances is clearly improved. The Council therefore agrees that Member States implementing such reforms should be allowed to deviate from the adjustment path towards the MTO [mid term objective], or from the MTO itself. The deviation from the MTO should reflect the net cost of the reform to the publicly managed pillar, provided the deviation remains temporary and an appropriate safety margin to the reference value is preserved.

This initiative created a prime incentive for the development of funded systems. While social contributions earmarked for PAYG pension schemes will continue to be seen as feeding public deficits, tax exemptions granted to retirement savings systems and employer contributions to specific reserve funds will look like investments for the future, and this despite the financial risk that even the Commission itself acknowledges. The mechanism constitutes a particularly harsh blow for PAYG systems in that the notion of "public deficit" not only applies to state budgets but also to social security deficits. In other words, reductions in social contributions and tax exemptions for savings systems will be seen as mechanisms for limiting public deficits.

The aim seems to be to undermine the financing of PAYG systems, and thereby justify new reforms… to save these systems by reducing their sources of financing even more.

From an institutional point of view, it must be noted that the legal status of the provisions adopted gives particular force to the mechanism:

- Formally speaking, the reform does not call into question the myth of Member State autonomy to manage social protection systems. However, the development of funding, although not compulsory, provides the means to avoid certain penalties (such as those stemming from failure to comply with the Stability and Growth Pact).
- The mechanism introduces a political orientation – developing funded systems – into the scope of Community law. It has been widely shown (see in particular Weiler, 1981, Streeck, 1995, and Scharpf, 2000b) that law is a key political issue. Weiler, for example, has analysed the dual nature of European construction and demonstrated the effectiveness of norms applied by the ECJ, and

the break away from intergovernmental rules. Both Streeck and Scharf have stressed, with the notion of negative integration, that the norms establishing the market have generally been those that are legally binding. The path followed by the Stability and Growth Pact illustrates this duality as well as the flexibility of the mechanism: beginning as a purely incentive tool, and sometimes presented as the first expression of the open method of coordination, it was progressively given legally binding strength.

As for the actors, as Antoine Math (2001) has noted, this key innovation illustrates how the champions of the doctrine of budgetary orthodoxy have dominated social affairs officials.

Above all, it illustrates that one of the fundamental strengths of the advocates of budgetary orthodoxy is the capacity to intervene in multiple fields and on varied legal bases. For, if the EU is sometimes presented as a multi-level governance, not all the actors are multi-level.

The central role of the Economic Policy Committee (ECP) (and its membership of state macro-economists) must be stressed here. This body, which once functioned in the shadow of the Economic and Financial Committee, has made pensions a key issue for its own promotion. The argument used is that the entitlements of future pensioners constitute a "hidden debt" which is not sufficiently recorded by the Economic and Financial Committee's accounting criteria. The ECP initiated the open method of coordination on pensions, and has also been able to introduce the question of pensions, as well as the solutions it recommends, in other areas that are not accessible to social affairs personnel, such as the reform of the Stability and Growth Pact.

This basic thrust of EU policies to promote implementation of a mandatory funded pension system was confirmed in the economic governance reforms introduced in 2011. The package of six legislative texts (called the Six-Pack) – presented as a response to the crisis affecting European public finances – increases the pressure exerted by the EU on Member States to comply with the criteria of the Stability and Growth Pact (in terms of debt and deficits), and strengthens the powers of the Commission with regard to the Council in applying sanction procedures. However, it is notable that in this overall austerity programme, the exception introduced in 2005 for second pillar schemes is maintained. Council Regulation (EU) No. 1177/2011 of 8 November 2011 contains the provisions in question:

> When assessing compliance with the deficit and debt criterion and in the subsequent steps of the excessive deficit procedure, the Council and the Commission shall give due consideration to the implementation of pension reforms introducing a multi-pillar system that includes a mandatory, fully funded pillar and the net cost of the publicly managed pillar. In particular,

> consideration shall be given to the features of the overall pension system created by the reform, namely whether it promotes long-term sustainability while not increasing risks for the medium-term budgetary position.

Inclusion of this provision is presented as a concession to the countries of the former eastern European bloc (notably Poland and Hungary) who have already introduced this type of reform. In assessing Poland's budgetary situation for 2011, the Commission applied this rule in order to avoid "proceeding to the next stage of the excessive deficit procedure". But this provision can be applied in the future to any country seeking to limit its public deficits.

And above all, with the Six-Pack and the European Semester, the Commission now has the means to push for reforming PAYG schemes in line with the aims of the OMC. The introduction to the 2010 Joint Report on Pensions, in summarising the EU instruments, notes (p. 12): "Moreover, the fiscal framework in the UE – the Stability and Growth Pact (SGP) – has been strengthened, including the need for pursuing structural reforms in the field of pensions that contribute to long-term fiscal sustainability." And continues on page 17:

> Recently Member States have agreed detailed principles on the revision of the medium-term budgetary objectives in order to ensure that the Member States' budgetary strategies reflect real medium-term needs, by taking account not just of debt levels but also implicit liabilities, notably costs related to ageing populations, in particular projected pension and healthcare expenditure.

Conclusion

It is important not to lose sight of the obvious – that the European Union is not a state. Its fields of competence are assigned by treaties that also define its modes of action. Nonetheless, this diversity should not mask the constancy of the political goal pursued with regard to pensions, via European Court of Justice case law, the open method of coordination, the IORP directive and the reform of the Stability and Growth Pact (stepped up since 2007). By making freedom of competition for financial operators in the European pension market a central issue in reforms (whether these operators manage individual savings products or occupational schemes), these Community instruments attempt to significantly modify national pension systems. Expressed in terms of resource regimes, the changes concern socialised wage and public service pensions, which are to be frozen in the name of the equation "public=solidarity=basic", while promoting pension forms sustaining the pursuit of the capitalist subordination of labour, that is, the deferred wage, wage-earner savings, and the tutelary allowance. It can be expected that pensioners, rather than being able to continue experimenting with emancipated work relations on a vast scale, will be maintained in a status of "inactive" consumers of leisure activities or put back to subordinated work. All this explains the apparently contradictory attitude of the EU since 2007. On the one hand, it acknowledges the fragility of funded schemes, and the need to "review [their] regulatory framework and design". On the other, using a corpus of prudential or fiscal rules, it continues, *mutatis mutandis*, in the name of the "demographic problem" and the fight against budgetary deficits, to pursue the same policy of freezing PAYG and developing funding through a market for occupational pension schemes. This is because the reform is not primarily aimed at technical changes. It is a political undertaking to maintain work within the capitalist convention of value. It thus attacks any pension scheme which, by continuing the wage for life thanks to social contributions, defines pensioners as workers liberated from the labour market and profit-making property. And it aims to replace these with schemes which are based on a longer presence on the labour market, a deferred income linked to past employment, solidarity with the poor, and retirement savings, and which thus serve to reaffirm the centrality of capitalist labour institutions.

Annexes

The IORP Directive:

– preparatory documents

European Commission (1990) Completion of the internal market in the field of private pensions, 15/224/90.

European Commission (1991), Proposal for a Council Directive relating to the freedom for management and investment of funds held by institutions for retirement provision, COM (91)301 final.

European Commission (2000), Proposal for a directive relative to the activities of institutions for occupational retirement provision, COM (2000)507 final, Official Journal C 96 E, 27.03.2001.

European Parliament (2001), Report on the proposal for a directive of the European Parliament and the Council relative to the activities of institutions for occupational retirement provision, Official Journal C 65 E, 14.03.2002.

European Council (2002), Common Position on the proposal for a directive of the European Parliament and the Council relative to the activities of institutions for occupational retirement provision, Official Journal C 299 E, 03.12.2002.

– legislative documents

European Commission (1994), Communication on an internal market for pension funds, COM (94/C 360/08) (annulled).

Communication on the elimination of tax obstacles to the cross-border provision of occupational pensions (COM) (2001), 214 final.

Directive 2001/108/EC of the European Parliament and of the Council of 21 January 2002 amending Council Directive 85/611/EEC on the coordination of laws, regulations and administrative provisions relating to undertakings for collective investment in transferable securities (UCITS), with regard to investments of UCITS, Official Journal, L41 of 13.12.2002.

Directive 2003/41/EC of the European Parliament and of the Council of 3 June 2003 on the activities and supervision of institutions for occupational retirement provision, Official Journal L 235 of 23.9.2003.

Presidency Conclusions, European Council of Brussels, 22 and 22 March 2005, 7619/05.

Euro-unionism and the Wage

Anne DUFRESNE

Researcher, Fonds National de la Recherche Scientifique, Université Catholique de Louvain, Belgium

Introduction

The past 30 years have seen a massive redistribution of the income from wages towards capital.[1] This raises the question of what could be done to promote a more equitable redistribution of wealth. In other words, what kind of structures and strategies could be developed at both national and supranational levels that would be able to counter the policy of wage restraint enforced in Europe since the beginning of the 1980s?

This chapter will show how state opportunism and the absence of solidarity are the order of the day in the European Union (EU), and how German doctrine has progressively succeeded in imposing its model. The combination of the new obsession with competitiveness and monetary and budgetary austerity – those fundamental principles of economic orthodoxy enshrined in the Treaty of Maastricht – has taken economic governance to such heights today that even the autonomy of national collective bargaining processes is being threatened. The possibility of an equitable sharing of wealth seems to be receding further and further away.

I will begin by examining the convergence towards wage restraint in Europe. In the second part of the chapter, I will then trace the history of wage co-ordination processes organised at EU level despite this difficult context. In reviewing the various initiatives undertaken since the 1990s, I will analyse the ground the trade unions have already been able to cover and the extent of their accomplishments. My aim is to better understand what instruments can be developed to limit the anti-cooperative wage strategies that contributed to the crisis sparked off in 2008.

[1] In Europe, as Michel Husson (2010) has shown, the share of wages in national income dropped by 8.6% (9.3% in France) between 1983 and 2006.

The political and ideological obstacles to realising wage coordination today are numerous. I will thus examine alternative paths, such as the introduction of a European minimum wage, and look into possible options for attenuating the boundaries that exist between national collective bargaining systems.

I. The History of Wage Restraint

In the 1980s, the countries in the European Monetary System (EMS) began using non-cooperative strategies to enhance their competitiveness. National governments seeking to improve their relative production costs either opted for "competitive devaluation" (via exchange rates) as in Italy, or "competitive disinflation" (via wages, taxation, etc.) as in France. But beyond these strategies, governments had little leeway to influence the major macroeconomic orientations. Since the EMS imposed the Deutsche mark as the nominal anchor currency, they were already subject to the monetary and budgetary orthodoxy dictated by the German monetary authorities. After the 1980s, these orientations would be reinforced by the process of Europeanisation. Thus in 1991, the Treaty of Maastricht, through its structural adjustment criteria,[2] enshrined a liberal approach to the coordination of economic policies. The choices made were shaped by the balance of power existing between the major countries: France wanted the euro, which it saw as the means to guarantee the integration into Europe of a newly unified Germany; but Helmut Kohl succeeded in imposing his model of central banking. And that is how, due to Germany's anti-inflationist obsession, monetary stability was established as the primary goal of the European Central Bank (ECB) launched in January 1999.

The birth of the single currency – as the end goal of economic and monetary union (EMU) – corresponded to a fundamental turning point that modified the policy instruments in the hands of the state. Joining the eurozone "club" meant definitively abandoning the use of "competitive devaluation" to increase national competitiveness. Wage "moderation"[3] thus became the last remaining option that governments could use to improve their relative production costs. As a result, the wage became the only adjustment variable in the EMU system. Furthermore, the ECB has used the argument of monetary stability to impose wage restraint as a "necessary" policy. This key premise of orthodox monetarism paved the

---

2 Participating countries had to comply with such criteria as: "achieving a 'high degree' of price stability, that is, an inflation rate which was not to exceed 1.5 over the average rates of the three Member States presenting the lowest inflation rate"; maintaining public deficit below 3% of GDP, and public debt under 60% of GDP.

3 Wage "moderation", that is wage restraint, is an economic measure aimed at slowing down real wage progression (purchasing power).

way for the progressive implementation of the EU's macro-economic straightjacket.[4]

The linkage between wage and employment is another argument used to justify the "necessity" of cost competitiveness, even if there has been no empirical evidence to show that reducing wages leads to job creation. During the 1980s, wage bargaining in Europe underwent a fundamental turn around, switching from productivity-oriented to competition-oriented bargaining. Under pressure from restructurings and the emergence of mass unemployment, many European trade unions followed the German example and lowered their claims. Bargaining under the threat of endangering national competitiveness, they switched their priority from wage increases to safeguarding jobs. Finally, within the framework of the EU, the dogmas of monetarism and competitiveness exerted a strong political pressure on the wage, affecting its very nature. How indeed can the wage – a quintessentially political topic – be reduced to a simple indicator of "labour costs",[5] that is, to no more than a factor for reducing inflationist pressure or improving competitiveness?

Following on several decades of wage restraint, today's European economic governance will amplify this move to denature the wage. Previously, the calendar of wage restraint apparently remained under national control. Now, however, pursuing the EMU framework and using the financial crisis as an excuse, European governments have, for the first time, decided to allow the EU authorities to intervene in the field of wages at national level. A competitiveness and convergence pact, called the "Pact for the Euro", was signed by the 17 eurozone countries in March 2011, at the instigation of France and Germany. After six non-eurozone countries (Bulgaria, Denmark, Poland, Romania, Estonia and Lithuania)[6] voluntarily signed the pact, it was renamed the "Euro-plus Pact".

The pact speeds up the introduction of concomitant changes in national models of collective bargaining. In addition to the requirement that strict public debt and deficit rules be transposed into national legislation, it allows the EU to intervene in national-level bargaining processes and impose a "method" for wage discipline. Thus, the Pact for the Euro stresses three key recommendations: 1) "Review the degree of centralisation in the bargaining process". This simply formalises at

4 Definitive abandonment of the exchange rate instrument, limiting inflation, and competitive policies.

5 For an analysis of the policy options implicit in the construction of European indicators on employment and wages, as well as the absence of the expression of social conflict in this construction, see Anne Dufresne, 2012.

6 The five Member States that did not sign the pact were the UK, Hungary, the Czech Republic, Cypress and Malta.

European level the decentralisation of collective bargaining underway at national level since the 1980s. It will entail, for example, increasing the number of sectoral collective agreements with opening clauses (already a particularly widespread practice in Germany); 2) "Ensure that wage settlements in the public sector support the competitiveness efforts in the private sector". In other words, governments are required to compress public sector wages in order to establish a weak standard for the private sector as well; and 3) "Review the wage setting arrangements". Combined with the first two points, this relatively general recommendation constitutes a particularly strong attack on the unions since it means intervening in their bargaining autonomy. The plan to cap the outcomes of national wage bargaining rounds will undermine union power, as bargaining is so central to their identity. These recommendations and methods of wage restraint are already partly applied in the "peripheral" countries where a series of austerity programmes have been enforced.[7]

The purely political commitment of the governments who signed the Euro-plus Pact contrasts sharply with the legally binding measures introduced six months later. The "economic governance" package, called the "Six-Pack" because it includes six European legislative measures, was adopted early October 2011 in a rushed process and as discretely as possible. For indeed, as Commission President José Manuel Barroso had declared the previous year, "What is happening now is a silent revolution – a silent revolution, moving step by step towards stronger economic governance. The Member States have accepted – and I hope they have understood this – to grant the European institutions considerable supervisory powers."[8]

This package is steered by the Directorate General for Economic and Financial Affairs, the Ministers of Economy and Finance, and the ECB. This dominant position of economic actors in the decision-making process is indicative of an increasing loss of democratic sovereignty. The outbreak of the financial crisis in 2008 provided a "dramatic" context which has enabled the EU authorities to short-circuit Member State sovereignty. The Treaty on Stability, Coordination and Governance (TSCG) adopted in March 2012 illustrates this particularly forcefully. It requires Member States to introduce "provisions of binding force and permanent character, preferably constitutional, or otherwise guaranteed to be fully respected and adhered to throughout the national

---

7 In Greece, for example, the European Commission has already directly intervened in the bargaining process by imposing a cut of about 20% in civil service wages and a decrease in minimum wages for young people and the unemployed. For more details, see the ILO Report on the High Level Mission to Greece, Athens, 19-23 September 2011.

8 José Manuel Barroso, at the European University Institute, Florence, 18 June 2010.

budgetary processes". Why devise such a complex institutional arrangement instead of opting for a mandatory inclusion in national constitutions? Because some countries require a referendum to amend their constitution, which was precisely what the movers behind the budgetary pact wanted to avoid. This choice of procedure was designed to limit public debate, and speed up the adoption and implementation of the Treaty. The attack on the wage under way here is thus part of a broader plan instituting a radical, counter-democratic regime change (Gobin 2005).

To come back to the Six-Pack, "economic governance" not only further strengthens budgetary orthodoxy,[9] it extends the European system of constraints to include social and wage policies. Member States' national economies will be monitored on the basis of a scoreboard that identifies countries "guilty" of "macro-economic imbalances" and/or "gaps in competitiveness". Each year, the Commission will monitor certain indicators country by country, and in particular, where wages are concerned, their Unit Labour Cost (ULC): if the latter exceeds a given threshold,[10] the Commission will compare it with the eurozone average. If the "guilty" country then fails to comply with EU recommendations, it will have to pay a financial penalty amounting to 0.1% of GDP. The ULC indicator reflects a country's competitiveness trends, which means that wage trends are assessed according to the sole criterion of competitiveness. This amounts to organised wage dumping, and a policy coordination aligned on countries with low-wage policies: Germany, to be specific (see box below).

Economic governance has thus evolved from the non-cooperative national strategies of the past to today's wage-dumping explicitly organised by the EU – a development that would have seemed unthinkable not that long ago. One reason for this is that, under the Treaty, there is no possibility of creating a legal framework at EU level for European collective bargaining or an upward harmonisation of wages.[11] As if it would be out of the question to imagine that claims for higher wages – the unions' prime tool for redistributing wealth – could be coordinated at European level. And yet, this is precisely what a number of unions have been striving to achieve for over 20 years now.

---

9 The 1997 Growth and Stability Pact, a follow-up to the Maastricht convergence criteria, had already reinforced budgetary constraints prior to adoption of the Six-Pack and the fiscal pact.

10 The ULC over the previous 3 years are not to exceed 9% in the eurozone countries, or 11% in the others.

11 Article 153.5 explicitly excludes pay from the EU competence.

Box 1. A decade of social collapse in Germany

Since 2003, Germany has experienced a considerable rise in poverty as a result of policies to flexibilise the labour market (Harz Laws). Temporary work has become a full-blown sector, earnings-related unemployment benefits have been abolished, and "mini-jobs" (flexible employment paid 400 euros a month) have made their appearance. In 2011, 40% of German workers were hired on precarious contracts, and 6.5 million were "low-wage" employees (earning under 10 euros/hour).[12] Collective agreements have also been rendered particularly vulnerable. Germany experienced the slowest wage progression of all OECD countries between 2000 and 2009: real wages (taking inflation into account) dropped by 4.5%, whereas they rose by 8.6% in France and by 22% in Finland during that same period.[13]

II. The Difficult Task of Constructing Transnational Wage Claims

In the historical overview that follows, I will seek to explain how the concept of coordinating collective bargaining took shape during the 1990s. The starting point for wage coordination initiatives dates back to the launching of EMU in 1993, and the growth of international competition.

These initiatives all share an overall ideological function, with a short-term goal of fighting wage dumping, and a longer-term goal of building up sufficiently robust coordination between the unions in order to negotiate European collective agreements. However, their motivations have been diverse, depending on the level concerned (cross-border or EU-wide, sectoral or cross-sectoral), as well as the particular period during which they were launched.

Coordination initiatives operate at two distinct levels beyond the "national" level: the cross-border level and the "Community" level. The cross-border level can be either transnational (involving a few neighbouring countries) or transregional (involving neighbouring regions). Four "forms of Europeanisation" can be identified with regard to the coordination of wage bargaining, as shown in Table I below. These processes are closely linked in terms of their members as well as their content.

12 For more details, see Reinhard Bispinck and Thorsten Schulten, 2011.

13 International Labour Organisation (ILO), 2011.

Table 1: The different levels of Collective Bargaining Coordination Committees (CBCCs)

Bargaining level	Cross-sectoral	Sectoral
Community	CBCC European Trade Union Confederation (ETUC)	CBCC 8 European Industry Federations (EIFs) (Metals, Textiles, etc.)
Cross-border	Doorn Group	Inter-regional networks
National	Confederations	National federations

Source: Personal compilation

Whatever the bargaining level, coordination fosters a process of "Europeanisation" that can be defined as the development of a transnational nexus of union actors, structures and processes set up within the European space and interacting with national actors. The approach is bottom-up, since it is based on the bargaining capacity of unions that already exist at national level. It is also an internal process of the union movement that takes place despite the absence of counterparts on the employer side.[14] The trailblazers (indicated by the grey areas in Table I) were the European Metalworkers' Federation (EMF) (followed by other EIFs) and the Doorn Group. I will present these two processes in some detail below, before examining their difficulties in progressing towards their respective goals.

At the intersectoral level, the cross-border coordination of collective bargaining known as the "Doorn regional initiative" was launched in 1998 and involved unions from four countries (Germany plus the three Benelux countries).[15] The impetus for the Doorn Group came from Belgium, where the unions were confronted with a national "law on competitiveness" adopted in 1996, which provided for the systematic comparison of Belgian wage levels with pay trends in the country's three main trading partners (Germany, France and the Netherlands). In 1997, the two major Belgian unions (the CSC and the FGTB)[16] took the initiative of calling a meeting between the German, Belgian and Dutch confederations (soon to be joined by their Luxembourg counterparts)[17]

14 No explicit wage coordination process has been initiated by European employer organisations. Indeed, they reject any idea of negotiations or even social dialogue on wages. For example, BusinessEurope is satisfied with the increased pace of wage restraint resulting from the Pact for the Euro, but refrains from engaging in dialogue on the topic with its "partner".

15 For more information on the Doorn Group, see Anne Dufresne, 2009.

16 Confédération des Syndicats Chrétiens, and Fédération Générale du Travail de Belgique.

17 The initial absence of the French unions was partly due to disagreements on the issue between the CFDT, CGT and FO confederations, and partly to the lack of interest

along with their main sectoral unions, with a view to setting up a group of experts to exchange information and make policy decisions on a regular basis. For the first time, unions from different EU countries agreed on joint guidelines for wage claims. In their 1998 declaration, the unions from these four countries committed to a "joint orientation formula" for national bargaining, in other words, a wage standard (taking account of inflation and productivity) (see below). This pragmatic and combative cross-border initiative stimulated union debates across the EU and played a leading role in clarifying and strengthening goals. It provided the impetus for the European Trade Union Confederation (ETUC) to set up a Collective Bargaining Coordination Committee (CBCC) in November 1999 (see Table above).

Table 2: The 8 European Industry Federations involved in coordination

EFFAT	European Federation of Food, Agriculture and Tourism Trade Unions
EMCEF	European Mine, Chemical and Energy Workers' Federation
EFJ	European Federation of Journalists
EMF	European Metalworkers' Federation
EFBWW	European Federation of Building and Woodworkers
EPSU	European Federation of Public Service Workers
ETUF-TCL	European Trade Union Federation – Textiles, Clothing and Leather
UNI-Europa	Union Network International (Services and Telecommunications)

Note: The EFM, EMCEF and ETUF-TCL merged to form industriALL on May 16, 2012

At the sectoral level,[18] Europeanisation of collective bargaining follows two routes: union initiatives can be either cross-border (such as the three- or four-country interregional union networks), or Community-level within the European Industry Federations (EIFs). The focus here will be on the latter. Since the beginning of the 1990s, and following on the pioneering initiative of the EMF, seven other Federations[19] have stepped up their efforts to create collective bargaining coordination structures.

The method of coordination used by these Federations is based on a political process linking the national and EU levels in order to imple-

shown by some of their representatives. On the insistence of the ETUC, they were nonetheless invited to the 2001 meeting as observers. They then became full members of the group in 2002.

18 It should be noted that there have been very few studies on the sectoral level. The most recent doctoral theses addressing this level are by Nadia Hilal (2005) and Anne Dufresne (2006).

19 Food, Agriculture and Tourism; Mine, Chemicals and Energy: Textiles, Clothing and Leather; Building and Woodworkers; Journalism; Public Services; Communications.

ment common standards. It can be broken down into three phases as follows:

a) Once a formal structure (coordination committee) has been set up, the first phase consists of an exchange of information with a view to comparing national collective bargaining systems (on wages and working time in particular), and establishing personal contacts between union staff from the different Member States.

b) Then, when a strategy has been developed, the second, tricky phase focuses on drawing up common criteria that will be formalised in policy documents (wage norms and/or minimum social standards). The EMF led the way by establishing the following wage norm:

Diagram: EMF proposal for a wage norm

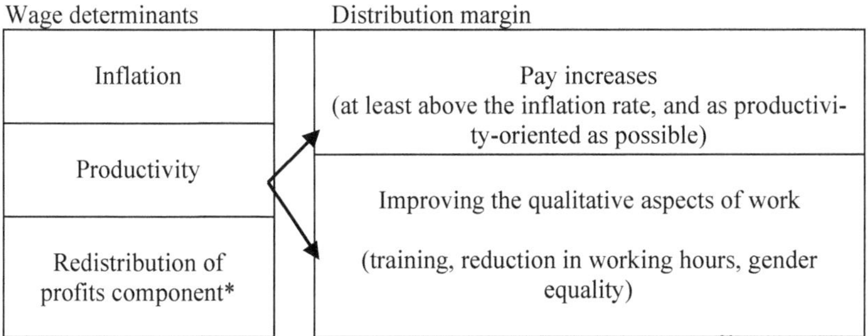

Source: Personal composition based on EMF resolutions of 1993 and 1998[20]
*This determinant only appears in the 1993 proposal

The criteria for determining claims for pay increases and improving "qualitative" aspects are inflation and productivity (the redistribution of profits component and the emphasis on the autonomy of collective bargaining at national level disappeared between the first and the second drafts of the proposal, that is, between 1993 and 1998). It can be seen that the advocated wage policy is based on productivity and is neutral in terms of competition and costs, and thus in terms of redistribution. The policy explicitly refrains from acting on wage discrepancies between countries within the European space. Its primary goal is to avoid "a wage policy oriented towards further redistribution of income in favour of capital gains".[21] It thus clearly diverges from the standard proposed in

[20] EMF, "Collective Bargaining Policy in a Changing Europe", Statement of Principle approved at the 1st EMF Collective Bargaining Conference, Luxembourg, 11-12 March 1993, and adopted by the Executive Committee, Luxembourg, 25 March 1993; EMF, "Collective Bargaining under the Euro", Resolution adopted at the 3rd Conference on Collective Bargaining, Frankfurt-am-Main, 9-10 December 1998.

[21] EMF, 1998, p. 3.

the recent Pact for the Euro, since the Pact requires the signatory governments to adopt measures ensuring that increases in nominal wages be consistent with productivity gains, inflation ceases to be a wage determinant, and this serves to encourage redistribution in favour of capital.

In addition to the wage norm, the EMF and other EIFs have also adopted a specific strategy on minimum social standards. First, the various unions draw up a common policy position on a minimum standard that they find appropriate for all the EU countries. The European Secretariat then decides on what would look like a "European average", the idea being to combine a politically defined minimum with a longer-term goal. In the next stage, it is up to the national unions to work towards getting these standards included in their collective agreements. For most of the sectors, social standards have been defined in two key fields: working time (based on the EMF norm of an annual maximum of 1,750 hours plus 100 hours overtime, and a 35-hour working week as the goal); and training.

c) The third and final phase of the process, which connects the first two phases (comparison of national negotiations and creation of common criteria – wage norm or social standards), consists of an *ex post* assessment of the outcomes of national bargaining rounds on the basis of these common criteria. The wage "norm" is thus intended to be used as a tool for monitoring the actual results obtained at national level.

However, a detailed analysis of the process launched by the EMF reveals an interesting contradiction. Whereas some EIF-affiliated unions follow a bottom-up approach and work together to draft common declarations in their collective bargaining coordinating committees (CBCCs), these declarations have no explicit effect on their respective national bargaining rounds. For the most part, the documents they produce appear to remain mere declarations of intent. Why are they not put to use? And why are the rules developed used more for analytical purposes than as a political tool? In other words, what are the obstacles to wage coordination? Some possible answers to these questions are provided below.

III. Obstacles to Wage Coordination

The Europeanisation of trade unions appears to be unable to get beyond a stage of "regulating diversity" (Gollbach, 2000), as regards both bargaining levels and topics. For example, in multi-employer collective bargaining systems, negotiations are essentially conducted by union and employer organisations, whereas in single-employer systems, they take place between the unions, staff representatives or individual workers and the company. In the Central and Eastern European countries (CEECs), collective bargaining structures are weak and decentralised, which limits union control over wage formation processes. Wage claims are negotiated at company level only, where rights to union representation are weak. More often than not, there are no bargaining structures at a higher level. These systems thus have a lower and less stable rate of coverage compared to multi-employer processes. The topics that can be addressed and the duration of collective agreements also vary widely between countries. These structural differences make data collection and comparison difficult. Furthermore, given the diversity of national judicial and political systems, work relations and union cultures, it is impossible for any national regulation to be directly applied in other countries. As a result, in each case, it will be the specific characteristics of the participating unions that will determine the way in which their particular transnational group or EIF coordination committee is organised. If even the Doorn Group countries found it difficult to coordinate their practices despite their similar cultures, it is easy to imagine how difficult coordination must be between the 27 nationalities currently represented within the EIFs.

Thus, the heterogeneity of bargaining systems and practices in the various Member States undoubtedly constitutes an obstacle to their coordination. But another important barrier lies in their current evolution. The macro-economic framework imposed by EMU has contributed to the erosion of national collective bargaining systems. The expansion of the low-wage sector has led to a decline in the bargaining power of the unions with regard to overall wage determination, while the strong trend towards the decentralisation of wage formation has become even more pronounced since the onset of the crisis (Glassner and Keune, 2010), making comparison of the wage increases obtained in sectoral agreements all the more difficult (Glassner and Pochet, 2011). All these changes have had a *de facto* effect on the unions' ability to coordinate collective bargaining systems at a transnational level.

The trends described here are particularly marked in Germany, and this is the source of another major difficulty facing union coordination. It will be seen that in the end, German leadership has contributed to creating a destructive standard for the other Member States. For indeed, the German union movement – which plays an influential role in Euro-unionism thanks, in part, to the political and economic weight of their country – appears to act as the "centre of gravity" for the determination of a transnational bargaining model.

Box 2: German trade unions, the driving force behind the coordination of collective bargaining

The German unions are at the hub of the EMF, Doorn and interregional network initiatives. They played a key role in the emergence of European coordination strategies, particularly IG Metall, which initiated the launching of the EMF Coordination Committee. The EMF's union membership is concentrated in Germany, and the powerful IG Metall, its leading union, plays a decisive role in the formulation of proposals. The Doorn Group was formed by the *Deutscher Gewerkschaftsbund* (DGB) (together with all the other German sectoral federations), following up on the Belgian proposal. Although the downward pressure on wages after the establishment of the Single Market and the introduction of the euro clearly had a European dimension that affected all the Member States, the idea of starting with concrete results in a small number of countries evidently appealed to the German unions. This also corresponds to Franz Traxler's view that bringing a number of small countries to coalesce around Germany would make it possible to achieve a critical mass large enough to guarantee European leadership on wage issues (Traxler 2002). He argued that leadership on wages would not require representing all workers, but that a grouping together of some 15% of workers would be enough to influence wage norms (Traxler and Bernd Brandl 2009/10). Finally, it was also IG Metall that launched cross-border wage cooperation (interregional networks) in June 1997, as part of the EMF's coordinated approach: the German union invited labour representatives from 14 neighbouring countries to attend its collective negotiations. Since bargaining is conducted at regional and sectoral level in Germany, the coordination strategy adopted was based on a regional networking of sectoral actors. IG Metal remains the hard core of these initiatives.

The German unions' leadership is fairly well accepted by its neighbours – the Benelux countries and Austria – since Germany's wage policies are likely to serve as benchmarks for the former Deutsche mark zone, and comparisons with its wage trends have always played an important role in Belgium and the Netherlands.[22] On the other hand, although on the decline, the predominance of the German system as the driving force behind coordination has been problematic for the Mediterranean countries. This is why, in 2009, the EMF adopted a position on the economic crisis which listed several guidelines for ensuring "solidarity in collective bargaining at EU level". Whereas until then, the German and Benelux unions had tended to impose their vision (with the wage norm based on inflation and productivity), the new declaration sought to reconcile positions stemming from cultural and socio-economic differences among EMF members (and in particular, to attenuate the North-South divide). This is no easy task, for even if EU eco-

22 This is why the Doorn Group was formed and also why German-Belgian-Dutch interregional sectoral cooperation developed more rapidly than in other European regions.

nomic governance means that responsibilities and political powers as regards collective bargaining are no longer solely determined at national level, unions are still reluctant to give up a national bargaining system that at least guarantees a known set of rules and actors.

Germany has been following a stringent wage restraint policy for over 10 years. And, not surprisingly, it displayed the most adverse wage trends of all the OECD countries between 2000 and 2009.[23] By asserting the virtues of German competitiveness – achieved thanks to the collapse of its wage model – the last two Chancellors succeeded in progressively establishing their wage restraint policy as the example for the rest of the EU. In practical terms, this has exerted a downward pressure on wages in the eurozone countries. A decade of German wage restraint has thus prevented any attempt to coordinate wage increases in Europe.

IV. Conclusions and Future Perspectives: What Prospects for European Wage Policy under European Economic Governance?

Given the difficulties in establishing inter-union solidarity in Europe, the question of how to promote an agenda for the redistribution of wealth to counter over 30 years of wage restraint – and its negative effects on wage relations in all the Member States – remains an open one. For indeed, in this regard, union organisations have not succeeded in developing a new vision of their political role. Thus far, their coordination meetings to set a common wage norm have simply not enabled them to develop a more combative union policy on wages.

The chances for wage coordination in the near future seem even further off after the launching of European economic governance in 2011. The adoption of an authoritarian system of wage monitoring by the EU has brushed aside any plans for the introduction of wage norms beyond setting up a European minimum wage rule. What then are the prospects and what European-level demands can be envisaged on this issue?

A. The European Minimum Wage: Better Than Nothing? Or a Dangerous Option?

Could the European minimum wage, as a second-best option for the coordination of collective bargaining, be a starting point for defining wage trend norms within the eurozone or the EU? Or would it, instead, be a dangerous option if the trend is towards lowering existing minimum wage levels? The Germans, who are campaigning for a cross-sectoral minimum wage in their own country, have been the main driving force

23 Real wages dropped by 4.5%. For more information on German trends, see Reinhard Bispinck, Heiner Dribbusch and Thorsten Schulten, 2010.

behind the demand, which they presented as a theme with a promising future at the Seville ETUC Congress of May 2007. They received support from delegates from two other major countries, France and the UK, as well as from the European Federation of Public Service Unions (EPSU). But the delegations from Italy and Scandinavia, where minimum wages are negotiated at sectoral level, categorically refused to follow this route, fearing that it would mean handing the power of their unions – which is based on their bargaining capacity – over to the state. The key issue in this debate is not so much the idea of a minimum wage, but the autonomy of the social representatives as regards pay bargaining. The opposition front feared creating a downward pressure on wages where the situation was better. Given these numerous divergences, the unions were not able to reach agreement on a common principle for a European minimum wage at the Seville Congress, and failed again to do so in Athens in May 2011. Little progress was made between these two congresses, with the same unions sticking to their initial positions, despite the increasing threat of wage dumping and the continuing expansion of low-wage sectors in the Member States.

Box 3: Minimum wage campaign in Germany

The German debate over a minimum wage began to emerge in 2004 (Hege 2005). It is revealing of the difficulties now facing the German union movement in pay bargaining. But it has always been a tricky issue because the autonomy of collective bargaining, as a constitutional right, has primacy. Wage bargaining in each branch and each region is thus left up to the sectoral unions. Yet, given the declining number of companies that have concluded a collective agreement, the expansion of low-wage sectors, and the downward pressure on social standards, the collective bargaining system seems increasingly less in a position to set minimum standards. This is why unions such as the NGG (food industry and Horeca) and Ver-Di (private services) launched a campaign in 2006 for a statutory hourly minimum wage of 8.5 euros. Specific minimum wages (at a higher rate) are planned for branches where sectoral collective agreements on pay structures still exist, but which companies are attempting to opt out of. This campaign re-politicises the issue of wages, and seeks to offset Ver-Di's weak organising power by mobilising public opinion.

In 1998, Pierrre Bourdieu suggested that different minimum wage rules could be set for different groups of countries at similar levels of economic development (Bourdieu *et al.*, 1998). In 2005, a network of researchers close to the unions[24] set a target for minimum wages in Europe at 60% of the average national wage, with a short-term interim

[24] From Germany (WSI), Switzerland (Denknetz), and France (IRES). The network aims to promote its "Theses for a European minimum wage policy", and generated a book by Schulten *et al.* (2006). See also IRES 2006.

target of 50%. Given that current legal minimum wage levels range from 30% to 48% of the average wage – corresponding respectively to 1.82 euros in the Czech Republic and 9 euros in France – this European rule would produce a relative pay rise across the EU.

On the other hand, if a less protective rule is adopted, rather than that based on these percentages of the average wage (50% or 60%), then it could present a danger for national minimum wage levels by promoting a downward harmonisation. In 2011, in the context of the crisis and under pressure from the EU authorities, a restrictive minimum wage policy became part of the package in the overall austerity programme adopted by the Member State governments (Schulten, 2009, 2012). Then, for the first time, in April 2012, the European Commission called on the Member States to introduce a minimum wage, arguing that "Wage floors need to be sufficiently adjustable, with the involvement of the social partners to reflect overall economic developments. Differentiated minimum wages […] can in that context be an effective means of upholding labour demand."[25]

The Commission thus gave its backing to Germany, where the system already provides for negotiating a minimum wage in certain sectors, and the Christian-Democratic Union (CDU), the major governing party, has precisely agreed to introduce minimum thresholds in industrial sectors where these do not exist. This approach to a European minimum wage contrasts sharply with the trade union proposal, which had, until then, called for a harmonised floor with a precise threshold.

The current inability of the Euro-unions to agree on the need for European social legislation on a guaranteed, cross-sectoral reference wage level shows how much remains to be done before joint demands with a mobilising force, that go beyond simple rhetoric, can be developed at transnational level.

B. Transnational Mobilisation: a Necessary Condition

A collective, transnational mobilisation is essential to the construction of a combative wage policy. For indeed, the whole point of coordination is to promote the creation of a European industrial relations system in which collective bargaining is predicated on the political recognition of the autonomy of the bargaining parties, the essential conditions for any deliberation. Lowell Turner (1996) has shown that transnational cooperation develops via networks (the CBCCs in this instance) and new institutions (here, the ETUC and EIFs) set up by structures belonging to organisations that already exist. But he noted

[25] European Commission, Communication "Towards a job-rich recovery" 18.4.2012, COM (2012) 173 final, Strasbourg, p. 11.

that, in the long term, these structures cannot act effectively without popular mass demands or protest to back them up. Although cruelly lacking in the last decades, transnational social mobilisation has somewhat mounted in pace since the onset of the crisis. On 5 April 2008, the ETUC mobilised 30,000 unionists from all over Europe for a Euro-demonstration at Ljubljana (Slovenia) in support of two demands: improved pay and purchasing power, and a more equitable distribution of profits.[26] The European trade unions also organised a strong reaction to the Pact for the Euro signed in March 2011, with a common Franco-German declaration in response to Sarkozy-Merkel, and a series of Euro-demonstrations in Berlin, Brussels, London, Budapest, Luxembourg and Wraclow (Poland).

At the ETUC Athens Congress in May 2011, the debate was clearly dominated by the question of how to respond to economic governance. From all the countries across the spectrum of today's two-speed Europe – from Greece to Germany – support emerged for the idea of the need for a paradigm change, with an upward coordination of wage, fiscal and social policies. It can be seen that Euro-unionism was, at that moment, seeking a return to what originally lay at the heart of union identity – the defence of wages – even if, by February 2012, the wage had once again disappeared from the slogan adopted for the Euro-demonstration, "For jobs and social justice".

The demand for securing a pay rate at European level which would effectively raise the majority of minimum wages – in other words, the introduction of a European minimum wage – could provide a strong incentive for collective mobilisation on a European scale. The EIF Collective Bargaining Coordination Committees and/or the ETUC Committee on the Promotion of a European Minimum Wage could then become the "suitable political structures facilitating the emergence of a transnational union protest movement" for which Turner (1996) had so forcefully pleaded.

---

26 The demonstration was part of the ETUC campaign for more equal pay, adopted by the 2007 Seville Congress. For a detailed analysis of this Congress, see Dufresne and Gobin (2007).

Should Fiscal Policies Be Included in a Labour Market Policy Database?

Ana Paula RIBEIRO
Assistant Professor, Faculty of Economics
University of Porto, Portugal

Margarida RUIVO
Assistant Professor, Faculty of Economics
University of Porto, Portugal

I. Introduction[1]

In the context of the Europe 2020 strategy, the implementation of the European Employment Strategy (EES) requires a variety of interventions ranging from traditional employment policies targeted at disadvantaged groups to broader interventions through employment, social, welfare and fiscal policies.

The monitoring of the EES has been gradually reinforced through the adoption of a common list of indicators to assess outcomes regarding implementation of the Employment Guidelines. At the same time, progress has been made with regard to harmonising data on the labour market interventions undertaken by national public authorities in their efforts to pursue these guidelines. The major contribution in this regard has been provided by the Eurostat labour market policy (LMP) database, which is designed to record labour market expenditures and participants and "aims to provide comparable data for the follow-up of some aspects of the Employment Guidelines whilst taking into account national specificities" (European Commission, 2000, p. 3).

However, the Eurostat LMP database has a narrow scope: it covers "public interventions[2] in the labour market aimed at reaching its efficient functioning and to correct disequilibria, and which can be distin-

1 This chapter draws on the helpful contributions of RESORE network researchers, in particular Peter Urwin, Adreana Khristova and Jean-Pascal Higelé.

2 "*Public interventions* refer to actions taken by general government [...] which involve expenditure, either in the form of actual disbursements or of foregone revenue (reductions in taxes, social contributions or other charges normally payable). *General government* should be understood as including central, state/regional, local government and the social security funds." (European Commission, 2006: § 2 and 3).

guished from other general employment policy interventions in that they act selectively to favour particular groups in the labour market" (European Commission, 2006: 6, §1). These target groups are defined by the European Commission as comprising persons facing difficulties in the labour market such as the unemployed, people in work but at risk of involuntary job loss, and economically inactive persons who would like to enter the labour market and are disadvantaged in some way. This definition is said to "facilitate a distinction between labour market policies and more general employment, social protection or fiscal policies which may have similar aims in terms of promoting employment, but which act in a non-selective way across the population" (European Commission 2006, §13).

Consequently, some public interventions covering large portions of the population, involving significant outlays from state budgets and playing a crucial role in the EES are not recorded on a harmonised basis. Fiscal policies such as the working and child tax credits in the United Kingdom (UK), and the *prime pour l'emploi*[3] as well as general reductions in employers' social contributions in France, are notable examples.[4]

This chapter will argue that given the aim, coverage and labour market impacts of such policies, they should receive the same in-depth statistical treatment as those included in the Eurostat LMP database. Indeed, the UK tax credits and the French *prime pour l'emploi* and general reductions in employers' social contributions are all explicitly targeted at the labour market with a view to enhancing its efficiency: the tax credits are aimed at fostering labour supply and employment through in-work benefits, and reductions in employers' social contributions at favouring labour demand for low-paid workers. Moreover, since these policies also benefit particular groups (unemployed and inactive persons, low-wage and low-income workers and disadvantaged people), the distinction between general policies and policies targeted at particular disadvantaged groups is somewhat debatable.

This chapter also seeks to contribute to one of the core topics of the present book, in that it addresses the question of the massive flows of public resources towards the financing of private employment channelled through reductions in employer contributions and the topping-up of workers' wage income. We argue in favour of making available com-

3 The French in-work tax credit measure.

4 Tax credits are an example of interventions considered to fall outside of the scope of the Eurostat LMP database "Interventions that provide in-work benefits based on levels of income may be used as an incentive to facilitate the transition from welfare to work but the benefits are equally available to persons already in low-wage employment and are thus not specifically aimed at an LMP target group" (European Commission, 2006: §23).

parative cross-country and cross-time data on the relevant public expenditures financing employment in Europe.

We thus propose to detail the tax-benefit measures introduced in the UK and France: the British tax credits are examined in Section 2, and the French *prime pour l'emploi* in Section 3. Section 4 analyses the general reductions in employers' social contributions implemented in France. The chapter concludes with some final remarks in Section 5. We suggest that, given their design, aims and impacts on the labour market, these measures meet several of the general objectives of the European Employment Strategy, as stated in the Employment Guidelines. Consequently, general government resources allocated to these measures could also be accounted for in a harmonised database that would complement the existing Eurostat database.

Our line of argument is reinforced by the relevance of these policies in terms of expenditure and number of participants involved, as they are among the most representative categories of active measures in the European Union (European Commission, 2000). Table 1 shows some indicators of their relative importance.

Table 1: Brief overview of the relative importance of tax credits and general reductions in social contributions, UK and France

		Participants		Public expenditure	
	Measure	millions	% labour force (1)	million euros	% total ALMP expenditure (2)
UK	Working Tax Credit (2009-10)	3.4 (3)	10.9% (3)	8,614.5	1,101.3%
	Child Tax Credit (2009-10)	7.4 (3)	23.6% (3)	13,704.6	1751%
France	"*Prime pour l'Emploi*" (2010)	7.5 (4)	20.7% (5)	3,610 (6)	22.4%
	General reductions of social contributions (2010)	10.5 (7)	36.8%	21,900 (7)	136.1%

(1) Eurostat on line statistics at http://epp.eurostat.ec.europa.eu/portal/page/portal/ (accessed in March, 2012).

(2) ALMP is the total of categories 2-7 at http://epp.eurostat.ec.europa.eu/portal/page/portal/ (accessed in March, 2012).

(3) Own estimations based on the number of in-work persons covered: couples (2 persons) plus single-person households (Source: HMRC, 2011).

(4) Number of beneficiary tax households in 2010 (République Française, 2012a, p. 76).

(5) Beneficiary tax households in 2010 as a % of total tax households in 2008 (INSEE).

(6) *République Française* (2012a, p. 76).

(7) ACOSS (*Agence Centrale des Organismes de Sécurité Sociale*) and CCMSA, in *République Française* (2012b), *Fiche No. 1*, "*Réduction générale des cotisations patronales de sécurité sociale, dite réduction Fillon*".

Since an LMP database should be comprehensive enough to provide comparative data to assess EES follow-through rates, excluding this information leads to biased monitoring and analysis, notably with regard to the relative weight of active *versus* passive measures. This latter issue is of particular relevance since the activation *versus* support distinction is central to most of the indicators used for monitoring and analysing Employment Guideline 7 (former Employment Guideline 19); however, only 6 of the 16 indicators are drawn from the Eurostat LMP database (even the follow-up of participants in active measures relies on national data sources), and no other Employment Guideline is assessed using this database (Employment Committee, 2009). Moreover, since LMP database publications are widely used in both official and academic studies, this can lead to partial or inaccurate results in assessing the functioning of the labour market.

II. The UK Tax Credits

This section will discuss the importance of monitoring the impact of UK tax credits on the functioning of the labour market in the context of the European Employment Strategy (EES). We focus on the Working Tax Credit (WTC) and the Child Tax Credit (CTC), two in-work measures introduced in 2003 upgrading their forerunners, Family Income Support (1971), Family Credit (1988) and the Working Families' Tax Credit (1999).

We begin with a brief description of the UK system of tax credits in order to show how their formal design fits into the EES. We then proceed to analyse their major effects on the labour market, and end this section with a tentative exercise to show how including tax credits would improve on the active LMP figures currently recorded in the Eurostat LMP database.

A. Design and Aim of Tax Credits within the EES Framework

Official European Council documents concerning the Employment Guidelines and specific recommendations for each Member State tend to support our argument for using information on tax credits to complement the Eurostat LMP database.

It is our contention that tax credits meet the general horizontal objectives of "full employment" and "strengthening social cohesion". These objectives were laid down in the 2005-2008 Guidelines, in which the European Council recommends that policies should be pursued to improve the overall employment rate through more inclusive labour markets in the European Union (OJEC, 2005, L 205/23). These objectives are still present in the European Council decision on the new Employment Guidelines: "Member States' reforms should therefore ensure access and opportunities for all throughout their lifecycle, thus reducing poverty and social exclusion through removing barriers to labour market participation, especially for women, older workers, young people, people with disabilities and legal migrants." (OJEC, 2010, L 308/47)

Tax credits fit in particularly well with Employment Guideline 7, which stresses the importance of financial incentives to encourage taking up and remaining in work (OJEC, 2010, L308/49):

> Policies to make work pay remain important. […] Member States should review tax and benefit systems, and public services capacity to provide the support needed, in order to increase labour force participation and stimulate labour demand. They should promote active ageing, gender equality including equal pay, and the integration in the labour market of young people, people with disabilities, legal migrants and other vulnerable groups. Work-life balance policies with the provision of affordable care and innovation in the manner in which work is organised should be geared to raising employment rates, particularly among young people, older workers and women. Member States should also remove barriers to labour market entry for newcomers […].

The Working Families' Tax Credit (WFTC) was included in the Government's 1998 "*Making Work Pay*" reform package, which was intended to provide a comprehensive strategy to move people from welfare into work (Peer Review, 2000, Brewer, 2003). It was replaced by the Working Tax Credit (WTC) in 2003, in order to "relieve in-work poverty and enhance work incentives for workers facing disadvantage with more financial help to those in low-paid work, whether or not with children" (Inland Revenue, 2002a, p. 1). To qualify for the WTC, households must have at least one member in work (working at least 16 hours a week) (HMRC, 2012). According to HMRC (2012), in 2012, single people without children were entitled to a credit of £1,920 per year (~ £36.92 per week), while couples with or without children and lone parents were entitled to a credit of £3,870 per year (~ £74.42 per week). In addition to increasing the support provided to lone parents, the WTC includes a childcare element which offers families with children where all adults are working, caring or disabled, help with up to 70% of approved childcare costs limited to a substantial maximum amount (£175 per week for one child under 16, and £300 for two or more children in 2012). Additional amounts are provided to adults with disabilities and people aged over 50 returning to work (50+ return to work element). The WTC is thus clearly an active LMP measure as it provides financial support to in-work situations that is proportionally higher for particular groups experiencing disadvantages in entering or re-entering the labour market, and contrasts, for example, with what is considered as the passive nature of the unemployment benefit.

The other measure introduced in 2003 as a successor to the WFTC is the Child Tax Credit (CTC), intended to "tackle child poverty and provide financial support for households with children, by providing a seamless, portable and secure system of support for households with children" (Inland Revenue, 2002a: 1). The CTC is paid to the main carer, irrespective of employment status, and consists of two components: a family element of £545 per year (~ £10.45 per week), doubled in the financial year of a child's birth, and an amount per dependent child of £2,690 per year (~ £51.73 per week, and higher for disabled children) (HMRC, 2012).

By providing additional financial support to households with children, both the WTC and the CTC contribute to reconciling work and family life. In this regard, they are also in line with the records of the Council's specific recommendations to the UK, which pinpointed the concentration of inactivity and long-term unemployment amongst particularly disadvantaged populations such as lone parents and jobless households (OJEC, 2003, L 197/30, among others). Lone mothers, in particular, display the lowest employment rates, substantially below the European Union (EU) average. Council recommendations include improving the access and affordability of childcare with a view to making it easier for parents to take employment (OJEC, 2001, L 22/37 and European Commission, 2011: 6, among others), and reducing the gender gap in terms of full-time equivalents in view of the particularly high rate of part-time work among women in the UK (OJEC, 2000, p. 40). In order to promote full-time employment, the WTC also includes a bonus for those working 30 or more hours per week (HMRC, 2012).

Families with annual gross income below £15,860 (CTC) or below £6,420 (WTC) are entitled to the full amounts (HMRC, 2012). Above these thresholds, the tax credit is progressively reduced. Thus, these measures are broadly targeted at low-income households with or without children, and are designed to increase financial support to enhance employability.[5] They correspond to a negative tax mechanism applied according to the level of earned income, hours worked and family composition, and use resources from general taxation under the management of the UK tax system (Peer Review, 2000).

---

5 Eligibility: persons with childcare responsibilities (CTC); individuals and couples without children working at least 30 hours a week, and families with children or a disabled member, provided that one of the persons works at least 16 hours a week (WTC) (Brewer, 2003, p. 5).

B. Impacts of Tax Credits on the Labour Market – a Tentative Assessment

In order to assess the relevance of these measures in terms of meeting the aims of the EES, we will now attempt to assess the effective impacts of tax credits on the labour market. Rather than presenting an exhaustive analysis, we will draw on several studies from official or independent sources (mostly concerning the WFTC) to illustrate the impacts of tax credits on three target variables: employment, income and gender equality.

Employment Effects

According to Peters *et al.* (2004, p. 344), "the literature has shown that family tax credits can be effective at combating unemployment and also long-term unemployment". A review of several in-work benefit programmes in Brewer *et al.* (2009) also shows that, in most of the cases, such policies increased the employment opportunities of low-income families (generally with dependent children). Take-up rates increased steadily after the introduction of the WFTC according to ECOTEC (2002), with higher rates being observed among those most in need (HM Treasury, 2005). The more recent CTC and WTC also simplified the claims processes, making it easier for families to apply (Inland Revenue, 2002a, p. 4) and thus improving take-up, with rates close to 90% compared to 70% for the WFTC (HM Treasury, 2008, p. 20).[6] Table 2 shows the evolution of WFTC/WTC recipient households between 1997 and 2011.

Table 2: WFTC/WTC recipient households, 1997-2011 (thousands)

1997 (Nov)	790	2006 (Apr)	1,884
1999 (Nov)	965	2007 (Apr)	1,988
2001 (Nov)	1,294	2008 (Apr)	2,091
2002 (Nov)	1,376	2009 (Apr)	2,259
2003 (Jul)	1,586	2010 (Apr)	2,458
2004 (Apr)	1,824	2011 (Apr)	2,593
2005 (Apr)	1,813		

Sources: ECOTEC (2002), Inland Revenue (2002b, 2004), HMRC (2006, 2011a).

It can be seen from the table that the highest increases in the number of recipient families occurred at the time of the launching of the WFTC and then the WTC.

With regard to employment status, data for November 2002 (Inland Revenue, 2002b) show that most of the families were receiving the

6 Take-up rate refers to the proportion of families within the eligible population who take up, or claim, their entitlement to a positive tax credit award.

additional 30-hour (full-time) element. For fiscal years 2003-04 to 2009-10, 38% to 47.2% of the households awarded in-work tax credits (CTC and WTC) received this element (HMRC, 2011b). Awards of the disabled worker (and severely disabled adult) and the 50+ return to work elements have remained roughly stable since fiscal year 2003-04, covering respectively about 3% and 0.3% of in-work tax credit recipient households. The second main additional element, the childcare element, was awarded to 9.7% of in-work tax credit recipient families in 2009-10, roughly 3.5 percentage points higher than in 2003-2004 (HMRC, 2011b).

There are few available studies on the impact of tax credits on employment. Blundell and Reed (2000), in summarising the results of three studies,[7] predicted that the overall impact of the WFTC on employment would be roughly 3%, and that higher employability gains would accrue to lone mothers and married women whose partners were not working. In a more recent review by Brewer and Browne (2007),[8] the results suggest that the WFTC improved the lone parent employment rate by approximately 5 percentage points between 1999 and 2002 and reduced the proportion of workless households. The aggregate employment effect was not as strong, possibly because of the negative effect of the WFTC on married women with children and employed partners (Peer Review, 2000, p. 4; Brewer and Browne, 2007, p. 15). According to estimates in Brewer *et al.* (2006), between 1999 and 2002, the WFTC slightly reduced the labour supply of mothers in couples by 0.6 percentage points while it increased that of fathers in couples by 0.8 percentage points.

Moreover, Blundell (2006) reported a 3.5-4 percentage point increase in lone parent labour supply attributable to the WFTC policy.

Figure 1 illustrates how the introduction of tax credits contributed to an increase in employment rates, particularly for lone parents and workless families with children, a dynamic supported by the results in the empirical literature (see Brewer *et al.*, 2009). These are the typical disadvantaged groups with higher than average unemployment and long-term unemployment rates that are frequently targeted by the European Council in its labour market policy recommendations.

---

7 Paul Gregg, Paul Johnson and Howard Reed, funded by the Joseph Rowntree Foundation (1999); Richard Blundell, Alan Duncan, Julian McCrae and Costas Meghir, funded by the Bank of England and the ESRC Centre for the Microeconomic Analysis of Fiscal Policy at IFS (1998); and Gillian Paull, Ian Walker and Yu Zhu, funded by the Nuffield Foundation (1999).

8 Concerning research by: Gregg and Harkness, funded by the Leverhulme Trust (2003); Francesconi and Van der Klaau, funded by the Economic and Social Research Council and the University of Essex (2004); Leigh (2005); Blundell, Brewer and Shephard, funded by the ESRC, the Inland Revenue and the Bank of England (2005); and Brewer, Duncan, Shephard and Suárez, funded by the Inland Revenue (2005).

Figure 1: Employment rate for lone parents and workless households with children

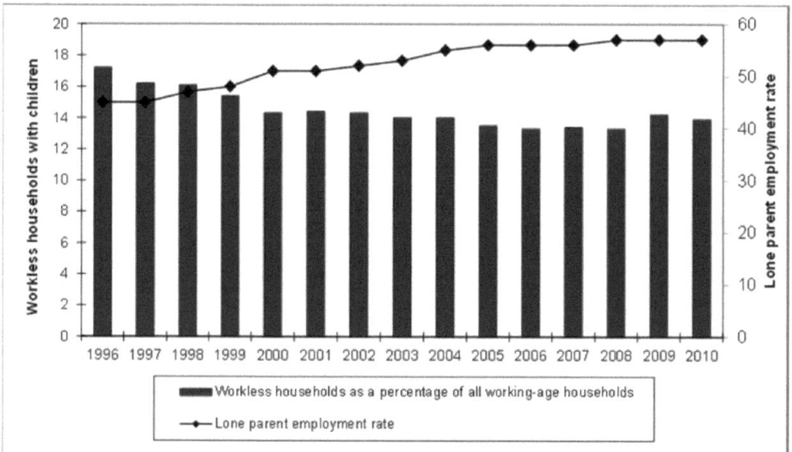

Source: http://www.poverty.org.uk/46/index.shtml?2 and http://www.statistics.gov.uk/downloads/theme_labour/Worklessness/ (accessed in March, 2012).

Income Effects

The employment effects noted above derive essentially from the improved in-work financial support provided to low/moderate-income families. This support is also designed to reduce poverty and inactivity traps.

Primarily targeted at low-wage workers and low-income families with children, the WTC and CTC are mostly awarded to employees in the service and public sectors. WFTC data provided by the Inland Revenue (2002b) show that "nearly half of lone parent recipients had administrative, secretarial or personal service occupations. For couples, over half the main earners had skilled trades, were process, plant or machine operatives or had elementary occupations"; individuals in the top 3 occupations also received the WFTC, although they represented under 5% of the employed persons in this category (Inland Revenue, 2002b: 17). Thus, the tax credits clearly appear to benefit low to mid-skilled (and, thus, low to mid-paid) occupations.

Compared to its predecessor, the Family Credit (FC), the WFTC increased the generosity of in-work support, even for typical entry-wage jobs. This, according to Strickland (1998), means that "families need lower wages than they would otherwise to be better off in work than on Income Support – their 'replacement ratio' will be lower". HM Treasury (2005: 28) data for 2000 showed that the WFTC improved average income by 14.1% among the families receiving the FC in 1999, increased the income of lone parents who entered work by 44% for those receiving Family Income Support in 1999, and sharply reduced the risk of severe hardship for both lone parents and couples compared to the FC.

In addition,

> The Working Tax Credit (WTC) has improved work incentives for workers aged 25 and over without children. From October 2003, a childless or disabled couple aged 25 and over in full-time work will be guaranteed at least £187 per week. This represents an increase in gains to work to £40 per week, compared with £15 per week before the introduction of the WTC. The reforms also mean that a single person aged 25 or over without children working full-time on the National Minimum Wage will be more than £25 a week better off from October 2003 compared with the previous system – an 18% increase in income (UK NAPE, 2003, p. 36).

Based on the Inland Revenue data (2002b), weekly WFTC awards averaged £86.78 (£178.3 including childcare charges) in November 2002. At their inception, WTC awards ranged from £29.2 to £169.2 per week, and for the CTC (adding the highest additional element), from £10.45 to £51.75 per week, according to HM Treasury data (2002, p. 32). Average awards have clearly followed an important growth path since the introduction of the WFTC in 1999: in 1989, average FC payments were slightly above £25 per week whereas for fiscal year 2009-10, the average entitlement (CTC plus WTC) was close to £85 per week (HMRC, 2011b).

Table 3: Effect of Government reforms on high Marginal Deduction Rates

Marginal Deduction Rate*	Before Budget 1998	system of tax and benefits		
		2002-03	2005-06	2008-09
Over 100 per cent	5,000	0	0	0
Over 90 per cent	130, 000	45, 000	30, 000	30, 000
Over 80 per cent	300, 000	210, 000	165, 000	150, 000
Over 70 per cent	740, 000	255, 000	235, 000	200, 000
Over 60 per cent	760, 000	940, 000	1, 730, 000	1, 875, 000

* Marginal Deduction Rates are for working households receiving income-related benefits or tax credits where at least one person works 16 hours or more a week, and the head of the household is not receiving pension or disability allowance.
Figures are cumulative. Before Budget 1998 data are based on 1997-98 estimated caseload and take-up rates; the 2008-09 system of tax and benefits is based on tax credit caseloads in April 2007, and earlier data for housing and council tax benefits.

Source: HM Treasury (2005, p. 30; 2008, p. 17).

It should be noted that the reforms to National Insurance Contributions (NICs) and income tax included in the overall reform package were also in line with Employment Guideline 7 (former Guideline 19): the number of families facing marginal deduction rates in excess of 70%, and particularly those facing rates above 90%, has fallen substantially since 1997-8. Table 3 shows the effects of the overall reforms on marginal deduction rates.

Tax credits constituted the most important policy measure contributing to an increase in the number of households with marginal deduction rates falling between 60 and 70% (UK NAPE, 2003, p. 37).

According to HM Treasury estimates (HM Treasury, 2008, p. 23) the reforms, taken overall, improved the average income for families with children by about £1,950 (£4,100 for families in the poorest fifth of the population) in real terms, relative to the previous 1997-99 system. The Treasury also estimated that if the system had been maintained unchanged, there might have been 1.7 million more children in poverty than at the time of the report (HM Treasury, 2008, p. 16).

However, some studies provide a critical assessment of the work incentives attached to the UK tax credits. Blundell and Meghir (2001) point out that the tax credits are means-tested and have no time limit, and argue that these schemes "reduce human capital accumulation and may thus create a culture of dependency on the programme". They also draw on studies testifying that wage progression is low and thus that exiting low-pay jobs and the tax credit programme has proven to be difficult. In addition, they suggest that the lower incentives to work compared with the US Earned Income Tax Credit may result from the fact that British tax credits are considered as income for determining eligibility for other transfer programmes, thus reducing net benefits. Hoynes and Blundell (2001) note, moreover, that the UK's in-work schemes were implemented alongside stable or even improved out-of-work benefits, inducing "rather modest increases in the incentives to work."

Gender Effects

Figure 2 shows that women represent almost 50% of the in-work parent recipients of both tax credits (CTC and WTC).

Data from the Impact Evaluation Report (ECOTEC, 2002) show that from the introduction of WFTC up to 2001, an additional 129,700 lone parents were claiming WFTC, of whom 94% were women. After peaking at 97% in 2002, the proportion of females among in-work lone parents receiving WTC plus CTC dropped back down to 93% in 2011 (Inland Revenue, 2003; HMRC, 2011a).

According to the same ECOTEC report, there were 78,000 fewer unemployed women of working age in 2000 compared to 1998; however, these figures reflect the overall effects of the reforms introduced in 1999, and assessment of individual policies is difficult.

Figure 2: Distribution of in-work families receiving WTC and CTC by type, April 2011

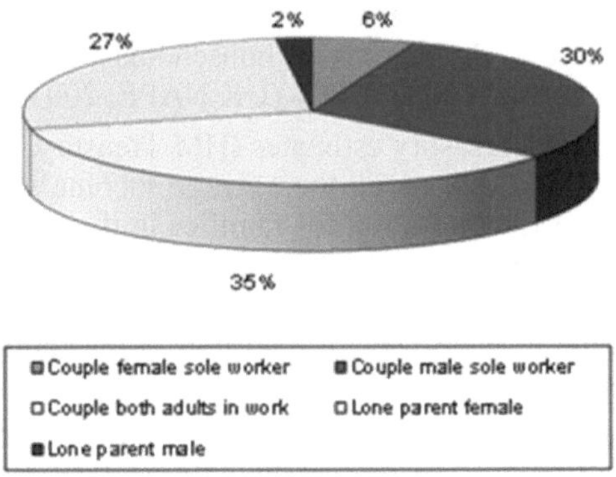

Source: HMRC (2011a).

The WTC provides help in covering up to 80% of childcare costs, thus encouraging even parents on the lowest incomes to work (HM Treasury, 2005, p. 29). This support helps to reduce one of the highest gender gaps in employment attributable to the impact of parenthood in the EU countries, an explicit recommendation of the European Council in 2001 (OJEC, 2001, L 22/37). Tax credits have indeed provided low-income support to encourage female work: Leigh (2005) found that the WFTC had a superior effect on the earnings of mothers compared with those of fathers.

In addition to improving the reconciliation between work and family life, in particular for women, the WFTC/WTC also includes a 30-hour element to encourage full-time employment. This feature is important as the gender gap in employment is biased towards women in part-time jobs in the UK. Alleviating such a disparity was a concern of the European Council in the policy recommendations of 2000. The review by Brewer and Browne (2007, p. 15) suggests a considerable shift from part-time to full time work among lone mothers.

C. Tax Credits versus Targeted LMPs: an Exercise

Although tax credits are geared to improving work attractiveness and remedying structural imbalances in the UK labour market, they have never been included in the Eurostat LMP reports. Use of these Eurostat data thus clearly underestimates the role of active labour market policies (ALMPs) in the UK and distorts results in cross-country comparative studies. In particular, the Eurostat LMP statistics show that, in 2009, the UK had one of the lowest expenditures on ALMP (categories 2-7) – roughly 0.05% of GDP – when compared to the EU15 average of 0.6% of GDP (Table 4, below).

Table 4: Eurostat statistics on LMP expenditures, 2004-2009 (%)

LMP database categories	2004	2005	2006	2007	2008	2009
(2-7)/(2-9) UK	25.0	21.7	18.2	23.8	20.0	13.2
(2-7)/(2-9) EU15	29.9	28.6	30.8	32.4	32.0	27.2
(2-7)/GDP UK	0.06	0.05	0.04	0.05	0.05	0.05
(2-7)/GDP EU15	0.60	0.53	0.52	0.48	0.48	0.55
(2-9)/GDP UK	0.24	0.23	0.22	0.21	0.25	0.38
(2-9)/GDP EU15	2.01	1.85	1.69	1.48	1.50	2.02

Source: Eurostat on line statistics: http://epp.eurostat.ec.europa.eu/portal/page/portal/ (accessed in March, 2012).
Notes: Category (2-7) includes "*LMP measures*" (European Commission, 2006), *i.e.*, public employment services are not included; category (2-9) also includes "*LMP support*" (European Commission, 2006), *i.e.*, passive LMP measures.

When tax credits are excluded, ALMP expenditure in the UK falls below the EU15 average: in 2009, it corresponded to 13.2% of total LMP expenditure (categories 2-9) compared to the EU average of 27.2%. Melis (2005, pp. 4 and 7) shows that between 1998 and 2003, total expenditure in the UK on both active and passive LMPs dropped by an annual average of about 7% in *per capita*[9] real terms, with expenditure attached to Employment Incentives exhibiting an estimated 33% annual decrease in *per capita* real terms. Strikingly, however, the overall unemployment rate in the UK fell from 6.2% to 4.9% during that same period.

Table 5 provides information on total in-work tax credit expenditures and participants.

Table 5: Expenditure on in-work tax credits (£ million) and participants (thousands)

	2003-04	2004-05	2005-06	2006-07	2007-08	2008-09	2009-10
Total expenditure	11314	12356	13111	14585	15609	18306	19885
% GDP	0.99	1.03	1.05	1.10	1.11	1.28	1.43
Participants (*)	7571	7836	7824	7829	7832	7914	7988
% Labour force	25.6	26.3	26.0	25.6	25.5	25.4	25.5

* Own estimations based on the number of persons covered: couples (2 persons) plus single-person households.

Source: Eurostat on line statistics at http://epp.eurostat.ec.europa.eu/portal/page/portal/ (accessed in March, 2012) and HMRC (2008, 2009b, 2010, 2011).

9 For the population aged 15-64 years.

From the examination of Tables 4 and 5, we conclude that:

- tax credit expenditure, alone, represents between 1 and 1.43% of GDP in the UK;
- if tax credit expenditure is added to expenditures effectively recorded by Eurostat categories 2-7, total spending on ALMPs in the UK would, in 2004 and 2009 for example, have represented 85% and 82% of LMP expenditures (categories 2-9) respectively;
- between 2003 and 2009, in real terms *per capita*, annual average expenditure on tax credits grew by 4.5%.[10]

Finally, regarding participants, the in-work CTC together with the WTC covered around 26% of the UK labour force from 2003 to 2009. These figures can be compared with those recorded in the Eurostat LMP database: in 2009, participants in total LMP (categories 2-9) represented, on average, 13.7% of the total labour force in the EU15 (12.2% for the EU27); of the seven countries whose coverage rate was higher than average (Belgium, Spain, Ireland, Luxembourg, Germany, Finland and France), only Belgium exhibited a value (30.4%) higher than that recorded for the in-work tax credit system in the UK.[11]

III. The French *Prime Pour l'Emploi*

In this section we will analyse the French tax credit, the *prime pour l'emploi* (PPE). It differs in some aspects from the UK system, but is also designed to act as an incentive to work.

A. Design and Aim of the PPE within the EES Framework

The PPE fits in with Employment Guideline 7, former Guideline 19. It is described in the National Action Plan for Employment (NAPE) as "the primary tool for making employment more remunerative, designed to help offset the higher tax rates and reduction in social security assistance[12] that accompany a return to work" (French NAPE, 2003, p. 116). It is intended to favour transitions from inactivity and unemployment to employment by increasing disposable income instead of reducing social transfers (*Evaluation de la Stratégie Européenne pour l'Emploi*, 2002, p. 22). Council recommendations on the implementation of Member States' employment policies emphasise pursuing the reduction of the marginal effective tax rate to encourage workers to seek and remain in

10 Expenditure in real terms was computed using the final consumption expenditure of general government deflator.

11 Source: http://epp.eurostat.ec.europa.eu/portal/page/portal/labour_market/labour_market_policy/database (accessed in March 2012).

12 For instance, the complete loss of the minimum income benefit (*RMI*) and loss of part of the individual housing benefit (French NAPE 2004, p. 66).

work, particularly those who are unskilled and low-paid (OJEC, 2002, L 60/75).

The PPE tax credit was launched in 2001 with the aim of increasing net earnings for low-income working people. It applies to persons earning above 0.3 times and below 1.4 times the full-time equivalent of the annual minimum wage (SMIC) for single people, or 2.1 times for lone parents or couples. The amount awarded depends on hours worked, family composition, individual earnings and total household income. The tax credit consists of two components: a variable component, which increases with earnings up to SMIC level, and then tapers off up to the ceiling of 1.4 times the SMIC; and a lump-sum component based on the family situation, with additional amounts for single-worker couples and persons with dependents.

The PPE has been reformed a number of times. The reform of 2003 slightly improved the situation of people working part-time or only part of the year. Another improvement was the establishment of a cash advance for persons meeting certain eligibility requirements, in order to offset the delay in payment since the tax credit is based on the earnings of the previous year and thus only disbursed in the year following job take-up. In the summer of 2006, the option of receiving payment in twelve monthly instalments was introduced. The amounts awarded were raised substantially: the maximum amount of the variable component progressed from 467 euros in 2002, to 538 euros in 2005 and 948 euros in 2007 (*République Française*, 2006 and 2007; Cochard *et al.*, 2008: 64). However, the freeze of the PPE after 2008 together with its new articulation with the RSA (*Revenu de solidarité active*)[13] initiated a decline in the generosity of the measure.

B. Assessment of the Impacts on the Labour Market

There have been extensive debates over how appropriate a measure such as the PPE is for the French labour market, which has a complex architecture of incentives, is far from achieving full employment, and where minimum wages are relatively high.[14] The problems associated with the fact that the PPE has a two-fold aim, as an incentive to work and as a means of income redistribution, have also come under discussion (Fitoussi, Pisani-Ferry and Le Cacheux, 2003).

In this section, we will attempt to provide a summary assessment of the effectiveness of the PPE with regard to these two aims, based on some of the debates and research results reported in the literature.

13 The *RSA* is a guaranteed income mechanism that replaces the *RMI*.

14 See, for example, Cahuc (2002).

Incentive Effects

Theoretically, the PPE offers a financial incentive to take up employment and increase the length of time worked by providing a supplement to raise work-related income above an individual's reservation wage. However, as will be seen below, evaluating these incentive effects is a complex exercise. The presentation that follows is largely based on the review of several *ex ante* studies by Stancanelli and Sterdyniak (2004), as well as on that by Cochard *et al.* (2008), who also present an *ex post* study on the topic.

Some of the studies reviewed by Stancanelli and Sterdyniak (2004) measured the incentive and disincentive effects of the PPE by estimating the financial gains and marginal effective tax rates for different categories of beneficiaries (typical-case method) taking up a job or increasing the length of time worked. These "typical" cases were defined on the basis of composition of the household (single, married, with dependents, etc.), labour-market status (unemployed, employed, RMI recipient, etc.) and working-time status (full time or part time). No general conclusion can be drawn from the results of the studies. For instance, it was found that the PPE, in its 2003 version, slightly increased the gain of moving from a half-time to a full-time SMIC job for a single person, and for the first individual in a workless couple entering employment. However, since eligibility is based on total household income, the PPE was also found to have disincentive effects in some situations (Stancanelli and Sterdyniak, 2004, p. 26).

Cochard *et al.* (2008) cite other studies using the same approach which have shown that after introduction of the PPE together with other incentive measures, there was no longer a loss of income on job take-up. However, they express strong reservations with regard to this typical-case approach, and discuss the use of other methodologies. They note that micro-simulation models have the advantage of being based on representative surveys rather than arbitrarily defined typical profiles, and thus permit more realistic assessment of the financial gains offered by the PPE. Here again, no unambiguous conclusions could be drawn, with results showing losses or only weak gains for some categories of beneficiaries. The authors also cite studies using structural models of labour supply which aim at explaining the participation behaviour of individuals. These models are of very difficult construction given the complexity of the French tax-benefit system and of the functioning of the labour market, the intra-household character of participation decisions, and the perceived disutility of work, etc. Because of these difficulties, the structural models adopt a number of controversial hypotheses that have important impacts on the results.[15]

Stancanelli and Sterdyniak (2004) surveyed five studies that used these models[16] and Cochard *et al.* (2008) selected three among the same *ex ante* studies. Again, weak incentive effects of the PPE were noted.

The original contribution in the paper by Cochard *et al.* (2008) is the *ex post* study of the effect of the PPE on participation decisions using a difference in differences method and data from the 2001 fiscal revenues survey.[17] The authors compared a group of potential PPE beneficiaries (treated group) and a control group whose members were not affected by the measure but had similar characteristics to those of the treated group. They found that the employment probability for the potential beneficiaries of the PPE between 2000 and 2001 was not higher than that of the persons not covered by the PPE (2008, p. 70). There was no significant effect of the PPE on employment. The authors suggest that the weak impact observed in 2001 could result in part from the low levels of the tax credit awards, delayed disbursement and insufficient information about the measure at the time of its introduction.[18]

There is still room for improvement in the assessment of the employment effects of the PPE, to which a new generation of *ex post* studies integrating the most recent reforms to the policy device will certainly contribute.

Although the PPE may not be very effective in achieving its aim of generating meaningful incentives to work, it covers a large proportion of total employment and of the labour force. According to some estimations (Bonnefoy and Robert-Bobée, 2008),[19] 9 million persons received the PPE for their revenues of 2006, which represented 32% of total employment.

---

15 For instance, it is commonly assumed that increasing the labour supply will induce an equivalent rise in employment, ignoring the shortage of available jobs. Another example is the assumption that individuals are free to choose their working time.

16 It is difficult to summarise the results of these studies. In their abstract, the authors state: "Overall, the effect on labour supply appears to be positive, but very weak (from 0.2 to 0.4%)" (Stancanelli and Sterdyniak, 2004:17).

17 *Enquête Revenus Fiscaux* (ERF), INSEE-DGI, 2001.

18 In 2007, the *Direction de l'Animation, de la Recherche, des Etudes, et des Statistiques* (DARES) and *Direction de la Recherche, des Etudes, de l'Evaluation et des Statistiques* (DREES) conducted a survey on potential PPE beneficiaries in relation to the revenues of 2005. A large majority of the respondents were found to be informed about the general principles of the measure, but not about its modalities (Mikol *et al.*, 2008).

19 Using as sources the *Enquête Revenus Fiscaux* 2004 (updated 2006), INSEE-DGI, model INES, calculations DREES.

Income and Redistribution Effects

The second objective of the measure is to raise the income of working poor/low-income families. Its redistributive effect has been analysed in most of the studies monitoring the impacts of the PPE on the labour market.

The characteristics of the recipients are revealed in some studies. INSEE (2002) data for 2001[20] show that more than one third of the beneficiaries were under 30 years old and 34% had worked less than full time (part-time or part of the year).[21,22] About two thirds declared earnings of between 1 and 1.4 of the SMIC. The study by Cochard *et al.* (2008) based on data from the 2001 fiscal revenues survey confirms the low-wage profile of the recipients: they were younger and had less schooling[23] compared with the total working age population (excluding students and retirees); 86% were blue-collar or white-collar workers (compared to 62% for the total active population) and 2% were managers or executives (compared to 15%); 12% were employed under fixed-term or temporary contracts and 20% held part-time jobs (compared to 9% and 16% respectively for the total wage-earner population).

The PPE mobilises a large amount of public resources (see Table 1 in Section I, above). The total amount of tax credits progressed from 2.1 thousand million euros in 2002, to 4.5 in 2007 and 2008, and reached 3.6 thousand million in 2010. The estimated value for 2012 is 2.8 thousand million euros. The total amount in 2010 represented 0.19% of GDP, while public expenditure on active measures in France (categories 2-7) recorded in the Eurostat LMP database was 0.83% of GDP.

The increase in the disposable income of recipient households is quite modest. In 2007, based on the revenues of 2006, the beneficiaries received, on average, 480 euros, corresponding to slightly under 4% of their earned income. This proportion goes up to 9% for those earning between 0.3 and 0.7 of the annual minimum wage. If we add the poorest workers earning below the entitlement threshold, the PPE represents a rather modest redistributive device.[24] It lowers the overall poverty rate of

---

20 The data are extracted from an analysis of a random sample of 500,000 fiscal declarations of PPE recipients concerning revenues for the year 2000.

21 In 2000, part-time jobs represented 16.7% of total employment (European Commission, 2004).

22 It should also be noted that the award for persons employed part-time was increased by the reform of 2003, as mentioned earlier.

23 75% had no diploma (or only a BEPC or CAP-BEP) compared to 63% of the total population (Cochard *et al.*, 2008, p. 62).

24 According to Cochard *et al.* (2008: 63), 70% of the total amount of PPE paid out in 2001 went to the half of the population with the lowest revenues. However, the target income deciles were 2 to 6, with only 9.7% of the recipient households being in the

employed persons by 0.5 points, and by more than 1 point for those earning close to the SMIC. The contribution of the PPE to the reduction of income inequalities is estimated at 3%, far below the 31% estimated for income tax before PPE (Bonnefoy and Robert-Bobée, 2008).

In conclusion, the PPE is a measure intended to improve the functioning of the labour market, along the lines defined by the EES and using the recommended instruments: making work pay by enhancing in-work revenues. There have been attempts over time to improve targeting in order to enhance the employment and redistribution effects, but these are still under debate. Moreover, assessment is difficult and the effects seem, for the moment, to remain somewhat modest. There are few *ex post* studies with recent data permitting better evaluation of the impact of these improvements. This notwithstanding, the point we wish to make here is that, regardless of whether tax credits are more effective in the UK or less effective in France, there is no reason for excluding them from harmonised statistical monitoring. Substantial budgetary expenditures intended to enhance work attractiveness should not be neglected when assessing implementation of Guideline 7.

IV. General Reductions In Employers' Social Contributions on Low and Mid-level Wages in France

While the idea that the French labour market was affected by supply-side problems emerged at the beginning of the 2000s, leading, for instance, to the introduction of the PPE, demand-side policies based on reducing labour costs through reductions in employers' social contributions have been promoted – and strengthened – since the beginning of the 1990s. We analyse below the role of this policy in the functioning of the labour market and discuss its status as labour market policy.

A. Design and Aim of the Measure in the Context of the EES

The measure discussed here concerns general reductions in employers' social contributions – in the sense that they apply to all private sector workers, irrespective of industry, geographical location or age.[25] But they are also targeted at low-level wages, up to a ceiling that has varied over time.

---

first decile. The 2003 reform, which increased the amount for part-time workers, operated a redistributive effect towards the first decile according to Legendre *et al.* (2004, p. 53).

25 Reductions in contributions also apply to target groups such as young people, the unemployed, certain geographic areas, and personal service occupations. These groups are not considered here because they are already included in the Eurostat LMP database.

General reductions in employers' social contributions are a policy measure that fits the EES for France, especially under former Guideline 22. Several issues of the French NAPE express the assumption that decreasing labour costs will create jobs for low-skilled workers. In the 2005 National Reform Programme for Economic and Social Growth,[26] the first measure in "the battle for jobs serving economic growth" is defined as "Promoting the employment of the least skilled by lightening payroll taxes".[27] This is one of the key employment measures in France in terms of participants and public expenditure (see Table 1 in Section I above). Public expenditure on foregone contributions was about 1% of GDP in 2003, and 1.1% in 2006 and 2010.

General measures reducing employers' social contributions were first introduced in France in 1993. Since then, several modifications have been made regarding the wage levels covered (ranging from 1.1 to 1.7 times the minimum wage), the extent of the reduction (from 5.4 percentage points to 26 percentage points of contributions),[28] and the form of reduction (from a ladder-type decreasing scale to a linear decreasing scale).[29] As suggested by L'Horty (2006), understanding the "demography" of these reforms helps to clarify the objectives of the measures. The reductions are often presented as aiming to encourage the hiring of low-skilled workers (see, for example, the French NAPE 2003, 2004), but their motivations have been more complex and varied. The first law introduced under Prime Minister Balladur initially intended to reduce labour costs in general, but for budgetary reasons, its scope was limited to low wages. The Juppé reform of August 1995 was designed to avoid a hike in labour costs stemming from the increase in the minimum wage that was set at the time; this type of reform is now referred to as a "defensive reduction". The reform of 1996, designed to simplify and harmonize the system – a reduction of 18.2 percentage points in social contributions at minimum wage level and a linear decreasing reduction for higher wages – was also limited by budgetary constraints, leading to a ceiling being fixed at 1.33 times the minimum wage. This was reduced to 1.3 times the minimum wage in 1998 for budgetary reasons once again. Under Lionel Jospin, the measures were reformed in order to

---

26 *République Française* (2005). This document replaces the previous NAPE.

27 Official translation of the French version, "*Promouvoir l'emploi des moins qualifiés par l'allègement des prélèvements sociaux*" (p. 25).

28 In July 1, 2007, the reduction was differentiated again, according to company size (*République Française*, 2007: 35). For further information on recent modifications up to 1 January 2012, see Ourliac and Nouveau (2012, p. 6).

29 The presentation of these measures is based on L'Horty (2006). The modifications do not include specific measures related to the reduction of working-time policy (known as the "*Robien*" and "*Aubry I*" measures).

offset the costs induced by working time reductions (2000). The reform of 2003 (the Fillon law) that unified the systems (now no longer linked to working time) was also a defensive measure to offset the rise in minimum pay, with a ceiling set at 1.7 times the minimum wage. The 2005 reform dropped to 1.6 times the minimum wage, again for budgetary reasons. In contrast with the aims declared in the NAPE, L'Horty (2006, p. 3) argues that "None of the reforms have organised an offensive reduction of the labour cost of low-skilled work with the aim of reducing the unemployment of low-skilled workers" or, in other words, "to optimise employment effects" (Gafsi *et al.*, 2005).

B. Assessment of the Labour Market Impacts of General Reductions in Social Contributions

Evaluations of the impact of these measures on low-skill employment present contrasted results.[30] The disparities can be explained by the use of different evaluation methods (*ex ante* or *ex post*), different hypotheses on the behaviour of firms and employees, different macroeconomic links, and the nature of data (firm or household-based). However, the main source of disparity is the definition of low-skilled employment. The criterion used can be based on a scale of wage levels, schooling or level of qualifications, or on an occupational hierarchy scale. This choice has important consequences on the degree of substitution between different categories of workers, a crucial factor in the estimation of employment effects. Finally, another source of disparity between the results in the studies is the variety in the design of the measures over time.

On the basis of the results of the assessment studies for the first ten years of the policy, and taking into account the macroeconomic links, it appears that the impact on employment is modest relative to the budget involved (Gafsi *et al.*, 2005). It is estimated that with a budget of 5,000 million euros, 250,000 full-time jobs paid the minimum wage could be created or maintained. With the 19,422 million euros spent in 2006 on reductions in social contributions for 9.4 million employees, almost one million jobs could have been created or maintained. What conclusions can be drawn as to the effects on low-skill employment? Reductions seem to provide a powerful explanation for the increase in the share of low-skill employment in total employment since 1992, but they are far less able to explain the rise in total employment and low-skill employment (Gafsi *et al.*, 2005). More recently, Ourliac and Nouveau (2012) reviewed the studies on the effects of the measures for the period 1993-2009. In particular, while stressing the substantial methodo-

---

30 A review of over 14 studies by L'Horty (2006) shows that employment may be multiplied by a factor of 1 to 4.5.

logical difficulties encountered, they reported that the conclusions from the estimations of the impact on employment of the Fillon reform of 2003 pointed to fairly modest net employment effects.

Although economic evaluations point to less optimistic results than were expected given the large group of beneficiaries and the high budgetary costs, this does not invalidate the fact that reducing employer contributions is one of the major employment measures used in France. It appears that if these measures are to improve the employment of low-skilled workers, low-wage/income populations and those at a higher risk of unemployment, they should be further targeted to these groups.

These measures are mainly targeted at specific groups, namely low- and mid-wage jobs. Is this degree of targeting too broad for Eurostat to include them in the LMP database? A harmonized statistical system with coherent and comparable data able to include all public interventions in the labour market would contribute to a better assessment of the actual weight of the state in the financing of employment in Europe.

V. Final Remarks

In this chapter we suggest that the UK and French tax credits and general reductions in social contributions in France should be recorded as a complement to the Eurostat LMP database, particularly given the levels of public expenditure and the number of participants involved. Furthermore, these measures are explicitly designed to impact on the functioning of the labour market, that is on labour supply and demand, as well as on employment and workers' income. The weight of these measures warrants their inclusion in a harmonised European statistical system. Several other policies[31] in the EU countries should be carefully analysed in the same light – should they be included?

Tax credits, traditionally classified as fiscal measures, are not explicitly considered as labour market policies, but they do have effects on the functioning of the labour market by increasing incentives for taking up and remaining in employment (targeting the unemployed and inactive). Reductions in employers' social contributions, which act as a demand-side device reducing labour costs, are intended to promote employment for low-wage earners.

The complex set of public interventions characterizing the present orientations regarding labour market institutions and the patterning of workers' resource flows cannot be fully perceived by exclusively examining traditional target labour market policies. The current narrow scope of the Eurostat LMP database fails to contribute to a full understanding

[31] For examples, see European Commission (2007).

of ongoing transformations. Researchers are obliged to use non-harmonised national sources for data on participants and expenditures, and this detracts from the value of the current Eurostat database as a meaningful instrument for monitoring the EES.

Part III

Back into the Labour Market!

Unemployment and Active Labour Market Policies in Austria

Roland ATZMÜLLER

Assistant professor, University of Linz, Austria

Introduction

In a general context marked by far-reaching restructurings of social protection systems and persistent labour market problems in Europe, active labour market policies (ALMPs) have come to play an increasingly important role. While political debates over welfare reforms are dominated by neoliberal concepts of lean government, welfare retrenchments and cost reductions, restructuring strategies have in fact brought about an expansion and multiplication of the institutions, governance mechanisms and programmes regulating the unemployed. Thus, a growing number of people are exposed to an increasingly differentiated set of labour market policy measures. The overall goal of these policies is to "activate" the unemployed and improve their employability and adaptability in order to reinforce the flexibility of labour markets and boost the economy. It was only in the 1990s that these trends became predominant in Austria.

It is of interest to note, however, that Austria features less prominently than other EU countries in current debates about reforms of welfare systems and labour markets. This is due not only the fact that it still has one of the lowest unemployment rates in Europe, but also to its quick recovery from the impact of the most recent crisis. Even though Austria's economic position and development are of course affected by economic imbalances within the Euro-zone (its economy belongs to the German block), the specificity and ostensible stability of its employment and welfare regime (Atzmüller *et al.*, 2012) must be highlighted. The Austrian model of development has not (yet) been subjected to radical legal and institutional ruptures such as the Hartz IV reforms in Germany. The collective bargaining coverage rate remains high, and there is still a dense institutional web linking the social partnership and the government. Notwithstanding the most recent pension reforms, which included massive cuts as well as the introduction of "additional" funded pillars, Austria's welfare system is still dominated by social insurance.

Even though the years 2000 to 2006 were marked by a more intensive period of social struggle, when the conservative/far-right government of the time attempted a full scale attack on the welfare state including the role of the "social partnership" (in particular the participation of employee organisations in policy making), the transformations of the domestic economy (growing internationalisation) as well as of the employment and welfare systems were more the outcome of a negotiated adaptation to changing national and international power relations than open confrontations and deep ruptures. However, more in-depth analyses reveal far-reaching cracks and subsurface erosions of the traditional configuration of this regime which are indicative of fundamental transformations of the institutional setting in some areas. These transformations have also involved the creation and implementation of new institutions and activities, as can be shown in regard to the development of ALMPs.

In the context of a neo-liberally inspired critique of the alleged rigidities of state administration, Austrian labour market policy was subjected to far-reaching reforms in which the former state-run *Arbeitsmarktverwaltung* (labour-market administration, AMV) was contracted out to a decentralised public employment service, the *Arbeitsmarktservice* (AMS). The approach to unemployment and the reintegration of the unemployed became increasingly shaped by the assumption that an overgenerous system of social transfers prevents the unemployed from taking up available jobs, leading to widespread welfare fraud. Thus, in the past years, the benefit system has undergone changes which have been dominated by reductions in unemployment entitlements as well as a tightening up of eligibility criteria and rules on "acceptable" employment. ALMPs are now essentially designed to reintegrate the unemployed into the labour market as fast as possible and to adapt "human capital" to changing labour market requirements. Recent reforms have continued to reinforce the restrictive and disciplinary character of the Austrian system of unemployment insurance and ALMP. While the expansion of activation policies has led to the creation of a market for all kinds of integration programmes, an analysis of the trend reveals a differentiated picture according to the type of measure involved. Moreover, even though the number of people participating – or obliged to participate – in such programmes is rising, this is not clearly reflected in the evolution of expenditure levels.

This chapter will analyse the evolution of the unemployment insurance system and active labour market policies in Austria. To begin with, I will give a short overview of unemployment trends since the 1980s and a brief description of the history of Austria's unemployment insurance system, in order to contextualise the nationally specific path of

ALMP development. I will then focus on the major policy shifts since the late 1980s that have impacted on labour market institutions and governance structures, the benefit system, and the expansion of ALMPs. The chapter concludes with a brief analysis of the reactions of the ALMP regime to the recent crisis.

I. Growth of Unemployment

Unemployment began to rise in Austria in the early 1980s, ending the consensus among the leading political parties on full employment. In the face of mounting economic and budgetary problems, Austro-Keynesian policies were abandoned in the second half of the decade after changes in the political power relations (Grand Coalition of the socialist/social-democrat SPÖ and the conservative ÖVP[1] from 1986). The Austro-Keynesian strategy, which had dominated the 1970s, had succeeded in temporarily stabilising employment by increasing public spending and measures to compensate for drops in private demand. This was flanked by hard currency policies (tied to the German mark) and wage restraint guaranteed by the social partnership (Talos, 1987, Unger, 1999).

The economic crisis that hit in the early 1980s led to a massive rise in unemployment, with figures shooting up from 1.87%[2] (or 50,000 people) in 1980 to 5.2% (151,000 people) in 1986 (for a more detailed analysis, see Atzmüller, 2009). Since then unemployment has risen steadily, notwithstanding cyclical reductions in periods of stronger economic growth. A first peak was reached in 2005, prior to the current crisis. That year the annual average unemployment rate climbed to 7.25%[3] or 252,654 persons. After dropping considerably in the following years, unemployment levels rose again to about 7.2% in the crisis year 2009. It should be noted that on an average some 800,000 people (of a total of about 3.3 million employees) experience at least one spell of unemployment annually. From an international perspective, however,

---

1 SPÖ: Sozialdemokratische Partei Österreichs (social democrat party), ÖVP: Österreichische Volkspartei (conservative People's Party).

2 Figures based on the national data provided by the AMS (Public Employment Service), where the indicator used to calculate unemployment rates is the number of unemployed persons registered at the Austrian PES (as a percentage of the total labour force). At European level, unemployment rates are calculated using Labour Force Survey data, which are based on a regular census and criteria that define the unemployed as persons who are working less than one hour per week, have looked for work in the last four weeks and are ready to start work within two weeks.

3 Data from the Arbeitsmarktdatenbank (AMDB) of the Federal Ministry for employment, social affairs and consumer protection which collects and publishes all available national data on the labour market and unemployment (e.g. from the AMS): http://www.dnet.at/bali/Default.aspx.

unemployment rates in Austria remain fairly moderate, and when calculated according to Labour Force Survey (LFS) criteria, did not exceed 5.5% in 2009, compared to the EU-27 average of 9% (European Commission, 2009). Since then, unemployment has fallen to 6.7% according to national calculations (4.2% according to the LFS).

It is important to add that unemployment affects certain social groups more than others, pointing to a high, and rising, level of labour market segmentation. Migrants (non-Austrian nationals) are traditionally more strongly affected than Austrian nationals, but the unemployment rates of these two populations have begun to diverge more sharply since 2000. Thus, while joblessness among Austrian nationals seems to remain more or less stable – albeit at a relatively high level – the rate for migrants has been increasing steadily and has been 50% above the average rate for Austrian nationals in the last years (Biffl, 2007, p. 75). Moreover, during the most recent crisis, unemployment rose by about 2.2% to 10.2% for migrants, whereas for Austrian nationals, it only increased by about 1.2%. The subsequent fall of unemployment has been more pronounced for migrants than for Austrian nationals, indicating that the former group is used as a flexibility buffer in the Austrian economy.

Furthermore, some age groups are more affected than others. Unemployment rates for persons over 55 are above the national average, with the 60-65 age group experiencing the most marked increase over the past few years. This rise is undoubtedly related to the pension reforms of 2002 and 2003, which led to the gradual abolition of early retirement schemes and related forms of withdrawal from the labour market (Mairhuber, 2009). Certain groups of young workers – in particular those aged 20-24 – also show higher levels of unemployment. This is particularly noteworthy because the rates for people under 19 are well below the national average, due to Austria's apprenticeship system and the continuing efforts of political actors to maintain it and provide apprenticeships or substitute programmes to as many young people as possible. Thanks to this, and to Austria's economic position, the overall rate of youth unemployment remains fairly low compared to other countries. Thus, the high figures for the 20-24 age group (notably for migrant youth, who account for two thirds of the unemployed in this age band) indicate that stable labour market integration after initial VET is proving difficult – which raises doubts as to the long-term viability of the training system. This population also experienced a more rapid rise in unemployment (+2.2%) compared to other age bands during the recent crisis.

Finally, the key factor associated with high risk of unemployment is low educational status. This is said to result from the alleged shift to a knowledge-based economy, which has led to the loss of jobs for low-qualified employees. The rate for people below apprenticeship level, who seem to be heavily affected by cyclical labour market downturns and subsequent unemployment growth, is twice as high as the national average, whereas it is below average for all other educational groups. According to AMS data, unemployment among the lowest educational group rose to 18.6% in the crisis year 2009, and reached over 25% or even 30% for males in urban agglomerations such as Vienna and certain peripheral regions. This group accounts for about 45% of all unemployed persons in Austria. Furthermore, the subsequent fall of unemployment was less pronounced in this group than for people at apprenticeship level, which is the only educational group on the Austrian labour market to experience a drop in absolute unemployment figures in the years following the crisis of 2008/9.

II. Evolution of Unemployment Insurance and ALMPs

The main traits of the Austrian unemployment insurance system were established in 1949, when the *Arbeitslosenversicherungsgesetz* (ALVG, bill on unemployment insurance) was passed (Schmidt, 1991). The original ALVG focused mainly on the unemployment benefit system, which to this day is financed by employer and employee contributions. Most of the central provisions – notably concerning the fundamental logics of the contribution and benefit system – are still in place, but others have been changed and amended considerably, as will be seen later. Briefly, all employees have the right to claim an earnings-related employment benefit after paying contributions for specified periods, which also determine the duration of the period of benefit receipt. Once entitlements have been exhausted, this unemployment benefit (*Arbeitslosengeld*) is followed by unemployment assistance (*Notstandshilfe*). Until the late 1980s the latter allowance, which – in principle – has no time limit, was not available to "guest workers" (mainly Yugoslavian and Turkish migrants), or to married people whose spouses were employed (i.e. essentially women) (Fischer and Talos, 1987).

Under the law of 1949, the unemployment insurance system became the responsibility of the labour market administration (*Arbeitsmarktverwaltung*, AMV) which was part of the Federal Ministry of Labour and Social Affairs (*Bundesministerium für Wirtschaft und Arbeit*). It thus remained under state control and was not returned to self-administration, which had been abolished in the period of Fascism (Wilk, 1991), because no consensus could be reached by the social partners and the Social Democrat/Conservative coalition government. From the beginning, the system's protective character was accompanied by strategies to pressure the unemployed to take up "acceptable" jobs. Rules regarding the acceptability of job offers provided some occupational protection for the unemployed, at least for a limited period of time.

In the early 1960s, however, prompted by the Swedish example, discussions on what later came to be called "active labour market policies" were initiated by the trade unions as well as the Ministry of Social Affairs, which has been run by a unionist for most of the time since 1945 (Schmidt, 1991). At first, the employers did not see the relevance of such policies as they believed that unemployment was a thing of the past. It was only in 1968, after accelerated structural changes of the economy had created frictions on the labour market, that they reached a compromise with the trade unions, and the first law on ALMP, called the "law to support the labour market" (*Arbeitsmarktförderungsgesetz*, AMFG), was passed. Due to the prolonged conflicts between the social partners and the parliamentary parties, the AMFG included no demand-side measures, but focussed almost exclusively on labour supply. The aim was to influence workforce size, quality and mobility by means of predominantly monetary incentives (Wilk, 1991) to support structural reforms and avoid frictional unemployment.

As the outcome of a consensual political approach, the AMFG obliged the labour market administration not only to implement active labour market policies so as to secure full employment, but also to prevent unemployment by taking macroeconomic and social dimensions into account (Schmidt, 1991). The participation of the social partners (and the trade unions in particular) in ALMP design was ensured by the creation of a number of advisory committees.

The ALMP measures introduced under the AMFG became an important component of Austro-Keynesian employment policy and economic growth strategy in the 1970s. They complemented the employment policies, which sought to limit and steer labour supply by reducing working time – and by reducing the migrant workforce. To secure employment and foster job creation, programmes offering structural aid to companies in regions with economic problems were also developed. As rather substantial funds were allocated to such measures, the importance of the labour market administration grew considerably.

In the second half of the 1970s, the labour market situation began to change and so did the character of Austrian employment and labour market policies. Expenditures on ALMP, could not keep up with growing labour market problems and fell far behind countries such as Sweden or Germany, a point that was to come under constant criticism from social scientists and the unions over the next 15 years.

Up to the mid-1980s, apart from the massive funds pumped into the nationalised industries and other nationally important companies – which had been hard hit by the crisis – the main focus was on developing new training programmes to cope with deteriorating labour market conditions. The first of these programmes targeted groups facing growing problems of labour market (re-)integration, such as young people, the long-term unemployed, the low skilled, etc. However, it is interesting to note that some groups, such as migrants and women, lost out because they figured less prominently in the political debates (Talos, 1987; Wilk, 1991).

In the second half of the 1980s, the Austro-Keynesian countercyclical strategy and the consensus on full employment were finally abandoned. The political priorities of the new Grand Coalition government between the Social Democrats and the Conservatives brought about a shift in focus to budgetary consolidation, tax cuts and supply-side-oriented structural policies aimed at improving the competitiveness of the Austrian economy. With the abandoning of macroeconomic-oriented employment policies, ALMPs came to play a more important role. Rather than full employment, priority was given to securing "high levels of employment" through policies of deregulation and flexibility which were claimed to foster a free functioning of the labour market.

A. Institutional Reforms

These shifts in the government's political priorities were accompanied by mounting criticism of the organisational structure of the state-run labour market administration, which was thought to be ill-adapted to coping with the problems of growing unemployment. The debates and conflicts around the AMV were underpinned by the neoliberal critique of welfare institutions which had taken hold in Austria since the early 1980s, under the influence of business organisations, parts of the conservative party, and the far right.

The dominant viewpoint in these debates interpreted regionally high levels of unemployment as problems in matching the unemployed with the needs of Austrian businesses, due in part to a lack of information about job opportunities and the kind of skills demanded. But it was the populist campaigns launched by the tabloids and right-wing politicians attacking the allegedly widespread welfare fraud among the unemployed that were to have the most effect on shaping the future reforms. Unemployment benefits were denounced as being too "generous", and this was said to encourage growing numbers of claimants to abuse the system and live as "welfare scroungers". Employment offices were said to be too accommodating in that they put too much emphasis on the acceptability rules for job offers.

In 1994, after some years of heated debate, the coalition government introduced a far-reaching reform of the Austrian system of unemployment insurance and ALMPs. The labour market administration was replaced by a public employment service, the *Arbeitsmarktservice* (AMS), which was contracted out and decentralised (Feurstein, 1998; Talos and

Kittel, 2001). The AMS was given company status and became a legal body of its own, overseen by the government or responsible ministry (Tritremmel, 1998). The outsourcing of the AMS was justified on the grounds that organisational procedures and management processes needed to be rationalised (Institut für Policy Research, 1992) in order to avoid overlap with other federal departments and to allow for a clear focus on core tasks (in particular, job placement). The reform included two other noteworthy provisions: first, the social partners were fully integrated into the governance structures of the new AMS, since conservative politicians claimed that this would secure their cooperation – in particular that of the trade unions – and thus serve to curb opposition to labour market policies; and second, the AMS lost the monopoly of placement services.

Decentralisation was seen as allowing for a differentiated implementation of labour market policy measures, tailored to tackle specific regional labour market problems and targets. The largely regionalised organisational structure of the AMS consists of units (*Geschäftstellen*) run along New Public Management lines based on management by objectives, contract management and output– or performance-related pay. The output targets are set by the Federal Department in agreement with the social partners represented on the AMS board. This means that the AMS units at federal and regional level (*Bundes- und Regionalgeschäftsstellen*) are required to devise programmes and targets based on labour market policy parameters and programmes developed by the government and the Federal Department. These programmes and measures are then implemented by the local AMS units (*Bezirksgeschäftsstellen*).

The primary aim of the reform was to ensure that the AMS focus on placing the unemployed and reducing the average duration of joblessness, and even seek to prevent unemployment altogether. Performance and output targets, in particular, force the AMS to develop and improve "early intervention" and activation instruments to keep claimants busy and prevent them from "getting used" to being unemployed. The AMS is thus required to offer the unemployed information and counselling as well as a number of so-called "support" measures to improve their employability, and to provide training schemes and help with job search efforts.

B. Cuts and Sanctions

From the late 1980s on, the unemployment insurance system became the target of cuts and cutbacks as calculation periods were lengthened, replacement rates reduced and eligibility criteria tightened.[4] Before 1987, the calculation of benefits was based on the last wage. After that, calculation periods were extended to the last six months, and since 1996, to the last calendar year (Spreitzer, 1999). This has led to a drop in benefit levels – in particular for the growing number of people with discontinuous employment histories due to the rise in atypical and precarious forms of employment.

The net replacement rate for unemployment benefits, which was originally fixed at 57.9%, was gradually dropped to 56% by 1995, due to budgetary cuts implemented to meet Maastricht criteria in preparation for EU entry (Talos and Wörister, 1998). It was then reduced to 55% in 2000 by the newly-formed Conservative/Far-Right coalition government, which pursued the cutbacks in the name of "offering incentives for taking up employment".

Reductions in unemployment benefits also implied reductions in the level of unemployment assistance, since the latter is calculated as a percentage of the former. However, the cuts in unemployment assistance were even more pronounced as the rate was decreased from 95% to 92% of the unemployment benefit. In addition, in 2001, family-related supplements to unemployment benefits were cut by about 40% for each dependent family member to ensure that recipients would not receive more than 80% of their last net income (Mairhuber, 2002a, b). To further reduce expenditure on unemployment benefits, the annual valorisation of the assessment basis for unemployment insurance as well as the valorisation of unemployment assistance for those already receiving the benefit (Fink, 2006b) were abolished after 2000.

Finally, eligibility criteria were tightened by extending the qualifying periods for entitlement. Whereas in 1981, young people could claim unemployment benefits after 52 weeks of employment during the previous 24 months, and could renew their entitlement after another 20 weeks of employment, this latter period was first extended to 26 weeks, and then to 28 weeks in 2000 (Fink, 2006b; Obinger and Talos, 2006).

In line with the assumption of widespread welfare fraud and benefit-related disincentives to take up available employment, the stricter eligibility criteria were accompanied, from the mid-1990s, by a considerable increase in the kind and number of sanctions imposed to discipline the unemployed. Sanctions mainly take the form of a temporary loss of

---

4 Only some measures have brought about an expansion of the system, for instance, for older workers who gained improved benefits and entitlements. Similarly, the eligibility criteria for claiming unemployment assistance were expanded (reduced importance of partner income), which benefited many women. The switch from gross to net replacement rates in 1989 brought some improvements in unemployment benefits for low-income employees.

payments, and are generally imposed to enforce the claimant's willingness to actively look for or take up employment. The legal criteria regarding "willingness to work" were tightened: whereas before the unemployed had to "credibly show" that they were trying to find a new job, since 2004 they have had to "provide proof" of their efforts by presenting a certain number of job applications. At the same time, rules on the acceptability of job offers were made stricter while occupational protection for the unemployed was reduced,[5] as it was claimed that these provisions give people the opportunity to avoid job take up.

Diagram 1: Sanctions

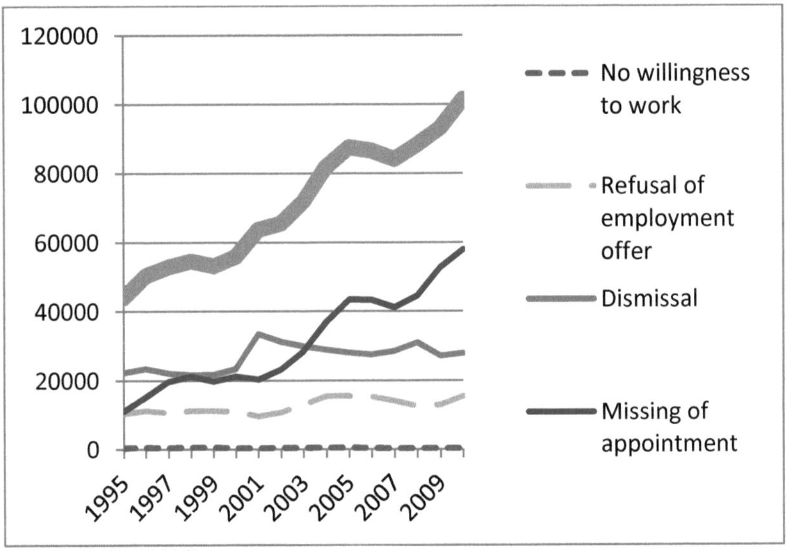

Source: AMS, BMAS

*Dismissal: people who terminate their employment contract or who are dismissed with instant effect have a waiting period of four weeks before receiving unemployment benefits.

Data from the AMS (2005) show that the number of sanctions imposed quintupled between 1990 and 2005. It is interesting to note that the increase was most pronounced after 2000 (Diagram 1), largely due to an increase in temporary payment stoppages for missing an AMS appointment. The AMS (2006) attributes this increase to two main factors: the growing number of unemployed, on the one hand, and improved controls – referred to as "more intensive customer care" – on the other. A comparison of the ratio of sanctions over time, however,

5 Occupational protection rules stipulate that jobseekers must be offered employment in jobs and at wage levels close to their former positions for a specific period of time.

shows that the increase cannot be attributed to the growth in unemployment. While in 1995, sanctions were imposed on roughly 6.5% of all people experiencing at least one period of unemployment during the year and 20.4% of the annual average number of unemployed, by 2006 these rates had risen to 10.8% and 36.2% respectively. Furthermore, during the recent crisis, whereas the total number of unemployed only exceeded the previous peak of 2005 by about 8,000 people, the increase in sanctions was far more pronounced (Diagram 1), suggesting a continuing expansion of the disciplinary aspect of Austrian labour market policies.

C. From "Experimental" to "Innovative" Labour Market Policy

The conflicts regarding the scope and orientation of ALMPs did not only revolve around allegations that overgenerous unemployment benefits were work disincentives and the cause of welfare fraud. The questions of how to reintegrate people and into what kind of employment were also of crucial significance for the emergence of the current ALMP structure in Austria. Not surprisingly, the most heated debates concerned groups at risk of long-term unemployment or facing problems on the labour market because of non-conforming lifestyles, etc. (Althaler and Dimmel, 1993).

The early 1980s had seen the introduction of "experimental" labour market policies which provided support for voluntary, non-profit and self-help organisations as well as self-managed companies (via employment subsidies). These experimental programmes were, from the beginning, the centre of intense political debate. There were several reasons for this, not the least being the relatively high cost of strategies seeking to combine guidance and support for the long-term unemployed with funding for certain projects. The latter aspect, in particular, led companies to fear possible competition from non-profit employment projects that could rely on public subsidies. The tabloids and right-wing politicians denounced these experimental policies for supporting a life on welfare and subsidising alternative political projects. The latter argument was not entirely unfounded as in the early 1980s the Federal Department of Labour and Social Affairs – run by a left-wing trade unionist at the time – used experimental labour market policy to provide support for a variety of "alternative projects" (civil society, 'self-managed' businesses, etc.)[6] and facilitate experimental bottom-up approaches to questions of social integration. Even today, representatives of employment projects point out that in the early years there were "no limits" to "creativity" and "imagination" (Zauner, 2006; Dorfinger, 2006).

---

6 Thus, for instance, an anarchist bi-weekly journal received funds through these programmes for many years.

One of the first experimental labour market policy measures was the AKTION 8000 programme introduced in 1983. A precursor of all today's employment projects and integration subsidies, the scheme targeted the long-term unemployed aged under 25 and aimed to create – transitory – employment opportunities in socially significant areas (ecology, urban renewal, social services, culture, and so forth). Between 1983 and 1994, about 40,000 jobs were funded through this programme.

AKTION 8000 was intended for the public sector and local councils, as well as voluntary and non-profit organisations. Private companies could not participate. The share of public sector organisations involved, however, soon diminished as Conservative-run Austrian provinces disapproved of the programme. Under AKTION 8000, unemployed people were to be hired for twelve months on standard employment contracts and paid according to the collective agreement covering the sector concerned. No other employee was to be dismissed during that period. The subsidy covered 100% of all direct and indirect wage costs for eight months, and the remaining time had to be financed by the organisation itself.

AKTION 8000 was considered to be a success because it provided improved employment opportunities and income for participants, particularly in the case of the long-term unemployed (>12 months of unemployment) (Lechner *et al.*, 1996; Fehr-Duda *et al.*, 1996). However, it predominantly benefitted people with relatively high skill and education levels. It was first complemented and then replaced in the 1990s by a number of other integration subsidies which were made available to the private sector as well. This also began to change the character of the "experimental" programmes which became more and more geared towards providing training to prepare integration into the labour market. In 2002, all forms of integration subsidies were merged into one device. The basic principle – temporary support for the employment of unemployed persons from certain target groups – remained intact. However, the requirement that pay be based on collective agreement provisions was abandoned. Participants now receive an unemployment benefit or unemployment assistance plus a top-up (Mitterauer *et al.*, 1999) for the duration of their contracts, resulting in considerably lower levels of income.

The evolution of experimental labour market policies and their subsequent metamorphosis into "innovative" labour market policies reveal interesting shifts in the dominant ALMP orientations in Austria. Whereas the experimental policies aimed at supporting integration into standard employment by creating scope for bottom-up experiments, ALMP measures today are increasingly geared to pushing people into any kind of job at the bottom end of the labour market, and thus serve to institutionally stabilise labour market flexibility rather than promote sustainable social cohesion and inclusion. Experts from the Austrian Chamber of Labour stress that, even though the average duration of employment contracts has not diminished, the "flexible segments" of the labour market offer little chance of entering into stable long-term forms of employment for a growing share of the workforce (at least one third).

III. Active Labour Market Policy Trends Today

Today, Austria boasts an extensive range of differentiated ALMP measures and programmes (Dimmel, 2000; Lutz and Mahringer, 2007). Absolute expenditures on ALMPs have grown considerably over the last years, with a notable rise during the recent crisis, when the funds dedicated to ALMPs were increased by about €400 million to counteract the most immediate effects on the labour market (Atzmüller *et al.*, 2012). As can be seen in Table 1, the numbers of unemployed subject to these unemployment measures have been increasing steadily, more or less independently of the cyclical development of unemployment, but crises on the labour market such as the most recent one, serve to accelerate the trend.

In the face of growing unemployment and a prolonged labour market crisis, a broad consensus has emerged among political actors in Austria regarding the relevance of ALMP and the need to introduce improved measures and programmes. The political parties and the social partners all agree on the importance of such policies, even though their approach to benefit entitlements or integration strategies might vary considerably. This consensus was also clearly shaped by the 1997 European Employment Strategy (EES) (Schweighofer, 2003). The programmes of the Conservative/Far-Right coalition governments of 2000 and 2003 referred explicitly to the EES and the National Action Plan (NAP) on employment; in the government programme of 2003, for instance, EU employment targets are said to form the parameters of Austrian employment policy because "full employment (!) continues to be our most important goal" (National Action Plan, 2003, 2). Full employment is also presented as the goal of the government programme of the 2006 Social Democrat/Conservative coalition.

Nevertheless it seems that the impact of the EES has diminished in recent years. According to Ministry of Work and Employment officials interviewed for the RESORE project, the EES has had little new to offer Austria as most of the measures and strategies would have been implemented without it (Atzmüller, 2006). Thus, in 2006 the government programme mostly referred to proposals put forward by national actors such as the social partners or the tripartite WIFO (*Wirtschaftsforschungsinstitut*, Austrian Institute of Economic Research), which published a

White Paper on employment and growth through innovation and skilling in 2006.

Table 1: Participants (persons) in ALMP

	Training	Employment	Support	**Total***
2001	150,342	25,806	33,360	**186,482**
2002	181,821	26,608	41,092	**219,173**
2003	210,519	30,330	46,421	**253,133**
2004	214,387	30,248	57,875	**266,191**
2005	247,681	35,052	51,953	**294,170**
2006	252,331	47,094	68,630	**308,530**
2007	284,541	71,567	59,836	**344,831**
2008	290,895	76,057	62,346	**357,684**
2009	336,355	125,606	85,885	**459,623**
2010	347,294	97,594	93,668	**441,052**

Source: AMS Jahresberichte

People who participated in more than one measure are only counted once. Therefore, the figures in the 'total' column do not correspond to the sum of the other columns.

In general, ALMPs oscillate between measures aimed at preventing the unemployed from making abusive use of what is seen as the "welfare hammock", and training strategies to help them adapt their skills to new demands in order to enhance their employability. As unemployment has increasingly come to be interpreted as a problem of the quality of labour supply, numerous measures have been introduced to enforce the reintegration of certain social groups (women, youth, the long-term unemployed, disabled persons, etc.). However, the particular problems these groups face on the labour market are increasingly seen as resulting from individual deficits in terms of work ethics, skills, behaviour, and such, rather than as the discriminatory effects of labour market segmentation and power asymmetries.[7]

The recent trends in activation measures have resulted in a range of new obligations being imposed on the unemployed, such as providing proof of job search activities or participating in coaching programmes during the early stages of unemployment. Since 2005, regional AMS units have been required to draw up a written support plan (*Betreuungsplan*) for each of their "clients" explaining the kind of advice, counselling and possible programmes they will be offered. This support plan is a kind of contract between the AMS and the unemployed person, setting out mutual rights and obligations. It is to be drawn up in agreement with the person concerned but does not give that person legal claim to particular programmes. However, if the parties are unable to reach agreement,

7 On the theoretical background, see Offe, 1984.

the AMS can draw up the support plan unilaterally – and the jobseeker has no legal means to contest its decision.

The current set of activation strategies is designed to encourage, or force, the unemployed to adapt to changing labour market requirements. Thus, on the one hand, the measures include information and advice to help jobseekers assess their future employment opportunities and develop adequate job search strategies or shift their career aspirations to new industries and sectors. On the other hand, coaching and job application training sessions are designed to make the unemployed adapt such aspects as their self-presentation – sometimes including their appearance – to the expectations of potential employers. Furthermore, the AMS uses low-cost "early intervention" measures (Bundeskammer, 2004, p. 68) as screening instruments to test the person's willingness to take up employment (Lutz and Mahringer, 2007, p. 204). Many unemployed people criticise these devices as lacking relevance and view them as instruments of discipline. Interestingly, interviews with employers have shown that companies are also critical of these measures as they feel job applicants are over-trained and their presentation in job interviews has been standardised (Atzmüller *et al.*, 2006).

There is general consensus that training and upskilling constitute the key labour market policy strategy. Thus, in order to achieve a better match between labour supply and demand, the AMS provides a range of VET measures and programmes for the unemployed as well as subsidies and allowances to cover the cost of training. Training ranges from very short courses in computer use or other basic skills, to high-quality arrangements such as the Work Foundations (Wagner and Lassnigg, 2005). Work Foundations (*Arbeitsstiftungen*) were first developed in the 1980s in response to the crisis facing nationalised industries. They are usually set up after intensive negotiations between the social partners, the AMS and local councils, and offer retraining and upskilling of up to four years and, in some sectors, even a job guarantee (for example in the care sector). Work Foundations are jointly financed by the AMS, local councils and employers. They have a success rate of 75% but have been criticised for creaming – that is, supporting primarily high-skilled, often male, employees in the manufacturing sector (Wagner and Lassnigg, 2005).

However, the expansion of ALMPs says little about the quality of the measures and devices they provide for, as has been argued in some recent analyses (Atzmüller 2009). First, none of the measures provide new social rights. The unemployed are not entitled to certain forms of support, but instead, are subject to new obligations, especially in terms of their willingness to find a new job and to behave and adapt accordingly. Second, apart from these cost-intensive programmes, the AMS support strategies mostly correspond to relatively short and not very intensive training measures. Thus, institutions such as the WIFO (Lutz and Mahringer, 2007) and the Chamber of Labour (Bundeskammer, 2004) criticise the lack of sustainability and narrow scope of training courses – which are often geared to the short-term needs of companies – and highlight their limited effectiveness for many unemployed groups. These measures therefore seem to support the flexibility of the labour market rather than sustainable integration into employment. These doubts about the quality of the available measures and programmes are supported by the fact that the number of measures and participants in ALMP grows faster than the sums dedicated to these policies, which means that the real value of expenditures per measure (when calculated after inflation adjustment) must be falling. This could be due to a number of reasons. It could result from an improvement in the effectiveness and efficiency of labour market policy measures. It could, however, also stem from lower prices paid for programmes and/or an ensuing reduction in their quality. As noted above, the growing market for ALMP programmes is putting increasing cost pressure on training organisations applying for projects and tasks outsourced by the AMS. However, as measures are frequently modularised and many unemployed people have to participate in more than one measure, it is still difficult to argue in a scientifically sound way that, individually, unemployed persons nowadays get less or worse support (for a detailed analysis, see Atzmüller, 2009). Thus, more in-depth analyses on the practices of ALMP measures would be necessary.

In addition to the measures geared to matching labour supply and demand, another major ALMP approach is to provide subsidies for companies and/or unemployed persons to support the job placement process. Some of these subsidies are intended to encourage employee mobility by offering relocation allowances, or to facilitate reconciling work and childcare responsibilities. Others are designed to temporarily subsidise new entrants' wages in order to help companies train and integrate people. Subsidies or fines are also used to safeguard the employment of certain target groups. Thus, companies benefit from a partial reduction in social contributions (in particular for unemployment insurance) when hiring an older worker, and are fined for dismissing one.

A last group of measures concerns a range of employment projects that are partially shielded from market pressures as they operate within the so-called second labour market. Projects such as SÖBs (*Sozioökonomische Beschäftigungsprojekte*) and GBPs (*Gemeinnützige Beschäftigungsprojekte*) offer temporary jobs financed by AMS subsidies, together with training and guidance, to promote the social integration and employment of people in difficult situations.[8] The training courses aim at preparing employees for the demands of the regular labour market and improving their skills, particularly in areas such as dependability, precision, independence and flexibility. These employment projects offer niche products and services and handicrafts in order to generate some income for their activities. Employment project jobs were initially limited to one year, but in 2007, their duration was reduced to six months.

Since the 1990s, when the experimental approach was dropped in favour of what was labelled "innovative" policy, projects have been increasingly subjected to benchmarking, guidelines and management by objectives. This has led to extensive intervention on the part of the AMS, which, according to people who have been working for such projects for a long time, has put a check on creative and innovative ideas (Dorfinger, 1998; Zauner, 1998). Since the integration of the social partners into the structure of the AMS and the implementation of management by indicators, pressures to perform efficiently and develop professional management structures have increased and the original "bottom-up approach", which allowed for many social innovations, has been replaced by a "top-down-approach". According to an employment project representative, the AMS claims to know which active measures are necessary and shops around for suitable offers on the market for labour market programmes that has emerged over the last few years. This has had severe negative effects for project operators because it forces them into precarious, insecure and/or atypical forms of employment. Their situation has deteriorated further due to the 2002 and 2006 amendments to public procurement legislation (*Bundes-vergabegesetz*), which oblige the AMS to put projects out to tender and ensure competition among applicants. A study conducted by FORBA on outsourcing strategies in adult education confirms the predicted developments (Eichmann *et al.*, 2008). Competition-based tendering puts strong pressures on applicants to reduce the price of their services. At the same time the costs of administration, infrastructure, documentation and participation in tenders have risen massively, and this favours the larger applicants while the two-year limit on contracts means that planning perspectives are somewhat narrow. These developments impact massively on the working conditions of coaches and trainers, who have to accept lower hourly rates and an increasingly precarious employment situation. Permanent employment contracts are now almost nonexistent in these sectors.

8 See: http://www.ams.or.at/neu/wien/4084.htm.

IV. Recent Developments

A. Amendments to Unemployment Insurance Legislation

The AMS's increasingly restrictive and disciplinary practices have given rise to a number of conflicts and protests in the past years. Interestingly, this led to the first attempts to organise the unemployed in order to raise public awareness of their situation. Complaints about AMS practices have been handled by the higher administrative court (*Verwaltungsgerichtshof*),[9] or taken up by the Austrian Ombudsman Board (*Volksanwaltschaft*)[10] and negotiated on television. The *Volksanwaltschaft*'s annual reports show that complaints about AMS practices and decisions have been on the increase since the second half of the 1990s. The fact that many of the high-court rulings effectively limited the practices of the AMS was an important factor prompting the government to amend Austria's unemployment insurance legislation (*Arbeitslosenversicherungsgesetz*, ALVG). Indeed, the nature of the complaints as well as the content of the high court decisions are essential to understanding many aspects of these recent amendments.

The complaints largely concerned the mandatory character of many AMS measures and programmes, but disputes over what constitutes employment also emerged. For instance, the question of whether an unemployed person is obliged to take up a temporary placement in an employment project was a central point of conflict. A number of people refused this kind of placement because, given the applicable calculation rules, they risked losing their benefit entitlements after completion of the programme. Since employment projects did not correspond to ALVG definitions of "job" or "training", unemployed persons who had been sanctioned for refusing a placement argued that the rules regarding acceptable job offers and the willingness to work did not apply. Furthermore, according to an administrative court decision, accepting a placement in an employment project was not mandatory, as this was neither defined as employment nor as training! Another issue that warrants mentioning here is the question of private non-profit work agencies to which the AMS has subcontracted placement of certain groups: a number of people who refused a placement claimed that, as private bodies, these agencies had no sovereign rights over the unemployed. Complaints were also raised about mandatory participation in coaching: the usefulness of these measures was questioned, and several people even referred to abasing experiences while participating in such courses. In

---

9 This court deals with public service disputes.

10 A collection of complaints can be found in the *Volksanwaltschaft*'s Annual Reports. http://www.volksanwaltschaft.gv.at.

particular they pointed out that the coaching frequently did not address their particular situation adequately.

In response to these developments, the government amended the ALVG in 2007. Most of the controversial practices are now covered by law. Thus, a person is now considered willing to work if he/she is ready to take up acceptable employment offered through a regional AMS unit or an employment service provider commissioned by the AMS; to take up VET; to participate in a labour market reintegration programme; or to use any other opportunity and undertake all possible efforts to find employment on their own according to their individual capacities. Generally, the AMS is now obliged to justify any placement in an ALMP programme, except in the case of the long-term unemployed where, the ALVG argues, the reasons are well known as laid down by the law. The 2007 amendment also sets out the rules of acceptability of employment offers and reduces occupational protection, on the basis of an agreement between the social partners concluded in 2004. Thus, the acceptable total travel-to-work distance was raised to two hours for full-time jobs, and to one and a half hours for part-time jobs; in exceptional cases, longer travel-to-work distances are allowed. Occupational protection provisions, another key issue in the agreement, were also changed: the duration of protection was reduced to 100 days, but complemented by an individualised protection of the wage level, which was set at 80% of the basis on which the unemployment benefit is assessed for the first 120 days of unemployment, and at 75% for the rest of the period of benefit entitlement (Obinger and Talos, 2006).

B. Reorganising Social Assistance

The approach to unemployment benefits and activation presented here is now increasingly being extended to the system of *Sozialhilfe*, or social assistance. People who are not entitled to unemployment benefits/assistance or whose transfers are below a certain threshold can apply for *Sozialhilfe* (the so-called second social net). In 2006, about 131,300 persons between 15 and 65 years of age received social assistance in Austria (of whom almost 84,000 were in Vienna). The *Sozialhilfe* system is decentralised and controlled by the Austrian provinces or, rather, municipalities. Thus, there are currently nine regional systems, and support levels vary from province to province. The current government has implemented a reform with a view to harmonising the social assistance system, and social assistance has been replaced by a new social transfer called *Bedarfsorientierte Mindestsicherung* (BMS, needs-based guaranteed minimum). The aim of the BMS measure is to create common minimum standards for all the provinces, to improve the situation of certain groups (such as lone parents), and to improve the legal situation of people entitled to the benefit. Most importantly, BMS recipients will be integrated into the healthcare system.

However, the main task of BMS is to move social assistance closer to labour market policy in order to end the separation between the two systems. To do so, a one-stop shop will be necessary where recipients will not only be able to apply for BMS, but also look for jobs, get advice and counselling, etc. Thus far, however, it is unclear whether a new institution will be created for this purpose or if one of the existing institutions will take on the task. This will depend on regional strategies to cope with the new regulation. A particularly important point is that BMS recipients who are fit enough to work will be included in the ALMP system. In Vienna, for instance, about 40,000 social assistance recipients are currently classed as ready for employment

At present, the AMS's prime focus on job placements and "work first" means that certain groups with very poor prospects of actually finding a job are pushed into social assistance. Thus, the question remains open as to whether the reform of the social assistance scheme will improve the prospects of social integration for BMS recipients, or just serve to add to the pool of heavily subsidised cheap labour available for the flexible segments of the labour market.

C. Reactions to the Crisis

The recent crisis of 2008/9 was an important test-bed for the Austrian ALMP regime and its role in the functioning of the labour market. Unsurprisingly, the evolving crisis triggered a phase of intense activity on the part of the government, the AMS and the social partners to develop and adapt a range of measures and programmes – based on a considerable if temporary increase in ALMP funding as well as two economic stimulus packages focusing on public investment. The discursive framing of these policies was to secure and stabilise employment, reintegrate the unemployed into the labour market as quickly as possible and offer enough apprenticeship positions for young people, but also to safeguard the industrial base of the Austrian economy (Hochrainer *et al.*, 2011, BMASK, 2012).

The main strategies to protect (highly) qualified employees (in particular in manufacturing) were focused, on the one hand, on supporting companies to temporarily reduce the available volume of work and to avoid lay-offs, and on the other hand, on expanding measures to help these employees to find a new job. In this context, it is interesting to note that some of the most important anti-crisis measures, such as short-time work or Work Foundations, date back to the Fordist era of full employment and social compromise.

Thus, since 2008, short-time work (STW) has become a key labour-market and employment policy instrument in companies' fight to overcome economic difficulties. It was presented as a major strategy for managing crisis-related restructuring. STW measures provide for a temporary reduction in standard working hours based on a contractual agreement between the social partners (company and works council) and are financed through the socialised funds of the unemployment insurance system. The works agreement concluded by the social partners aims at securing jobs and compensating for employees' wage losses by means of an STW allowance and a further training allowance. The further training allowance is aimed at encouraging persons on STW to make use of reduced working hours to participate in qualification programmes for the benefit of their company (for a more detailed analysis, see Atzmüller and Krischek, 2010).

Concerning the significance of reskilling highly qualified employees in times of crisis, the Work Foundations, which provide comparably high quality and sustainable further training and re-training, were expanded (to more than 10,000 places). These foundations present a way to deal with crisis-related staff cuts while avoiding the stigma of unemployment. Consequently, this labour-market policy instrument is characterised by the intensive involvement of the social partners at the regional and company level. This especially refers to the companies' contribution to financing the measures. Alongside these high quality measures for certain groups of employees, the AMS also considerably expanded VET courses. Evaluations of the effectiveness of these policies to tackle the impact of the crisis claim that between 35,000 and 42,000 jobs were created or maintained through the fiscal stimulus and ALMP measures (BMASK, 2012).

However, it can be argued that the claims of policy makers and the AMS concerning the goals and effectiveness of the policies to counter the labour market crisis only present half the picture at best. While the discourse tended to focus on measures such as STW and Work Foundations, these mainly protected highly qualified employees. Altogether in the crisis year 2009, short-time work measures (for at least one day) concerned about 66,000 employees. The average reduction of working time was about 25%. The net employment effect of this measure was estimated to concern about 3,500 to 6,000 jobs, which is far lower than in other countries such as Germany (OECD, 2010). A closer look at the employment effects of the crisis reveals a trend towards an increasingly polarised and segmented labour market. Furthermore, recent analyses by the OECD (2010) have shown that Austria was one of the countries with the biggest reductions of actual working time during the crisis, independently of any ALMP measure. Stiglbauer (2010) estimates that the reduction of working time volume amounted to 5.2%, which considerably exceeds the drop in employment (-1.8%). This reduction of working time is only marginally supported by short-time work measures, which, according to Stiglbauer, only concerned 0.26% of the 5.2% reduction. Rather, it reveals the high level of working time flexibility and overtime in the employment system which allowed companies to adapt the necessary volume of work and to embark on a strategy of labour hoarding while monitoring the evolution of the crisis (OECD, 2010). Another strategy adopted by companies was to get rid of temporary agency workers, i.e. to make use of the growing number of precarious forms of employment: these workers accounted for about one quarter of the total increase in the numbers of unemployed in 2009 (+44,000 in total). In addition to these strategies to make use of the built-in flexibilities of the Austrian employment system, the remaining options of early retirement were also increasingly used during the crisis (+6,000 entries), even though they are now linked to considerably reduced entitlements.

Final Remarks

In this chapter I have analysed the development of ALMP in Austria since the 1970s. The growing importance of ALMP is linked to an ongoing reconfiguration of the institutional borders of labour markets, and the evolution of employment conditions and the social security system. The so-called passive administration of unemployment and support of the unemployed by means of unemployment insurance transfers, whose decommodifying aspects are suspected of encouraging welfare fraud, is being replaced by an increasingly workfarist ALMP system (Dimmel, 2000). This is accompanied by a progressively more restrictive and disciplinary benefit system. Recipients of unemployment benefits and unemployment assistance are now seen less as people with social rights than as cost factors in tight social spending budgets. The unemployed have been redefined as active job seekers and clients of employment services. Any individual deficits they may have, due to personal problems or lack of marketable skills, are to be remedied by ALMP measures to keep them employable.

The recent crisis and its effects on employment put the ALMP regime to the test and sparked off a range of actions by the government, the social partners and the AMS to stabilise the Austrian labour market. The interplay between developments on the labour market and the instruments used to tackle the effects of the crisis revealed that the ALMP regime increasingly serves to regulate a segmented labour market through a polarised ensemble of strategies, programmes and measures. The contrast between this reality and the spotlight put on measures intended to secure employment and enhance human resources is striking. Furthermore, the linking of job protection measures to training programmes, and the expansion of re- and up-skilling measures, show that the crisis was also used to support structural change. All these developments have served to reinforce the polarised character of the Austrian ALMP regime. On the one hand, a range of measures provided through the AMS and the government support and protect highly qualified core employees of the Austrian economy; the social partners and the AMS seem willing and able to adapt and reform these devices quickly in order to respond to specific problems raised by the crisis. On the other hand, an expanded set of activation measures and disciplinary devices makes it possible to regulate and stabilise a flexible, segmented labour market based on precarious and low-wage employment and a growing population of working poor (Atzmüller *et al.*, 2012). These instruments are not only designed to serve in a period of crisis, but also to secure a docile workforce when the economy takes off again.

New Employment Forms

Reducing the Scope of the Wage

Martí LÓPEZ-ANDREU

Assistant professor, Department of Sociology, Universitat Autònoma of Barcelona, Spain

Andreu LOPE PEÑA

Associate professor, Department of Sociology, Universitat Autònoma of Barcelona, Spain

Joan Miquel VERD

Associate professor, Department of Sociology, Universitat Autònoma of Barcelona, Spain

Since the 1990s, the majority of European countries have seen the expansion of a range of forms of employment that are either subsidised through tax-based resources or associated with reduced wages and/or rights. The origin of the monetary resources flowing into the wage, one of its essential dimensions, has thus been significantly modified. A detailed analysis of these new forms of employment shows that it is the linkage between the wage and social protection centred on the socialised wage which has been most affected.

This chapter will focus on the transformation of the linkages between employment and social protection observed in a sample of four southern European countries. We will examine the development of mechanisms based on a logic of subsidising employment or reducing wages, and which are presented in government discourse as able to contribute significantly to employment growth. The results presented are based on the research conducted within the framework of the RESORE project,[1] but they have been updated to take account of the effects of the present economic recession. The aim of our study was to compare the ways in which the various mechanisms were implemented in order to see wheth-

[1] Employee's resources and social rights in Europe (RESORE), work package 4: Societal logics of linkage between resources, social rights and employment: institutions, actors and dynamics (2002-2005).

er, despite the different social realities of the countries analysed, common logics in the changes in workers' statuses, flows of financing and workers' rights over resources could be identified.

The type of policies presented here was initially developed in the wake of the employment slowdown that began in Western Europe in the mid-1970s, and the crisis of the "Fordist" model. At European level, however, the fight against inflation remained the primary focus until at the Luxembourg summit of 1997, and later, with greater vigour, the Lisbon Summit, employment was declared a key priority for the EU and its then 15 Member States. Since then, employment has featured prominently as a key strategic goal in EU discourse: the stress has been on job creation and the implementation of what are described as "active employment policies" (in opposition to so-called "passive" measures)[2] to which social protection policies are increasingly, and evermore tightly, linked. It is these employment policies that provide the framework for the promotion of *employment aid* schemes (Ramos, 2010; Auer, Efendioglu and Leschke, 2008) by governments and public administrations, often with the support of the social actors. The justification for these developments has been that the fact of being employed, regardless of the type of job, means that a worker stands a better chance of integrating the labour market than if s/he has remained jobless for too long a period.

This chapter will present (1) the analytical categories we developed with a view to classifying the various types of employment measures studied here; (2) an examination of the Spanish case, used as the basis for a comparison of the different measures adopted in our sample of countries (Spain, Portugal, Italy and France); and (3) the common trends we have identified, and which reveal the transformations underway in the subordinated employment relation and the approach to job creation, tendencies that have been reinforced with the current economic crisis.

I. Subsidised Employment and Reduced Wages: a European Reality

Our analysis of changes in employment forms and their financing takes as starting point the *resource regime* approach (Clasquin *et al.*, 2004; Friot, 1998, 2006, 2012, and in this volume), which provides a conceptual framework for investigating the ways in which different national employment and social protection systems have constructed different modes of access to resources for wage-earners. The reference here is to wage-earners, rather than citizens, since this theoretical approach defines the wage as the central institution channelling the flow of

2 For a discussion of policies designed to "activate" the unemployed, see Khristova, Moncel, Friot in this volume.

resources linked to work and social protection which, because of this, are closely interconnected.

Another noteworthy aspect of our analytical framework is that it breaks away from the dichotomies (commodification *vs.* decommodification, or market *vs.* state) established by Esping-Andersen (1990, 1999). This appears clearly in our approach to the active or activation measures that European governments are deploying to promote employment and that redefine certain wage rights by conditioning entitlements on participation in employment-related activities (workfare). Rather than the degree of commodification implied by these measures, or the level of interaction between market and state that they might reflect, our focus will be on their effects in terms of the reduction or loss of rights entailed, or the tightening up of the conditions of entitlement.

This will be our angle of approach to a range of employment forms found across the EU that entail a reduction of the total wage (direct wage plus social contributions) paid by the employer. This reduction, whether compensated for or not by other resources (usually from taxation), also leads to changes in the status of the workers concerned. In the discussion that follows, this kind of employment situation will be referred to as *reduced wage employment* (RWE). The term will be used here to cover all forms of employment for which the wage has been reduced below the rate set by collective agreements or that was standard practice in a given sector before the introduction of the measures. It will also be applied to cases where workers' entitlements to social benefits such as severance pay, unemployment or pension rights, have been reduced. RWE largely concerns situations in which the reduction in resources is of an individual nature, but it also applies to situations where, although the individual is not directly affected, the flow of socialised resources at a collective level has been diminished due to reductions in employers' contributions. Finally, while linked to the intervention of national authorities, these changes in employment forms must be placed in the context of the social and employment policies implemented in the EU over the past 25 years. Indeed, the subordination of social policy to economic policy has become a salient characteristic of Western capitalist societies today (Jessop, 2002), and modifying the social rights linked to employment is seen as a means to achieve economic goals, whether through employment, income, training or even industrial policies.

Although the periods of introduction and the modalities tend to vary, this kind of policy became predominant across the EU during the 1990s. The European Employment Strategy adopted in 1997 is underpinned by the assumption that responsibility for a particular situation of employment, and all the more so, of unemployment, lies with the individuals themselves (Watt, 2003). Indeed, notions such as *employability* and *activation*, both of which have ambiguous connotations (Serrano, 2003), have been integrated into European employment policies and are considered as core criteria for promoting job creation and full employment. As a result, the populations targeted by employment aid schemes, which are also those stigmatised by the employability discourse, appear as obstacles to achieving full employment. The EES also aimed at creating jobs for women, and the targets set for increasing employment rates across the EU include a strong growth in female employment, thanks in part to the development of legal measures and concrete policies to facilitate reconciling working and family life. All these policies also reflect the increasingly close links established between social and employment policies.

However, as foreseen by the Kok report (Facing the Challenge, 2004), the employment objectives established for 2010 by the Lisbon Summit were not achieved. In the last few years, economic recession and other factors have led to a change in the focus of European employment policy, which now places key emphasis on flexicurity. The notion of flexicurity covers different policies (Keune and Pochet, 2008) and includes the notions of employability and activation. These notions remain central in the Europe 2020 Strategy (*Europe 2020, A strategy for smart, sustainable and inclusive growth*, European Commission, 2010), but are subordinated to the Stability and Growth Pact.

As stated earlier, we will examine the modalities of RWE introduced in a sample of four southern European countries – Spain, Portugal, Italy and France – in order to draw out the key characteristics. We have adopted an asymmetrical approach to the comparison, in that the main focus will be on Spain, while the examples in the other three countries are drawn on, by way of contrast, to illustrate the varied forms that RWE can take. The measures examined were initiated in the mid 1990s and early 2000s and remain largely in effect.

Given national differences and the specific models of social relations within which employment policies are embedded (Bilbao, 1999), it is no easy task to undertake a systematic comparison of the various measures or to attempt to establish functional equivalents. The societal context within which the measures are implemented must thus be taken into account as an element of interpretation.[3] However, we were able to identify two dimensions that are common to all the countries examined here, and that permit classification of RWE. These are 1) the arguments used to justify their introduction, and 2) the type of public intervention involved.

[3] See Verd in this volume.

The official arguments used to justify and legitimate the various measures can be classified as follows:

1) Increasing the level of employment and/or employability: the claim here is that the measures concerned will facilitate the integration into employment of certain populations (who are thus defined negatively, by their lack of or difficult access to employment);

2) Improving skills and qualifications: these measures are presented as seeking to improve the match between workers' training and the specific needs of the enterprise;

3) Economic needs: the claim is that the measures will boost economic activity, by helping companies renew their workforce in order to adapt to changing markets;

4) Promoting self-employment: this concerns measures intended to enable populations experiencing difficulty in gaining access to employment, to become "independent" workers or "entrepreneurs".

The above arguments are all used to justify the introduction of schemes geared to reducing unemployment among target groups. The implementation of these measures involves different forms of public intervention in the wage relation and the distribution of resources that can be classified as follows:

1) Reductions in employers' social contributions: this means lowering "labour costs" for the employer;

2) Job subsidies: the public authorities directly finance a part of the wage, or a part of the cost of setting up as self-employed;

3) Reduction of social rights: this can concern any right associated with an employment contract (such as severance pay, unemployment insurance or pension entitlements);

4) Reduction of the direct wage: measures authorising pay levels below the statutory minimum wage or that defined in the sectoral collective agreement.

The relative weight of these forms of intervention varies between countries: reductions in employer contributions, for instance, play a significant role in Spain, Portugal and France where strong emphasis is given to the argument of job creation. In Italy, on the other hand, the creation of a new type of employment contract half-way between the wage relation and self-employment clearly expresses the attempt to sidestep the standard employment relation, in a context where it already appears relatively weak compared to neighbouring countries.

Table 1 shows that in Spain, Italy and France, to differing degrees and despite the changes, the relationship between the wage and employment corresponds to the continental model based on a linkage between the wage and social rights. Due to its extensive informal sector, Portugal presents a notable difference in that the share of financing from other sources (that is, neither taxation nor social contributions) is relatively high. Despite this marked difference, the Portuguese model of social protection can still be classed as continental since social contributions still constitute the major source of financing, and taxation represents a smaller share.

Table 1: The financing of social protection according to the source of funds. 2001-2009 (percentages)

	Social Security Contributions		General Government Contributions		Other receipts	
	2005	2009	2005	2009	2005	2009
EU15	58.77	56.63	37.92	39.57	3.31	3.81
Spain	63.54	55.53	34.30	43.06	2.15	1.41
France	65.62	64.61	30.57	31.91	3.81	3.48
Italy	57.01	54.60	41.39	43.81	1.61	1.9
Portugal	45.57	44.73	44.14	44.28	10.9	11.00

Source: Eurostat: Social protection receipts, 2005-2009.

In order to complete this overview, a brief statistical comparison of expenditures on employment policy in the four countries examined is provided in Table 2 for the years 2005 and 2009. It can be seen that public expenditure in France was clearly above the European (EU-15) average, particularly on so-called passive policies in 2005 (but not in 2009, when it dropped below the average because of the increase of the expenditure on "passive policies" in countries with higher unemployment rates). The Spanish case is also interesting: overall expenditure was above the EU-15 average, with spending on "passive" policies showing a marked increase in 2009 due to the rise in unemployment. Finally, in Portugal and Italy, expenditures on both active and passive policies were below the respective EU averages, with Italy showing the lowest total tax-spending on employment policy in our sample of countries.

Table 2: Public spending on employment policies (% of GDP in 2005 and 2009)

	EU-15		Spain		Italy		France		Portugal	
	2005	2009	2005	2009	2005	2009	2005	2009	2005	2009
Labour Market Services (cat. 1)	0.23	0.24	0.09	0.13	0.04	0.03	0.3	0.26	0.14	0.12
Active Policies (cat. 2-7)	0.53	0.56	0.8	0.65	0.48	0.36	0.66	0.72	0.50	0.63
Pass. Policies (cat. 8-9)	1.2	1.47	1.46	2.98	0.8	1.39	1.58	1.42	1.28	1.31
Total	2.07	2.27	2.14	3.6	1.29	1.78	2.48	2.40	1.92	2.06

Source: Eurostat, Labour Market Policy Expenditure by type of action, 2005-2009.

Cat 1: Labour market services.

Cat 2-7: Training, job rotation and job sharing, employment incentives, integration of disabled people, direct job creation, incentives for self-employment.

Cat 8-9: Benefits for unemployment, early retirement and other situations (pensions, sick leave, etc.) with social protection.

We will now examine the RWE measures introduced in each of the countries studied. We will begin with an examination of the Spanish case: the target populations and types of intervention will be analysed, and the measures placed in historical perspective. Then we will look at the cases of Portugal, Italy and France: here, the analysis will focus on a sample of measures in order to highlight the generalisation of RWE, as well as the specific forms developed in each country.

II. Employment Forms Derogating from Standard Open-ended Contracts in Spain

A. The Measures and Their Justification

An overview of the various measures in effect during the period of analysis (some of which were repealed or changed for new measures) is provided in Table 3. The table lists the full range of measures that can be defined as RWE in Spain, and classifies them according to the type of public intervention and the principle arguments used to justify their introduction. As stated earlier, RWE is taken to encompass all interventions leading to a reduction in the socialised wage. Thus, in addition to other temporary contracts, we have included the *contrato por obra y servicio* (contract for a specific project or service), which entails a reduction in severance pay compared to the open-ended contract (8 days less per year worked), and thus a loss of monetary resources for the workers. This contract is of particular interest since it is legally established for the performance of a specific job or service, with a certain degree of autonomy, and for a period of time that is limited, but of uncertain duration. This lack of clarity, which also allows the tasks covered by such contracts to be defined by sectoral or company agreements, has resulted in their widespread use, and in many cases, they have replaced the standard employment relation. In 2006, they accounted for 6,395,190 contracts,[4] and thus contributed to maintaining a high level of temporary employment, which affected 34.0% of the total wage-earner population in 2006.[5] By 2010, the number of these contracts had dropped to 5,623,676 due to the rise in unemployment, while the share of temporary employment – particularly affected by job destruction – was reduced to 24.9% of total wage-earners

Table 3 shows the predominance of measures providing for reductions in employers' contributions for *contingencias comunes* (common contingencies), mostly for employing certain populations on indefinite contracts. An example of this is the *Programa para el fomento del empleo estable* (PFEE; programme for the promotion of stable employment), initiated in 1999 with the agreement of the most representative unions (CCOO and UGT) and employers' organisations (CEOE) and renewed each year, with an extension of the target populations. Another notable feature is the high number of measures justified by the arguments of *employability* and *increasing employment levels.*

Table 3: Justification and forms of intervention. 2012

Increasing the level of employment and/or employability	
Reductions in Employers' social contributions	– *Programa para el fomento del empleo estable (PFEE)* (Programme for the promotion of permanent employment) (1999-2006) – *Contrato temporal y de interimidad para minusvàlidos* (Temporary and provisional contract for disabled people – *Incentivos conversion en empleo estable* (Incentives for conversion to stable employment) – *Contratacion temporal de personas en situacion de exclusion social* (Temporary contract for people in situations of social exclusion) – *Personas victimas de la violencia domestica* (Victims of domestic violence) – *Trabajadores afectados por ERE a los que se les haya reducido la jornada* (workers' affected by a redundancy procedure with working-day reduction)

4 Contract statistics, Spanish Institute of Employment: Accumulated data, 2006 and 2010. This measure allows contracts to be signed, even on a daily basis, in sectors as varied as construction, journalism, courier services, etc., the rationale being that the specific task concerned does not fall within the scope of the company's usual requirements.

5 Active Population Survey, Annual data 2006 and 2010.

Job subsidies	– *Contrato indefinido para trabajadores minusvalidos* (Indefinite contract for disabled workers) – *Contrato temporal de insercion* (Temporary integration contract) – *Bonificaciones Fomento del empleo 2006 – Acuerdo para la mejora del crecimiento y del empleo* (Employment incentive bonus 2006 – Agreement for the improvement and growth of employment) – *Contrato de trabajo por tiempo indefinido de apoyo a los emprendedores* (Indefinite contract to support entrepreneurs)
Reduction of Social Rights	– *Contrato para el fomento de la contratacion indefinida* (Contract for the promotion of indefinite employment) – *Contrato temporal de fomento del empleo* (Temporary contract for the promotion of employment) (1984-1997)

Economic needs	
Reductions in Employers' social contributions	– *Contratación interina por descanso de maternidad* (Contract for replacing employees on maternity leave) – *Contratacion interina en sustitucion de personas con suspension de contrato por maternidad, adopcion, etc.* (Replacement of persons on leave for maternity, adoption, etc.)
Reduction of Social Rights	– *Contrato de lanzamiento de nueva actividad* (Contract for launching a new activity) (1984-1997) – *Contrato de obra o servicio determinado* (Contract for a specific project or service) – *Contrato eventual por circunstancias de la produccion* (Contract to meet unforeseen production needs) – *Contrato en sustitucion por prejubilacion* (Contract for replacing early retirees)

Improving skills and qualifications	
Reductions in Employers' social contributions	– *Contrato para la formacion* (Training contract) (1993-2012) – *Contrato temporal para la formación y el aprendizaje* (Temporary contract for training and apprenticeship)
Reduction of Direct Wage	– *Contrato en practicas* (Work experience contract) – *Contrato de aprendizaje* (Apprenticeship contract) (1993-2012)

Promoting self-employment	
Job subsidies	– *Subvencion estatal a desempleados para que se establezcan como autonomos* (State subsidy for unemployed people to set up as self-employed) – *Subvencion estatal a los minus vàlidos para que se establezcan como autonomos* (State subsidy for disabled people setting up as self-employed)

Source: Own research/compilation

B. A Two-fold Approach: Pursuing Flexibility while Promoting Stable Employment

A high unemployment rate and high level of temporary employment have been the major characteristics of the Spanish labour market in the past 35 years. The series of reforms undertaken with a view to "modernising" employment and social policies to align with EU recommendations, and intended to "maintain international competitiveness", were also aimed at tackling these problems. They included the introduction of a whole range of RWE measures. The latter must be seen as part of a process aiming to break with standard employment (in the sense used by Rodgers, 1992)[6] and deregulate the labour market. They cannot be isolated from a generalised trend towards the extension of atypical forms of employment and the use of social policies to "manage" their consequences.

The beginning of this process dates back to the 1980s when, faced with a strong rise in unemployment, the first Socialist governments decided to intervene in the labour market by introducing more flexibility. A significant step was the reform of the Workers' Statute in 1984, which provided incentives in the form of subsidies (essentially reductions in employer contributions) for recruitment on temporary contracts called *contratos temporales de fomento del empleo* (which did not have to be justified by specific production needs).

During the subsequent period of economic growth between 1985 and 1991, employment increased and unemployment dropped (from 21.9% in 1985 to 16.3% in 1990), but as a result of these policies, worker turnover also increased and the share of temporary contracts grew, rising to 32% by 1991. Moreover, Segura *et al.* (1991) suggest that the job creation observed was attributable for the most part to economic growth, and that the contribution of these policies had been minimal.

The economic recession that began in 1992 brought a rapid destruction of the temporary jobs created during the previous period, and affected standard employment as well. In 1994, a new reform of the Workers' Statute introduced greater flexibility as regards redundancies, mobility, and company-level bargaining, as well as a legal status for temporary employment agencies (Sebastián, 1995); in addition, the *contrato temporal de fomento del empleo* was abolished and the *contrato para la formacion* (training contract) as well as the *contrato en prácticas* (work experience) were reformed. However, none of these measures had a real effect on the share of temporary contracts. The equation proposed by Bilbao (1994) sums up the logic underpinning this overall trend: the only way to integrate "outsiders" (young people, the unemployed, temporary workers, etc.) is to destabilise "insiders" (in permanent employment). The results of this approach are clear: a persistently high rate of tempo-

---

6 That is, on the lines of the Fordist employment model: an open-ended contract for full-time employment with a direct wage and social rights permitting the reproduction of labour power.

rary employment and a rhetoric that blames trade unions for only defending insiders (Banyuls *et al.*, 2009).

In the late 1990s, a major employment reform was introduced by the *Partido Popular*, then in power. In order to reduce the high rate of precarious, temporary employment (around 34% at the time), the leading trade unions and the employers' associations signed the *Acuerdo Interconfederal para la Estabilidad en el Empleo* (AIEE, Multi-Industry Agreement for Employment Stability), which the government then transformed into law in 1997 (Royal Legislative Decrees 8/97 and 9/97). These laws limited the duration of temporary contracts to two years (instead of the previous three), abolished seven types of such contracts, and established the *contrato para el fomento de la contratacion indefinida* (contract for the promotion of indefinite employment), intended to encourage recruitment on open-ended contracts by reducing severance pay for what in Spain is termed "non-justified objective dismissal" (*despido objetivo improcedente*).[7] We consider this measure to be particularly relevant in that severance pay was reduced by 12 days per year worked, compared to an ordinary indefinite contract. Furthermore, its use became widespread: data for 2005 show that despite its failure to contribute to reducing the proportion of precarious contracts, which still affected 33.5% of employees,[8] it accounted for 34.26% of open-ended recruitment that year.[9] Thus, although the measure was initially programmed to end in 2001, its duration was extended, and as will be seen below, this policy of reducing severance pay was pursued in the *Acuerdo para la mejora del crecimiento y del empleo* (Agreement for the improvement and growth of employment), signed by the social representatives and the government in 2006. In 2010, in a context of rising unemployment, Law 35/10 extended the contract for the promotion of indefinite employment (with reduced severance pay) to all workers except men between 30 and 45 years old who have been registered as job seekers for less than three months. Furthermore, the Royal Legislative Decree 3/2012 extended the reduction in severance pay for "non-justified objective dismissal" to all new indefinite contracts; thus, what was introduced as an exceptional measure has now been extended to all

---

7 Dismissal is defined as "objective" when for economic or company reasons and therefore not attributable to the worker. It is considered "justified" if the company can prove the cause (severance pay of 20 days per year worked), whereas "non-justified" dismissal implies the reinstatement of the worker or higher dismissal costs. The reform reduced the latter from 45 to 33 days per year worked for these new indefinite contracts.

8 Total temporary workers, Annual data 2005, Active Population Survey.

9 INEM statistics on employment contracts: Accumulated data December 2005.

new contracts. These last measures met with strong opposition and two general strikes called by the unions.

1999 saw the introduction of the *Plan para el Fomento del Empleo Estable (PFEE; Plan for the promotion of stable employment)*, which provided monetary incentives for recruitment on indefinite contracts. The Plan offered reductions in employers' social security contributions targeted to specific populations (young people under 30; people registered as unemployed with the Public Employment Service (PES) for over 12 months; and unemployed people over 45), with an additional reduction of 5% for women, and for a duration of 12-24 months depending on the population concerned. The measure was renewed in the 2000s, and in 2005, extended to new groups, such as female victims of domestic violence, and the reduction increased by 10% for hiring women full time. These reductions in employer social security contributions are compensated for by the state through the National Institute of Employment (INEM) budget.[10] With the number of contracts on the rise since 1999, the measure has lost its temporary, targeted nature to become a permanent device in widespread use. According to the CES (2005), in the period from 1997 to 2004, 86.8% of new indefinite contracts signed during this period were affected by reduced contributions or reduced dismissal costs.

In May 2006, with the Agreement for the Improvement of Growth and Employment, the PFEE was replaced by a new system of reductions which had the same stated goal of reducing precarious employment and increasing indefinite employment, and maintained the same target populations. This reform combined a generalised reduction in employer contributions for indefinite contracts with an extension of the cut-off date for the conversion of fixed-term or temporary contracts to a "contract for the promotion of indefinite employment" (*contrato para el fomento de la contratacion indefinida*, with reduced severance pay), and the replacement of the PFEE reductions in employer contributions by a programme of direct subsidies for hiring people from certain populations on open-ended contracts.

In June and September of 2010, in a context of a high increase in unemployment, two laws on Urgent Measures for Labour Market Reform introduced new reductions in employers' social security contributions for the recruitment of unemployed and self-employed workers, and for employers implementing working-time reduction schemes instead of dismissals in a redundancy procedure. In addition, employers were

[10] State resources account for at least 40% of the INEM budget, and are allocated to the financing of active labour market policies, with the main expenditure corresponding to compensation for reductions in social contributions.

granted reductions in social security contributions for hiring unemployed persons on training contracts. In 2011 (Royal Legislative Decree 1/2011) further reductions in social security contributions were introduced for indefinite or temporary part time contracts provided to workers under 30 years old, and to people registered as unemployed with the PES for over 12 months. The 2012 reform (Royal Legislative Decree 3/2012) introduced new subsidies and a new indefinite contract for enterprises with less than 50 employees (*contrato de trabajo por tiempo indefinido de apoyo a los emprendedores*). The stated aim is to encourage the recruitment of unemployed persons aged between 16 and 30, or over 45, and of women in mostly male sectors. Under this contract, the trial period will last one year.

The reform also increases flexibility by changing the rules for objective dismissal (with severance pay further reduced to 20 days per year worked). It establishes that economic reasons are considered valid "when a negative economic situation arises from the results of the enterprise, in cases such as the existence of current or foreseeable losses, or the persistent drop in its revenues or sales". In this case, a drop in revenue or sales is considered persistent when occurring over a period of 9 consecutive months.

Table 5: Target populations, amount and duration of aids. 2006, 2012

Target Population	Subsidy (annual amount)	Duration	Year of introduction
Women -Employed within 24 months of childbirth. -Employed after 5 years of inactivity, if they had worked for at least 3 years before stopping. -Re-employed after interrupting their contract (indefinite or temporary) to have a child.	1,200 Euros	4 years	2006
Unemployed women and female victims of domestic violence.	850 Euros	4 years	2006
Women over 45 years old	1,200 Euros	The full duration of the contract	2006
Young people between 16 and 30 years old	800 Euros	4 years	2006
People unemployed for at least 6 months, and people in a situation of social exclusion	600 Euros	4 years	2006

Conversion of temporary training, relief, or replacement contracts (including of retiring workers) into indefinite contracts	500 Euros	4 years	2006
Disabled people	3,000 Euros	The full duration of the contract	2006
Severely disabled people	3,200 Euros	The full duration of the contract	2006
Workers hired on an Indefinite contract to support entrepre-neurs	From 1,000 to 1,500 Euros (100 Euros more for women)	3 years	2012
Beneficiaries of the Plan for the conversion of work experience contracts to permanent contracts	500 Euros (men) and 700 Euros (women)	3 years	2012

Source: Ministerio de Empleo y de la Seguridad Social (2012): Bonificaciones/reducciones a la contratación laboral, available at:

http://www.sepe.es/contenido/empleo_formacion/empresas/pdf/ResumenBonificaciones Marzo2012.pdf

C. The Beneficiaries

As we have seen, the main type of intervention consisted in lowering employers' social contributions, but also the establishment of direct subsidies and the reduction of dismissal costs. The primary beneficiary in all cases, whatever the measure concerned – reduced social contributions, reduced social protection for the workers, or subsidised employment – is the employer, who is able to recruit workers at a lower cost. These aids are focused on employment creation, and are justified on the grounds that the only way to create jobs is to reduce wages – or lighten the so-called "burden" of social contributions, although these are of course a part of the wage.

The major role played by transfers to employers is revealed by the data in Table 6, which shows public expenditures on employment policies, and their beneficiaries. The figures are particularly telling in the case of employment incentives (which include reduced contributions as part of the PFEE and for the conversion of temporary to indefinite contracts). The increase in transfers to individuals from 2005 to 2009 is due to the lump-sum payment of the unemployment benefit as a start-up incentive.

Table 6: Expenditure on employment policies, by recipients (%) 2005-2009

	2005				2009			
	Transfers to individuals	Transfers to employers	Transfers to service providers	Total	Transfers to individuals	Transfers to employers	Transfers to service providers	Total
Training	0.7	1.8	23.0	25.5	0.8	3.5	22.7	26.9
Job rotation and job sharing		1.5		1.5		1.5		1.5
Employment incentives		49.7		49.7		40.0		40.0
Supported employment and rehabilitation		3.3		3.3		4.1	0.1	4.2
Direct job creation		11.3		11.3		12.3		12.3
Start-up incentives	8.8			8.8	14.9		0.3	15.1
Total LMP measures (categories 2-7)	9.5	67.5	23.0	100	15.7	61.3	23.0	100

Source: Own research based on Eurostat, Expenditure by Labour Market Policy interventions, 2005-2009

We see that in 2009, over 61% of total public expenditure on employment went to the employers, but if training and start-up incentives are excluded, this figure reaches 99.9% of expenditure on the remaining categories. Furthermore, the data provided by the Labour Market Policy database (2009) show that reductions in social contributions accounted for 92.89% of spending on employment incentives. The focus on reducing "labour costs" shows how the employer point of view has been integrated into the development of public policies. And these policies appear to be geared essentially to putting the unemployed back to work with little regard for the quality of the employment created.

The major trend in Spain has thus been to progressively extend reductions in employers' social contributions until these reductions were finally generalised to all indefinite contracts.

III. Portugal, Italy and France

We have chosen here to briefly present the most representative examples of measures geared to reducing "labour costs" in each of these countries for the period analysed. Our aim is to see how each country uses RWE mechanisms to regulate its "labour market". The following measures were selected:

- Temporary reductions in employers' social contributions in Portugal
- General reductions in employers' social contributions in France
- The *Collaborazione Coordinata Continuativa* contract in Italy

We find these measures particularly relevant in that they highlight the main approaches to employment with reduced wages and reduced rights, and, notwithstanding existing societal differences, are revealing of common trends as regards the distribution of resources, the mechanisms through which social rights are established, and the role of RWE in these processes.

A. Portugal: Seeking to Reduce Unemployment and Improve Training

Historically, the main RWE measures have been based on two stated objectives:

1) Improving workers' skill levels and "modernising the productive fabric". The 1990s saw the introduction of schemes for combined training and work experience in public or private enterprises, paid at minimum wage level plus a complement based on the worker's level of educational qualifications, and for which the employer received a subsidy.
2) The fight against unemployment, which initially targeted young people, but in recent years has been generalised to the whole population (due, it is claimed, to the crisis). Employment incentives are thus intended to increase the volume of employment; our focus below will be on the reductions in employer contributions.

Social Security resources have traditionally been used for employment policies in Portugal: a portion of the revenues from social contributions is allocated to the budget of the Institute of Employment and Vocational Training to finance the remuneration of workers participating in "work experience" programmes. In 1986, Decree-Law No. 257/86 authorised temporary reductions in social contributions – of around 20% for a maximum period of 24 months – in order to encourage the hiring of young people (from 16 to 30 years old) seeking their first job (Ruivo and Dias Da Silva, 2004). This measure was then extended in 1995 (Government Decree No. 85/95): the target population was broadened to include the long term unemployed and the duration of the reductions was prolonged to 36 months, but conditioned on a net creation of jobs. In 2002, the measures concerned a total of 141,623 workers, corresponding to an expenditure of 172.57 million euros. Labour Market Policy Database figures for 2003 show that employment incentives accounted for the major proportion of expenditures on employment policy overall, and for 64.73% of spending on "active" policies, thus far more than that on training or direct job creation.

These measures show how resources deriving from the total wage, in particular from Social Security contributions, were allocated to job creation policies. In contrast to Spain, the main justification used for reducing employers' social contributions in Portugal was creating employment rather than promoting indefinite contracts.[11] However, although these two countries have characteristically low levels of social spending,[12] both have used social protection resources to support their active employment policies. These resources go to the employer, directly or in the form of reductions that are compensated for by the state, rather than to the worker (in the form of training or social protection rights).

In 2011, in the framework of the labour reforms demanded by the European Commission, the European Central Bank and the International Monetary Fund, a number of measures to reduce public debt were introduced. These included a reduction of the duration of unemployment benefits and a reduction of severance pay from 30 to 10 days per year worked for indefinite contracts, and from 36 to 10 days in the case of temporary contracts.

B. Italy: Dependent Self-employment

Although the problems are defined in a similar way to elsewhere, the focus in Italy has been on a different type of mechanism to those observed thus far. We have chosen here, given the significant proportion of self-employed workers in this country, to examine an unorthodox measure in widespread use since the 1990s – the *collaborazione coordinata e continuativa (co.co.co.)* contract – which applies to the provision of services and combines aspects of subordinated and independent work. The principle features of this type of contract are:

1) It is not regulated by employment law, as it is defined as applying to an independent activity, but it is characterised by the same constraints for the worker as waged employment.

---

11 Although there is also a scheme for encouraging the creation of stable employment: a subsidy corresponding to 12 times the minimum monthly wage is offered to businesses with less than 50 workers for creating a new post, or those with more than 50 workers for hiring a person over 45 years old who has been registered as unemployed for at least 4 years.

12 Social protection as a % of GDP was 27.3% for EU-15, 30.3% in France, 25.3% in Italy, 23.5% in Portugal, and 20.3% in Spain for the period 2001-2003 (Eurostat, European Social Statistics, Social protection, Total Expenditure on Social protection. 2001-2003).

2) It is associated with limited social rights. Although the pension reforms of 1995 introduced a mandatory pension contribution of 10-12% of gross remuneration, paid by the worker into a specific separate Social Security fund (*Cassa de Gestione Separata*, CGS), and certain maternity and sick-leave benefits were extended in 1997, the benefit entitlements remain far more limited than those associated with standard employment.

This contract thus allows the enterprise to avoid the constraints of the wage relation, but has little resemblance to a simple business relationship since the conditions correspond to a situation of subordination: working at fixed hours, for a single enterprise, and so forth. We thus once again have a measure aimed at job creation – initially intended to provide young people with access to employment – but which, in sidestepping the characteristics of the wage, amounts *in fine* to a reduced total wage for the worker and therefore reduced costs for the employer.

Although the contract is associated with mandatory social contributions, these are paid into a distinct fund, and the entitlements are thus not the same (nor at the same level) as in the case of standard employment. Furthermore, by establishing a contract with limited social rights, associated with partial social contributions and the exclusion of certain risks (such as unemployment), and that does not recognise wage-earner status, the government achieved a second objective: setting up a permanent scheme that collects workers' resources for the financing of the Social Security system, and thus contributes to balancing the budget without increasing labour costs for the employer or needing to transfer tax funds (Fravega and Queirolo-Palmas, 2005). Data on the numbers of people registered with the *Casa de la Gestione Separata*, which grew from 1,008,115 in 1996 to 2,146,382 in 2001, provide an indication of the impact of this type of contract. According to data collected by Vasapollo (2006), over 2,400,000 people were working under this contract in 2002, and their numbers were still on the rise. This author also highlights the great diversity of activities, conditions of pay and of work covered by the *co.co.co.*

In 2003, as part of a general reform of employment policies (known as the *Biagi* Law), the *co.co.co.* was replaced by the *Lavoro e progeto* scheme. The reform strengthened all those aspects of the contract that enable employers to benefit from lower labour costs. The individual nature of the wage, which is not covered by collective agreements, was maintained, and as we have seen, the working conditions in force in the enterprise do not apply to the contracted workers.

The measure is still in force and is the main source of flexibility in the Italian labour market (Leonardi *et al.*, 2011).

C. France: the Silent Break with the Wage Norm

The *general reductions in social contributions* in France will not be examined in terms of one specific measure, but rather in reference to a range of measures for which the parameters have changed over time. Their application has spread across the labour market and they are no longer linked to particular target populations. In 2003, these reductions concerned over two-thirds of private sector wage-earners, according to official estimates (DARES, 2004, p. 63).

This policy of cuts in employer contributions was, to a large extent, developed during the 1990s for low-wage jobs (using the minimum wage as reference) and the negotiations on working time reductions. According to Daniel (1998), the measure marked the beginnings of a "silent revolution" in French social policy, which moved away from temporary schemes stigmatising certain target populations on the basis of what they "lack", towards a structural approach with the generalisation of the reductions to a significant share of waged employment.

Although certain reductions have existed since the 1980s, their generalisation took place during the 1990s. The Law of 31 December 1992 reduced employer contributions for part-time employment to begin with, and then for all types of contracts and various types of coverage (family benefits and sickness). In 1996, the range of existing measures were merged, and employer contributions further reduced. With the "Aubry Law" of 2000, the introduction of the 35-hour week was accompanied by an incentive based on a "reduction in labour costs", that is, reduced contributions conditioned on a company agreement including a commitment to job creation. The measures concerned wage levels up to 1.7 and then 1.6 times the minimum wage (SMIC) (Higelé and Khristova, 2005).[13]

Despite the uncertainty as to the effects of this policy, the 2003 "Fillon Law" extended it to low wage workers not concerned by the 35-hour week, thus dropping the conditionality of a reduction in working time or job creation. What had started out as a temporary, targeted strategy has thus been progressively transformed into a policy designed to limit the space of the wage, and undermine the principles of the wage relationship.

Thus, the "extensive cut in labour costs" called for by the employer world became established as the new norm, in the context of a general trend towards tightening the contributory nature of wage-based benefits and an increasing flexibilisation of workers' career paths. In 2000, the jobs of one-fourth of French wage-earners were covered by the reductions in employer contributions linked to the 35-hour week; this propor-

[13] See also Ribeiro and Ruivo in this volume.

tion had risen to about two-thirds by 2002-2003 (DARES, 2003). Since then, several new measures have served to progressively generalise these reductions. Recent data show that in 2010 the reductions amounted to 20.1% of total employers' contributions (Acosstat, 2011).

Conclusions

This chapter has shown how countries with different social realities have developed similar modes of public intervention in the field of employment. We see these interventions as mechanisms for reducing the cost of labour for employers, by reducing their social contributions or by permitting a reduction in direct wage levels. The most widely used measures in the countries analysed, and those with the greatest impact, concerned the two forms associated with reduced contributions – *reductions in employers' social contributions* and *a reduction in workers' social protection.*

This type of measure plays a contradictory role in the regulation of the links between the wage and social protection. While the public authorities have restricted workers' access to certain social benefits, arguing that available resources are insufficient, they have, at the same time, introduced measures intended to increase the employment level of target populations but that effectively reduce contributions to these same resources. Moreover, such measures serve to subordinate social protection to the "primary goal" of job creation. The level of social protection provided and the resources required are thus considered as elements of employment policy, and the aim has been to gain acceptance for the idea that the jobs could not have been created without some sacrificing of social protection. This is clearly the case in Spain for the numerous measures that jeopardise the source of resources for social protection, or directly reduce rights. The scope of the socialised wage is being reduced and absorbed by the economic sphere: those same institutions (such as Social Security) that were designed to provide social benefits (and continue to do so) are today being used as instruments for the construction of a "labour market" and to support employers. These policies have been maintained in the context of the public debt crisis, in spite of the reduction in public expenditures in many fields.

We would like to stress the point that the measures designed to reduce the cost of labour for employers and limit the scope of the wage have progressively been consolidated to the point of becoming structural. The most obvious example is the *co.co.co.* in Italy, where it is considered as an open-ended contract. The Portuguese measures described here have been expanded to cover increasing numbers over time. In Spain and particularly in France, what began as temporary mechanisms have taken on an increasingly permanent form, and employment policies that were initially targeted to stigmatised populations (young people, the long-term unemployed, women, etc.) have progressively been extended to cover majority segments.

In order to legitimate this drop in resources, the governments of these countries all use the argument of improving the *employability* of the worker, who needs to be "(re)integrated" – even temporarily (by reducing employers' costs). The approach to implementing these stated goals was found to differ between the countries, as reflected in the particular form of measure developed. The Spanish governments initially focused more on promoting open-ended contracts, but with the economic and employment crisis, subsidies have been generalised to any kind of employment situation. In France, the measures were designed to promote a reduction in working time, or to provide support for low-wage jobs. In Portugal, the focus was on targeting specific populations (such as young people, the unemployed, or low-skill workers); however, in the context of the economic crisis, measures reducing severance pay have also been introduced. The Italian case is unusual, as the measure with the most impact was not designed for any specific group or limited in terms of duration, and the argument of integration was not used to justify its introduction; the device has contributed to creating a type of employment which, by masking the subordinated nature of the work relationship, eliminates most of the obligations of the employer towards an employee, and considerably jeopardises the role of wage bargaining. Collective bargaining reforms introduced in 2010 and 2011 have made dismissals easier, reduced severance pay, and facilitated opting out of agreed working conditions.

The other line of argument used focuses on the *activation of resources*. Here, *activation*[14] means transferring social protection resources to the financing of employment policies, by disconnecting the former from the latter, or even opposing the two, as if diminishing these resources (and therefore the benefits) could contribute to raising the level of employment. According to this view, instead of serving to provide protection against risks, social security resources must be used "actively" (supposedly to increase employment) – which in reality means passed on to the employer, and essentially treated like tax credit.

Some of the measures analysed here have obvious consequences on the level of social protection, particularly in a context where the trend is

[14] As is well known, the dividing line between active and passive measures is arbitrary and semantically tendentious. For the EU, public expenditures that entail a transfer of resources are considered active (for example any type of subsidy or award provided to companies, or to workers to make them "employable" and therefore "active"), except of course unemployment and retirement benefits, which are not subject to the immediate subordination of employment.

to lower, rather than raise, tax resources. With the Italian *co.co.co.*, wages are reduced and unemployment benefits eliminated, and the contracts in Spain stemming from the AIEE (Agreement on the improvement of growth and employment) entailed reductions in severance pay that have been generalised to all new indefinite contracts. Furthermore, these measures must be placed in the broader context of the European Union, where the main thrust of national unemployment insurance reforms is to strengthen the contributory nature of benefits and tighten the conditions of access. A new model of society is emerging: instead of a wage society based on a wage that includes social rights, we are seeing one in which people are defined as more or less "employable" individuals who are to be "integrated" into a "labour market" where their pay will be individualised and its socialised component amputated. This transformation clearly reflects the move to *de-socialise* the wage, by reducing the scope of social rights and employers' social contributions (Friot, 2012).

The wage relation, which in the continental countries conditions access to socialised resources, is gradually being eroded by the introduction of evermore numerous exceptions to what had previously been constructed as the wage norm. All the measures analysed in this chapter – officially presented as part of a strategy to make the recruitment of certain categories of people (seen as *poorly employable*) "more attractive" to employers – have contributed to the development of a new model in which the rights linked to the wage relationship are becoming fragmented and progressively "de-universalised" (see Part I in this volume).

Furthermore, the essentially conflictual nature of the wage as the locus of the struggle for rights and resources is tending to disappear in the measures analysed since the total wage is no longer seen as a collective right but as payment for an individual effort (Friot, 2012). This logic corresponds to the principles of the European Employment Strategy, and is backed up by active employment policies that define individuals as solely responsible for their employment situation.

From the point of view of the distribution of resources, we have seen how the relative socialisation of risk that was constructed through the wage is being undermined. Collective risks are gradually being transformed into individual problems requiring individualised solutions. Indeed, the cuts in the socialised component of the wage essentially benefit the employer, whose responsibility for the risks linked to subordinated labour seems to be progressively shrinking. All this, together with an increasingly workfarist approach conditioning entitlement to certain social rights on the proactive behaviour of claimants, illustrates the extent of the changes produced. Employment, which once constituted the basis of the wage, has been turned into a tool for reducing "labour costs" and its previous range of attributes reduced to a single dimension – that of the subordination of labour.

Workfare or Social Security?

Labour Market and Social Policies in the UK

Roland ATZMÜLLER

Assistant professor, University of Linz, Austria

"Today the greatest challenge for any democratic government is to refashion our institutions to bring this new workless class back into society and into useful work, and to bring back the will to win" (Tony Blair, speech at the Aylesbury Estate, June 1997).[1]

Welfare-to-work was a key element in New Labour's government project of 1997 and one of the results of a radical overhaul of the Labour Party's political programme during the 1990s, when the party abandoned the socialist goal of replacing capitalism with a new economic order. This workfarist strategy to combat unemployment and welfare dependency by activating the unemployed (Gray, 2004; Peck, 2001) aimed to further social inclusion and overcome poverty by re-commodifying labour. The term "workfare" describes the realignment of social and labour market policies towards a stance that expects welfare recipients to do something in return for their benefits. This can include participating in information and counselling sessions, training courses or community work, and active job search – gauged, for instance, by the number of applications.

As New Labour's welfare-to-work programme illustrates, workfare can take different forms in different countries (Noel, 1995; Fink, 2006a). It cannot simply be reduced to the enforcement of neoliberal forms of increasingly repressive and restrictive labour-market policies, as a number of other measures must also be taken into consideration.[2] The developments in the UK since 1997 show that implementing a welfare-to-work strategy requires establishing new practices and institutions. The New Labour government promised to reconcile the goal of an inclusive society providing fair opportunities to all with the imperatives of a globalised economy. However, it reduced social inclusion and equal opportunities to a question of individual participation in employment

[1] Quoted in Peck (2001).

[2] For a similar viewpoint, see Adler (2004).

(and the individual's readiness to do so). Alternative models of society no longer had any place in the New Labour programme. In 2010, the incoming coalition government formed by the Conservative Party and the Liberal Democrats brought New Labour's attempt to reconcile flexibility and competitiveness with social inclusion to an abrupt end, and replaced it by a strategy geared to making "the UK model fit the textbook model of a liberal market economy with a residual welfare state" (Grimshaw and Rubery, 2012, 107). Despite the doubts raised as to the sustainability of the new government's policies, which it legitimises by an alleged necessity to bring down debt levels, the current attack on the welfare state not only aims at massive reductions in public spending but also at a fundamental overhaul of the benefit and tax credit system.

In the first part of this chapter, I will discuss the significance of workfare in the restructuring of the Keynesian welfare state. Part II will then outline the key elements of the Labour government's welfare-to-work strategy. These notably included the introduction of a national minimum wage (Part III), the expansion of in-work benefits (Part IV) and, more narrowly associated with a workfare approach, the New Deal labour market policy programmes (Part V). Finally, the Conclusion will address the question of the extent to which these measures can be regarded as a workfare-based alternative to the welfare state, and offer first insights into the strategies of the new government.

I. The Role of Workfare in the Restructuring of Social and Labour Market Policy Institutions

Workfare is a relatively recent term, a combination of "work" and "welfare" that in itself provides a rather apt description of the strategies involved. These rest on an increasing delegitimation of so-called passive benefits, which are said to permit a life on welfare. Thus, workfarist labour market and social policies increasingly tie benefit entitlements to the claimants' willingness to accept any "reasonable" (an increasingly elastic term) work, participate in training courses, etc. – unless they can prove they are engaged in other socially acceptable activities, such as raising a child. First introduced in the US in the late 1960s, the term "workfare" entered the broader political discourse when William Safire, (ultra-conservative) speechwriter to President Nixon, used it as a catchphrase to describe the Nixon administration's social policy plans. As Jamie Peck (2001) points out in his in-depth study of labour market and social policy restructuring in Anglo-Saxon countries, workfare has largely positive connotations in the US, especially among the conservative right, where it is seen as an alternative to "welfare" and a strategy for social policy reform. By the time the Clinton administration pledged to "end welfare as we know it" in the 1990s, workfare had achieved cross-party consensus in the US.

In Europe (including the UK), "workfare" is generally used in more critical terms to describe neoliberal labour market and social policies aimed at fighting alleged welfare dependency and activating benefit recipients. The political actors implementing such measures, such as the New Labour government, thus usually shy away from having their programmes labelled as workfare in the public debate.

Workfarist approaches are often claimed to spill over into other areas, including passive labour-market measures, when job acceptability criteria are loosened, for instance, or welfare recipients rapidly pressured into actively seeking a job. However, judging from the budget volume spent on active labour market policy, which in EU Member States amounted to just below 1% of GDP in 2000/2001 (compared to an average 28.8% of GDP going to total social policy expenditure), workfare seems to play a rather marginal – if, owing to Europe's persistent unemployment problem, highly symbolical – role in European social security regimes.

However, if we follow the line of argument advanced by Jamie Peck (*op. cit.*) or Bob Jessop (2002), who discuss the relevance of workfare in terms of regulationist debates around the disarticulation of the Fordist welfare state, these developments can be seen as a key dimension of neoliberal hegemony – originating in the Anglo-Saxon countries – in the restructuring and dismantling of the different European social security systems and the re-commodification of labour. In this context, workfare describes the public enforcement and safeguarding of the individual work ethos required for capitalist exploitation, and the integration of workers into increasingly flexible and deregulated labour markets: in other words, the public regulation of precarious forms of employment and working poverty.

In the conflictual dismantling of the Fordist-Keynesian welfare state and its replacement by a post-Fordist "welfare model", workfare thus has a strategic importance that clearly exceeds the narrow focus of labour market policy. What is actually at stake are the social regulation of labour markets, the associated social rights, and potential alternatives to having to accept wage labour under any kind of market conditions (Dimmel, 2000).

In the decades after 1945, the Keynesian welfare state contributed to stabilising productivity growth and to stimulating a period of economic boom. Through its institutions, which were based on a social compromise shaped by a strong labour movement, it was temporarily able to channel the contradictions between labour and capital and particularly the conflicts around wage increases. Social security systems minimised individual risks (unemployment, illness, and old age) and secured a decent standard of living for a vast majority of the population, while incidentally furthering economic stability. Keynesian demand-side policies, state redistribution and an expansion of the public sector ensured full employment and contributed to a massive rise in living standards (Jessop, *op. cit.*, *inter alia*).

The establishment of what have been labelled "workfare states", on the other hand, is based on a major shift in power away from trade unions and social movements. It entails the gradual subordination of social policy to economic policy imperatives and strategies aimed at maintaining competitiveness in globalised capitalism. As a result, there are constant pressures to cut social spending and social security costs – whether tax-based or wage-based – or to switch over to fully funded, and thus privatised, social security regimes. Workfare policies here strive for labour market and social policy reform in order to ensure the availability and willingness of the unemployed and the poor to accept precarious jobs in flexible labour markets. Integration increasingly focuses on the individual's readiness and capacity to participate in wage labour under the prevailing labour market conditions.

Workfarist restructuring of labour markets and social security regimes shows that the boundaries and transitions between (wage) labour, social rights and benefits, and other forms of socially acceptable work (such as childcare) are not static but perpetually redefined and institutionalised through social struggle. Government strategies and public institutions play a vital role in the construction and institutionalisation of different forms of (non-)participation in the labour market as well as in the definition of socially acceptable alternative commitments:

> Welfare-retrenchment and/or work-enforcement strategies do not simply shift the boundary between the employed and the non-employed segments of the labour market in some socially neutral manner. Because this boundary is socially constructed, its movement inevitably entails the reorganization of social relations. And when this boundary movement occurs in the context of liberal welfare/neoliberal workfare regimes, the outcomes are usually measured in terms of deepening social and economic inequalities. (Peck, *op. cit.*, p. 48)

In the institutions at the intersection of social and labour market policy, complex and conflictual processes are at work to assign individuals to different categories (unemployed, part-time workers, people on parental leave, etc.), grant resources (such as financial support or entitlement to services) and define social roles and tasks. These processes must be understood in material and ideological terms: they subordinate the individuals concerned to a variety of demands on their subjectivity, as the institutions' concrete practice is closely connected to the moral and normative construction of the rights and responsibilities of their "clients", their construction of specific groups of "clients" ("welfare scroungers" *vs*. globalisation victims, for instance) and their response to so-called welfare fraud (punishment, counselling, training, etc.).

> [T]here is a regulatory imperative not only to numerically adjust the flows of workers into and out of wage labour, but also to endeavour remaking workers themselves, their attitudes towards work and wages, their expectations about employment continuity and promotion prospects, their economic identities, and so on. (Peck, *op. cit.*, p. 52)

Joblessness and precarious working conditions become individual problems related to the personal attributes of the unemployed (behaviour, qualifications, work ethos as well as family duties, and so forth), rather than a problem concerning macro-economic demand and social security regimes. Workfarist "welfare-state" models thus claim to activate the unemployed, transforming benefits from a "handouts hammock for welfare scroungers" into a spring-board for personal responsibility and work (Ferrara and Hemerijck, 2003).

II. Workfare in the UK

When New Labour came to power in a landslide victory in 1997 after 18 years "in the wilderness", it was confronted with the far-reaching changes to the welfare system introduced by its Conservative predecessors, in particular as regards labour market and employment policies. The Thatcherite strategy to restructure this branch of the welfare state rested on a two-tiered approach. On the one hand, the benefit regime was increasingly tightened through measures to change eligibility criteria, reduce benefit levels, increase means testing and decrease contributory benefits; in particular, this process culminated in the unemployment benefit being redefined as a Jobseekers Allowance (JSA) in 1996. On the other hand, while the Conservatives were claiming to roll back the (welfare) state, they began to develop a new, increasingly differentiated public sector for active labour market policies (ALMPs) closely tied to the tightening benefit regime. Apart from activation measures such as mandatory job interviews and job coaching, training programmes for different groups of unemployed (in particular young people) were introduced in an attempt to address both labour market and skill problems through ALMPs. The Thatcherite government thus laid the cornerstone of a workfarist restructuring of the British welfare system even though at the time they shied away from making participation in ALMP programmes fully mandatory (Peck, 2001).

During the 1990s, party modernisers close to Tony Blair had convinced Labour to accept much of this Thatcherist legacy, and to move on to a new political programme, the so-called "Third Way". Critical voices from within the party were largely silenced. The programmatic reorientation left no doubt that there would be no return to the "tax and spend" policies of the past. Labour's tax-raising and squandering image had been identified by party strategists as one of the main reasons for its repeated defeat by the Conservatives. Instead, the tabloid public was to be convinced that the economy would be "safe in Labour's hands".

"Welfare-to-work", as the party's new labour market and social policy strategy was snappily named, constituted a core element of New Labour's government programme. Chancellor Gordon Brown summed up the strategy's key objective in his first budget address, "Employment opportunity for all", and its implementation was launched in 1997.

Ideologically, "welfare-to-work" reached well beyond labour market policy itself as it promised no less than social inclusion for all segments of the population and the victory over poverty. While the focus below will be specifically on labour market policy, welfare-to-work also underpinned other Labour government policies, such as education and training.

New Labour ideologists identified unemployment and welfare dependency – with their impact on personal dignity and the moral cohesion of communities – as a primary cause of social exclusion and poverty. This stance shows that New Labour had largely embraced the notion of "welfare dependency", as formulated by right-wing thinkers like Charles Murray. For this reason, inclusion into wage labour and job readiness formed the core social integration, anti-poverty and anti-unemployment measures. As noted by Peck (*op. cit.*, p. 359),

> Welfare dependency, rather than poverty *per se*, has become the explicit focus of policy: the poor behave 'inappropriately' because they inhabit a world of perverse incentives, an incentive structure that must be transformed if they are to achieve 'independence'. The solution must be about work and work ethics.

The Labour government's welfare-to-work strategy involved at least three policy areas. First, the introduction of a *national minimum wage*, for which the amount was not only set with a view to avoiding the feared economic consequences (inflation, loss of jobs) but was also fine-tuned with other social policy measures. A second policy strand concerned changes to the tax system and benefit entitlements, which were adapted to give greater priority to *in-work benefits*, a system that had already been developed by the Tory government. In-work benefits formed a core element of the government programme's objective to "make work pay", aimed at ensuring that certain groups of unemployed persons (such as lone parents) would not be discouraged from taking up gainful employment because of the alleged disincentives associated with welfare benefits. The third policy area discussed here concerns the *New*

Deal measures. These focused on the mandatory participation in labour market programmes – such as in-depth counselling and assistance with job search, (subsidised) placement in the private sector, and training or further education – targeted at certain groups of long-term unemployed welfare recipients (notably 18-24 year-olds and lone parents). The compulsory nature of most of these measures was a target for criticism, with the New Deal being condemned as Britain's first fully-fledged workfare programme.

The current Conservative-Liberal Democrat coalition has set out to further extend the workfarist character of social policy. Its agenda includes tightening eligibility criteria, reducing benefit levels (by linking these to the Consumer Price Index instead of the Retail Price Index – which includes housing costs – or capping total benefits per household) and further limiting the scope of contributory benefits (for handicapped people, the Employment and Support Allowance, and incapacity benefits where these still exist). Indeed, the new government aims at nothing less than a fundamental overhaul of the prevailing system of in-work-benefits, which will be replaced by a single *Universal Credit*, while all Labour's New Deal welfare-to-work programmes have already been merged into one *Work Programme*. The reforms are justified by the need to simplify the system (which should improve take-up), and to boost cost saving in times of austerity. These arguments are linked to a new framing of the notion of fairness: according to the government, no household on benefits should receive more cash transfers than people who go out to work.

III. The National Minimum Wage

The national minimum wage, a flagship policy of Labour's 1997 election campaign, was put in place in April 1999. Its introduction had been preceded by years of campaigning by the Trade Union Council (TUC) which, in view of declining unionisation and bargaining power, had opted to support juridical wage regulations for low-wage sectors in the second half of the 1980s. The Labour Party had also included the introduction of a national minimum wage in its programme in the late 1980s, but under Tony Blair avoided mentioning specific hourly rates, for fear their economic reputation might suffer. This naturally came under fierce criticism from trade unions and NGOs.

The introduction of a national minimum wage (NMW) was an historical event for the UK. In the decades after 1945, wages had been regulated in more than 60 wages councils comprised of employer, trade union and independent representatives and covering a total of 3.5 million workers. But since not all sectors were covered, large sections of workers in low-wage sectors were excluded and a general regulation for low-paid jobs was a long way from being fully realised. Under the Thatcher government, wages councils lost much of their significance and were finally abolished in 1993 (with the exception of the council for the agricultural sector).

The first NMW level was set at £3.60 for adult workers aged 22 and over, and at £3.00 for 18-to-21-year-olds. Although trade unions and anti-poverty movements generally welcomed its introduction, they were strongly critical of the level of hourly rates, and the fact that the government's fear of inflation took priority over improvements in the low-wage sector. As a consequence, initially only 1.15 million workers, about 5% of the labour force (instead of the expected 8.5%), benefited from the new regulations. According to the Low Pay Commission (2005), this proportion remained more or less unchanged after each subsequent rise. But alternative evaluations proposed by Richard Dickens and Alan Manning (2003), for example, produced far lower numbers. These authors also pointed out that the introduction of the NMW had little direct effect on poverty levels as it largely benefited the lower middle classes, whereas poverty mainly affects the long-term unemployed, jobless households (whose working-age members are all unemployed) and old-age pensioners. Nonetheless, Metcalf (2008) noted that wage dispersion and inequality among the lower income deciles was reduced and that, since 70% of the workers benefitting from the NMW were female (especially part-time workers), this had also somewhat reduced the UK gender pay gap.

After the government's initial caution, the minimum wage was progressively increased to £4.85 by 2004 (£4.10 for workers aged 18-21), which corresponds to a rise of about 35% between 1999 and 2004, compared to an overall average wage rise of 26% over the same period (Howarth and Kenway, 2004). In 2004 a minimum wage was also introduced for 16-17-year-olds. In 2011 the NMW stood at £6.08.

In their 2006 report, the Low Pay Commission had announced that increases would not be able to exceed that of average wages indefinitely. In 2012, they reported:

> However, most of the real and relative increases in the minimum wage occurred as a result of the comparatively large upratings from October 2001-October 2006. Since that time, the adult rate of the minimum wage has risen more or less in line with average earnings but has lagged [behind] price increases. The minimum wage increased by 13.6 per cent between October 2006 and October 2011. This compares with increases of 13.2 per cent in average earnings and higher rises of 17.2 per cent in CPI and 18.8 per cent in RPI.

Thus, it is noteworthy that after a hesitant start, the NMW increased faster than average earnings and inflation in the UK (Low Pay Commission, 2012, p. 28). This is undoubtedly linked to the fact that the absence of negative effects on employment and inflation allowed the government to adopt a bolder policy. As noted by Metcalf (*op. cit.*, p. 507), "Trends in aggregate employment and sector shares were unaffected by the introduction and uprating of the NMW. Similarly there is little or no evidence of employment effects in the many studies of individuals, areas and firms."

Given this success, the coalition government has decided to keep the NMW – which is quite a remarkable move on the part of the Conservatives. However, as Grimshaw and Rubery (2012) point out, the Conservatives' pre-election declarations suggest that they favour restricting the annual uprating of the NMW to below inflation.

IV. Expansion of in-work benefits: Working (Families) Tax Credit (W(F)TC), Child Tax Credit (CTC) and finally, Universal Credit

As indicated above, New Labour came to endorse the idea that poverty and unemployment "traps" riddled Britain's social system. The rationale being that these, rather than low wage levels, discouraged workers from taking up work, since the resultant loss of benefits would leave them little better off than when unemployed. The benefits system was thus held responsible for the high poverty rate and large number of workless households. In the late 1990s, about 20% of households were workless, and thus at risk of severe poverty. It was for this reason that in-work benefits formed an important part of government measures aimed at tackling poverty (especially child poverty) in the UK.

As part of its welfare-to-work strategy, Labour thus expanded the system of in-work benefits (transfer payments and tax credits provided exclusively to people in employment) previously introduced by the Tory government (Harvey and Urwin, 2006). In 1999, the Working Families' Tax Credit (WFTC) replaced the earlier system of Family Credits, and then in 2003, the WFTC was replaced by the Working Tax Credit (WTC) and a newly introduced Child Tax Credit (CTC). The new system was more generous than its Conservative predecessor and, owing to higher income thresholds, reached far larger numbers of people, extending even into the middle classes. The WTC can be considered a form of wage subsidy[3] since paid by the state through the tax system and thus handled by Inland Revenue rather than the Benefits Agency. Moreover, "Delivery through the tax system, rather than through the social security system was central to the design from the start, not least because the

---

[3] See J.M. Verd in this volume.

government was keen to associate tax credits with participation in employment" (Millar, 2008).

The system introduced by the Blair government was rather complex, as tax credits depended not only on individual income but on family situation as well. The aim was not to simply seek to alleviate the effects of a low wage economy, but was also a response to the crisis of the (male) breadwinner model/single-earner family resulting from the decline in wage levels for low income groups. Thus, the bulk of the recipients were to be people with family responsibilities.

WTC awards were fixed at a variety of different rates, corresponding to different "elements" for households with dependent children, lone parents, disabled persons working at least 16 hours a week and older workers (50+) returning to work.[4] People not falling into any of these categories were required to work at least 30 hours a week in order to qualify – a provision intended as an incentive to encourage full-time employment. Depending on the circumstances, people or households earning less than about £6,400 were entitled to the full amount of the relevant WTC element. For any additional pound earned this amount was reduced by 39%.[5] Thus, people earning up to around £16,000 a year (second income threshold) could qualify for WTC.

The Child Tax Credit was part of the national Child Care Strategy announced by the Labour government in 1998, in which they pledged an expansion of childcare facilities to enable women to participate in the labour market. The award was designed to be paid directly to the primary carer, who in 2009 received up to a maximum of £2,235 per year for one child, and £2,670 for a disabled child. Persons earning less than £16,000 were eligible for the maximum amount; this amount was then reduced by 39 pence for each additional pound earned up to £22,000. After this, claimants received only the Family Element, a flat rate tax credit of £545, up to an income of £50,000 (third income threshold), then withdrawal started again at a rate of 6.67%. The New Policy Institute calculated that tax credits could boost the household income of lone parents by almost 100% (Howarth and Kenway, 2004). In 2008, about 6 million people in the UK claimed tax credits, with the majority claiming the CTC (Millar, *op. cit.*). Some 1.8 million received both WTC and CTC, and slightly more than 300,000 single people and 120,000 couples without childcare responsibilities received WTC only. While take up of

4 For detailed information about thresholds and statistical data, see HM Revenue & Customs 2009: Child and working tax credit statistics. http://www.hmrc.gov.uk/stats/personal-tax-credits/cwtc-quarterly-stats.htm.

5 Millar points out that the rate of withdrawal is calculated according to gross pay, which means that the effective tax rate is 70% as people in employment also have to pay Income Tax and National Insurance Contributions.

the tax credits is not easy to ascertain, it was estimated at roughly 80-84% of the eligible population for the CTC, and at about 60% for the WTC before the 2010 elections.

The expected effects of the tax credit system were a controversial issue. While some critics feared that productivity may stagnate if employers can make use of cheap subsidised labour, others pointed to a potential negative impact on wage levels in low-wage sectors. The risk is greater

> (i) the more closely social welfare benefits are dependent on labour market activity; (ii) the weaker the bargaining power of the recipients of social welfare in the labour market and therefore the greater the chances that social welfare will enter into competition and drive down wages; and, (iii) the higher the level of unemployment and therefore the greater the possibility that workers with subsidised wages will be substituted for those without. (Wilkinson, 2001, p. 11)

Negative effects on wage bargaining have also been suggested (Howarth and Kenway, 2004), since wage rises no longer automatically entail higher incomes for workers because a higher direct wage reduces their eligibility for tax credits. At a more general level, in the debates about the significance of recent welfare “reforms”, tax credits are seen as a cornerstone of a new approach to social protection which has become more oriented towards employment and social investment (Adler, 2004). Millar notes that “Tax credits highlight the way that the UK income maintenance system is increasingly focused on wage supplementation rather than wage replacement, which was the rationale for the Beveridge welfare state” (*op. cit.*, p. 27).

The Conservative-Liberal Democrat coalition has announced a fundamental overhaul of the British benefit and tax credit system. It intends to replace the differentiated structure of means-tested out-of work-benefits and the tax credit system with a single Universal Credit (Haque, 2011). The main aims, it is claimed, are to simplify the system, to improve work incentives – by reducing marginal deduction rates and participation tax rates for people on benefits who want to take up employment, – and to cut costs. In general, the government wants to cut between 10% and 18% (depending on the calculation) of the overall expenditures for social security and tax credits by 2013/14 (Grover, 2011; Taylor-Gooby, 2012).

The implementation of Universal Credit is scheduled for 2013-2017. At this stage, the possible effects of this new system are not clear. The government claims that there will be a transitory period during which no benefit recipients will lose out. It has come up with calculations to show that overall, there will more winners – who will see their entitlements increase – than losers with the new system. This of course ignores the other measures affecting the benefit and tax credit system such as the decision to index entitlements to consumer prices instead of retail prices, which represents over one-third of the total savings planned for the welfare system (Grover, 2011). These claims aside, it is in fact possible that a simplified system would improve benefit take-up, which has traditionally been a severe problem in the UK. However, the general plan is to introduce an "individualised conditionality" designed to link all benefits more tightly to the employment system. This means that Universal Credit will be tailored to claimants' individual circumstances, and tied to more intense forms of personalised "support" as well as the requirement that people engage in activities which will bring them closer to or back into employment. Thus, Universal Credit further reinforces the workfarist character of the welfare system.

V. The New Deal

The "New Deal" programme of labour market measures is generally considered a flagship strategy of the Labour government's welfare-to-work policy. Its design and implementation were based on previous experiences with active labour market policies under Conservative rule. Experts also point to the influence of US policy and, to some extent, Swedish strategies (Cebulla *et al.*, 2005). The programme's sheer size as well as the volume of funds made available (initially financed by a one-off windfall tax on privatised public utilities), the wide-ranging connections with other policy areas and not least, the emphasis on mandatory participation for some target groups, identify the New Deal as a defining cornerstone of New Labour's government project. The policy's compulsory character underlines its workfarist nature.

The first programmes were launched in 1998 and targeted young people, the long-term unemployed, disabled people, and lone parents. In 1999, they were followed by New Deals for the over 1950s and for partners of the long-term unemployed. A New Deal programme for musicians was also introduced. Implementation at local level was, from early on, not only entrusted to public institutions and the voluntary sector, but also at times to private enterprises, which in some cases was a source of controversy.

The *New Deal for Young People* (NDYP) aimed at the long-term unemployed aged 18 to 24, and the *New Deal for Adults* (ND25+) targeting people between 25 and 50 who have been unemployed for at least 2 years, were the two major programmes. Participation in these was mandatory and refusal to comply could lead to a temporary withdrawal of benefits.

The Labour programme basically comprised two stages. The *Gateway* phase, lasting a maximum of four months, was intended to provide information about job vacancies as well as intensive counselling. The position of personal advisor was substantially upgraded, or created where it did not exist, for the purposes of delivering the latter. If participants had not found a job during this initial period, they were prepared for the next phase, where they were required to choose one of the following four options: 1) a subsidised job placement in the private sector (subsidised, for example, to the amount of £75/week for 6 months for an employment of at least 30 hours/week), paid at least the national minimum wage, and intended to lead to long-term employment; 2) full-time training or education (of up to 12 months); 3) environment task force and 4) voluntary work. The last two options were designed to improve participants' employability by providing work experience in "socially useful" activities, and included one day of training per week.

The compulsory character of the New Deal programmes, for which Labour spin doctors created the memorable slogan "There is no fifth option", provoked heated disputes over the policy's workfarist nature. The government itself eschewed the term "workfare" in describing their strategy because of its negative connotations. During the 1980s and 1990s, Labour had harshly criticised the "creeping compulsion" of Tory labour market and social policy programmes. New Labour ministers were thus keen to stress their programmes' reciprocal "something for something" approach based on formulating the rights and responsibilities of both the long-term unemployed and the state, and ensuring that each party would comply with them (Handler, 2004). To this end, the Public Employment Service and client were actually required to sign a contract laying down each party's rights and responsibilities. Contractual social rights, however, are but fiction. As Joel Handler points out,

> 'rights' in welfare contracts are not the same as rights in ordinary contracts where the parties have equal bargaining power. In ordinary contracts, the relationship is horizontal; in workfare contracts the relationship is vertical. The Third Way proponents [...] argue that because the clients have rights and the government workers have obligations to fulfil these rights, clients will be empowered. (Handler, 2004, p. 18)

Assessments of the New Deal programmes have been controversial and relatively unclear. As might be expected, the government hailed the programme as an all-round success. However, detailed analyses (Bivand, 2007, p. 21) of the evolution between 1999 and 2006 of the number of participants in the two major programmes – the New Deal for Young People and New Deal 25+ – reveal that after the initial high levels observed in the early years, the number of NDYP participants stabilised at about 80-100,000 after 2001. Participation in the ND 25+ ranged between 55,000 and 80,000 unemployed people.

It remains difficult to ascertain whether the New Deal programmes actually succeed in improving the long-term job prospects of participants. Diagram 2 shows that after participation in a programme, less than 40% of young people found employment lasting more than three months, although the rates were higher in the first years of the programme. Job outcome rates for older unemployed consistently oscillated between 30% and 40%. Given the narrow conceptualisation of sustained job outcomes, Field and White (2007) have expressed doubts as to whether the New Deals improved employment prospects for target groups. They note that some 420,000 of the 1.1 million NDYP participants between 1998 and 2007 went through the programmes for a second, third or even fourth time. These authors conclude, "The data suggest that the New Deal [...] seems incapable of adapting to the needs of those young people who find it most difficult to find a job".

Another controversial aspect was the question of job creation. Past assessments suggest that 17,000 new jobs were created in the early years of the programme (Blundell *et al.*, 2003), whereas the government originally expected over 340,000. The controversy about employment creation is due in part to the difficulty in making accurate assessments as the UK experienced continual job growth from the second half of the 1990s. Another reason is that supply-side programmes are incapable of actually creating jobs for certain groups of workers, but can at most contribute to reducing labour market frictions.

> What is more, the 'Third Way' 'welfare-to-work' strategy is not underpinned by generous income transfer programs. [...] Finally, and this in sharp contrast to 'Third Way' rhetoric of 'learning and education as the key to prosperity', the relative significance of vocation training, skill enhancement and upward mobility is rather limited. The emphasis on 'sticks' rather than 'carrots' implies that for those who remain [...] outside the reach of employment through employability measures and tax credits, poverty remains a persistent threat. (Ferrara and Hemerijck, 2003, p. 104)

Critics also argued that workfare programmes like the New Deal mainly tend to place participants in precarious jobs at the lower end of the labour market while paying little attention to their long-term career prospects. "Work first" – the overall thrust of the programmes, especially during the *Gateway* stage – means giving priority to placement over costly training schemes, thereby contributing to high labour turnover in low-wage labour market segments and leading to substitution effects. Another criticism was that the programmes also tended to "cream" clients, i.e. focus on the workers that were easiest to place while passing others over and assigning them to less interesting schemes, such as the Environmental Task Force, which came under sharp criticism for this reason (Gray, 2004). Overall, job instability and the associated precarious employment conditions appeared to remain unchanged, resulting in a "revolving door" effect, with workers moving continually between short-term jobs and labour market policy programmes.

In reaction to some of these criticisms, the government introduced a major reform of the New Deal programmes, called "Flexible New Deal". The aim was to modernise the "welfare-to-work" strategy by instituting a stronger "framework of rights and responsibilities to move benefit claimants from being passive recipients to being active jobseekers" (DWP, 2007, p. 10). This meant accelerating entry into activating measures, with "directed job search" activities after three months and "supported job search" after six months (DWP, 2009b). The overall intent was to make the system focus more on outcomes than on process, in order to increase the time people spend in employment after going through one of the New Deal Programmes. Jobcentre Plus staff and public, private and third sector providers of New Deal programmes were given greater discretion to handle their clients, in what was called a "personalised and responsive approach" (DWP, 2009a, p. 9). In general, the reform required that every unemployed person enter the Gateway after six months of unemployment "leading to more intense job-search activity and skills assessment" (DWP, 2007, p. 12); and after twelve months be transferred to a specialised provider under contract to organise the "Flexible New Deal" programmes and activities in close cooperation ("partnership") with the public employment service Jobcentre Plus. The reformed programmes included the obligation for the unemployed to sign in at Jobcentre Plus every fortnight and a mandatory four-week work-related activity (DWP, 2009b). The goal of the reform was to make each step taken by the unemployed towards employment "more active".

In 2010, the current coalition government announced a major reform to create a single welfare-to-work programme, along similar lines to its planned new benefit and tax credit system. Apart from some changes concerning the timing of referral of different categories of unemployed to certain measures, the most striking feature of this reform is the aim to create a fully developed welfare market, but with a reduced number of providers – which will affect the voluntary sector in particular. Based on debates which had already emerged under the New Labour government, the reforms are geared to changing the funding structure of labour market policy services provided by private, public and voluntary organisations. In the jargon of the DWP, the goal is summarised as follows: "The programme design combines strong long-term incentives with freedom for service providers to innovate. It is at the leading edge of wider government commissioning of payment-for-results public services." (DWP, 2011, p. 2)

Thus, the financing of measures has become outcome-oriented – outcome referring to successful job-placements – thereby transferring the risk to the service providers. This favours big providers as they are more able to advance the necessary investments for certain categories of unemployed. Pricing policies have been further differentiated to reflect the fact that some groups of unemployed are closer to the labour market than others. This links the Work Programme to the introduction of "individualised conditionality" in the welfare system in general. Also the length of contracts has been extended. However, given the strong focus on results, creaming of the most employable individuals can be expected, and has already been reported.

Conclusion

With the defeat of New Labour in 2010, the incoming coalition government's sweeping welfare reform programme revealed that despite the Third Way's claim to move beyond neoliberalism, it had failed to change the institutional setting of the British welfare system or the mindset of the other parties as Thatcherism had succeeded in doing in the 1980s. Thus, legitimated by the crisis and mounting public debts, the new government has been able to embark on a radical strategy to overhaul the welfare state and cut spending massively. Whether this strategy will be successful remains open at the time of writing. It is clear however, that it will once again reverse the tide, and put an end to Labours' attempts to curb the growth of inequality and poverty.

Recent studies (for example, Sefton and Sutherland, 2005; Brewer *et al.*, 2009) have shown that New Labour measures did little to reduce poverty or reverse the trend towards rising levels of inequality. However, some have conceded that the policies at least succeeded in stopping previously dominant trends – despite a continuous period of economic boom, which historically has always led to greater inequality in the UK. This assessment appears to hold if the development of real income (including earnings, benefits and tax credits but also savings) under the Labour government is compared with real income dynamics under previous Conservative rule. Thus, income growth by quintile group was more or less equalised under New Labour whereas higher income quintiles experienced far stronger growth under the Conservatives.

However, Brewer *et al.* (2009) also observe that, by 2008, income inequality had risen to its highest level since the early 1960s, while the drop in poverty rates could largely be attributed to benefit entitlements growing more than inflation. While noting that relative poverty had fallen sharply since Labour came to power in 1997, "with the biggest falls occurring for families with children and pensioners, groups favoured by recent tax and benefit reforms", they added that "relative poverty has risen for all groups over the last three years, and poverty for working-age adults without dependent children is now at its highest level since the start of our comparable time series in 1961." (*op. cit.*, p. 54)

Labour market integration and the fight against poverty played a key role in the moral foundations of New Labour's project and in its ability to deliver economic prosperity. On the one hand, the government aimed to draw support from "Middle England" by proposing to re-establish social cohesion ("one nation") and base wealth on effort, hard work and respect rather than individualism. In this context, welfare-to-work promised not only to discipline the jobless and the poor but also to reintegrate them into society.

> Thus, [...] New Labour [...] has clearly moved towards a more socially inclusive hegemonic project. This addresses the limitations of the possessive individualism favoured by neo-liberalism and recognizes the need to re-embed market forces into a broader, more cohesive social order. It aims to remoralize the neo-liberal accumulation strategy around a populist 'one nation' hegemonic project that will reduce social exclusion without undermining the economic well-being of 'Middle England'. (Jessop, 2003)

On the other hand, however, the institutions of the British workfare state only offer the poor and the unemployed highly specific channels for reintegration. Welfare-to-work seeks to change the socially excluded rather than changing society. It is in this way that Labour sought to combine the re-commodification of labour and its subordination to flexible labour markets with social integration and the fight against poverty, with the aim of crafting a sustainable British "workfare" model that would offer a viable alternative to the welfare state. New Labour's far-reaching acceptance of Thatcherist restructuring of the UK provoked immediate criticism condemning the "Third Way" as nothing but a continuation of neoliberalism with a Christian-Socialist face. While critics of New Labour, such as Bob Jessop, do recognize that the Blair government proposed to abandon Thatcherism's hegemonic project – aimed at social polarisation and confrontation with the trade unions – they stress that Conservative state reforms and accumulation strategy (flexible markets, and so forth) were left largely untouched. Nevertheless, while New Labour largely accepted the results of Thatcherism, it sought to transcend the latter by trying to offer individuals social inclusion and justice *within* post-Fordist capitalism. Therefore, I would rather suggest that the Third Way could be seen less as a continuation of neoliberalism than as an attempt to provide an anti-socialist "alternative" to neoliberal regulation, and that it was finally defeated because of its unwillingness and inability to implement changes designed to transcend the imperatives of flexibility and competitiveness.

In the 1990s, the Conservative government was finally replaced by New Labour because the encompassing success of the Thatcherite project to reorganise British capitalism undermined the sustained reproduction of its social preconditions. New Labour, on the other hand, was finally defeated some 13 years later because, among other things, its internal contradictions were exacerbated by the economic crisis. The idea to socially re-embed the market through the adaptation of individuals and social institutions to a new economic framework based on flexibility and free markets failed to offer a solution to the crisis or an alternative option to raising the deficit and defending the current state of welfare and public services. This, however, does not mean that the new coalition government will not face a range of problems if it wishes to undo the reforms discussed here and to implement a renewed "market-radical" project in the UK. To do this, they will have to shift the ideological ground away from New Labour's promise that social inclusion into post-Fordist capitalism is possible if people are willing and able to adapt and public policy is able to provide them with the necessary forms of support. In the 2010 election campaign, the Conservative party had to tone down its traditional neoliberal rhetoric to contend with the ideological success of New Labour, and with the Liberal Democrats who had presented themselves as a progressive alternative to Labour. However, in contrast to the success of Thatcherism which had forced the Labour party to change – which does not imply that these changes could only go in one direction – New Labour only appears to have succeeded in forcing the Conservatives to adapt their style and rhetoric. Indeed, Tory campaigns blaming the Labour government for "Broken Britain's" persistent social problems (crime, deprivation, poverty and such), and the budget cuts planned by the new coalition government, hold little promise for the sustained success of New Labour's idea of social cohesion and inclusion within post-Fordist capitalism.

Thus, it comes as no surprise that the new government immediately launched far-reaching strategies to cut public spending and restructure the (welfare) state and public services. But while New Labour tried to link a tightened benefit regime and a reliance on markets to the goal of social inclusion, the Conservative-Liberal Democrat coalition is much more bluntly focussing its attack on the welfare state on expenditure levels and the marketization of public services. This could lead to a systemic change of social security and public services in the UK.

> The immediate concern of the UK government's programme is with the first aim, to cut the annual fiscal deficit virtually to zero and reduce national debt. However, the policies go much further than this in launching major reorganization of virtually all public sector services designed to change the rules of the game and eliminate future pressures for welfare spending. (Taylor-Gooby, 2012, 63)

The Hybridisation of Worker's Resources

Wage Supplements and Wage Subsidies

Joan Miquel VERD

Associate professor, Department of Sociology, Universitat Autònoma of Barcelona, Spain

This chapter will focus on four measures that our research network has qualified as subsidised employment: the *Working Tax Credit* (WTC) in the United Kingdom, the *Prime pour l'Emploi* (PPE) and the *Revenu minimum d'activité* (RMA) in France, and the *Contrato para personas desempleadas en situación de exclusión social* in Spain. All four are "activation" measures intended to incite persons receiving social assistance benefits to take up and remain in employment. The aim is to highlight the shift that measures of this kind have introduced in the nature of the resources workers receive as a result of being employed.[1] As argued previously, addressing the question of subsidised employment leads us to examine the relations between employment and social protection. In our analytical framework, this means examining the institutional forms governing the circulation of resources flowing through the wage.[2] Thus, in the comparative analysis attempted here, particular attention will be paid to the effects of the measures on the articulation between the origin of workers' resources and their position with regard to employment.

Active labour market policies are usually presented in government discourse as a collection of measures oriented towards improving employment prospects for jobless or precarious workers. However, despite their stated goals, these policies have done little to improve the lot of the targeted populations, particularly women, young people and immigrants, whose chances of escaping precarious work or unemployment continue to be extremely limited (Leschke 2009). This situation, as will be seen,

1 Some of these measures are also examined elsewhere in this volume, from the point of view of their impact on the labour market or their results in terms of the intended policy objectives (see Ribeiro and Ruivo, Atzmüller, in this volume).

2 Unless specified otherwise, wage is used throughout to mean the total wage (direct plus indirect, that is, including employers' social contributions).

is the result of the profound changes the activation paradigm introduced long before the onset of the current economic crisis.

This is why we have chosen these four measures and situated our analysis in the period 2000-2005, just before the current crisis, when the second wave of labour market reforms in Europe had largely been implemented. The characteristics of the measures and the statistical data presented thus correspond to this period. The discursive context and policy recommendations that frame the measures are also taken into consideration.[3]

The difficulties facing any comparative undertaking are well known. Perhaps the best way to tackle these may be, following Dupré *et al.* (2003), to think of comparison as a research strategy. As Marry (2003) points out, there is no "one best way" to do comparative analysis. Maurice, Sellier and Silvestre (1982), in theorising the *societal approach*, have provided a valuable alternative to customary *cross-national* comparative studies characterised by a strong quantitative emphasis and low sensitivity to qualitative differences. The societal approach defends the idea of "comparing the non-comparable" by taking societal diversity as a fundamental principle, while at the same time seeking out comparable dimensions within a "coherent" societal space. This "societal sensibility" finds an echo in the work of a wide range of authors, such as Lallement (2003) who argues for a more interpretative and comprehensive (and less explicative) approach to comparative sociology. The proposal by Barbier (2007) to use "functional equivalents" instead of objects/phenomena belonging to different national realities that might appear to be similar in a de-contextualised approach is also in line with the societal approach. The position adopted by Marsden (1999) to compare different national employment systems by analysing the transaction rules on which labour contracts are based rather than "national institutional" effects, has its roots in the societal approach.

While the option adopted here draws on some of these proposals, this chapter will not seek to develop a full societal analysis in the strict sense, as the societal spaces will not be fully examined in the discussion that follows.[4] The angle of approach is to present a qualitative analysis of the characteristics and underlying institutional logics of the wage supplement and wage subsidy measures selected for study. The social protection systems in which these instruments are embedded thus also constitute an essential framework for the analysis. Two of the countries

[3] See also Gobin, Part II in this volume.

[4] This was undertaken in a previous European thematic network: The social construction of employment (IVth European Framework Programme, contract ERB SOE 2 CT 97 3041).

in the sample can be classified as Bismarckian (France and Spain) and one as Beveridgean (the UK). When the Bismarckian systems were established, a clear dividing line was drawn between social protection benefits channelled through the wage and tax-financed social assistance provision. In contrast, the Beveridgean system was built on two pillars: public social welfare provision financed by a mix of wage- and tax-based resources, and an occupational pillar financed through the wage.

The chapter comprises three sections. Section I begins with a discussion of the "activation" discourse in order to contextualise the measures examined. These will then be broken down into five different components using the variables we defined collectively (Harvey and Maier, 2004), before comparing them in Section II with the "passive" benefit schemes they were designed to replace. This analytical strategy permits continuities and discontinuities to be identified in order to establish a basis for evaluating the impact of the measures on recipients. The third section addresses the consequences of these "activation" measures for workers and the employment relation.

I. Wage Supplements and Wage Subsidies as "Activation Measures"

A. The Arguments Justifying 'Activation Measures'

In EU discourse, "activation" can be used to mean several different things (Serrano, 2005). When applied to the individual, it implies inducing jobless people (and not only the unemployed) to be available for and seek subordinated employment, of any type and regardless of the wage. Here, the desired effect of activation policies is to make target populations feel ashamed and guilty for not working, and responsible for their situation. On the other hand, when referring to resources, "activation" means transforming so-called "passive" measures, for instance by using resources to create employment (whatever its characteristics) instead of paying unemployment benefits. "Activation measures" such as wage supplements and wage subsidies are thus aimed at increasing employment rates. They provide a framework for transferring social protection resources to the financing of employment policies, and for using tax-based resources to finance a part of the wage.[5]

Wage supplements (in-work tax credits) as well as many wage subsidies paid to employers, and in general all the measures seeking to "activate" the population receiving social benefits, derive their theoretical justification from the neo-classical school of economics and related

[5] See Atzmuller's chapter on the Austrian case in this volume.

neo-liberal policy recommendations. Wilkinson (2001, p. 10-11) aptly sums up the essential line of argument as follows:

> [Neo-liberalism] predicts that monetary control will contain inflation, and that labour market deregulation combined with regressive tax and benefit reform will secure full employment. The expected result is that the more unequal redistribution of income and the freeing up of markets will dramatically improve economic performance, and that the benefits of this higher rate of growth will *trickle down* the income distribution, benefiting everyone.

More specifically, wage subsidisation is justified in the following terms:

> Labour market imperfection (social welfare benefits and institutional barriers to wage reductions) combined with poor skills and motivation has, it is argued, opened a gap between the supply price of labour, based on the income needs of the poor, and the demand price of labour, based on their low marginal productivity. A longer-term solution may be to raise productivity by education and training, and to inculcate an improved work ethics. But a shorter term solution is to either pay a wage supplement to workers to bridge the gap between their income needs and their marginal productivity, or a wage subsidy to employers to lower the cost of wages demanded to the level of the marginal productivity of perspective employees (Wilkinson, 2001, p. 11).

The above rationale underwrites the political arguments serving to justify introduction of the measures analysed here. The latter thus cannot be considered as isolated actions but must be placed in their historical context, that is, the overall reform process translating neo-liberal prescriptions into specific employment policies. A comparison of our research network's national reports (Verd, 2004) permitted identification of two periods of reforms corresponding to "turning points" in the way workers' resources are constructed: the 1970s to the early 1980s saw a first wave of reforms, and then the decade of the 1990s, a second wave, this time clearly linked to European integration.[6] As regards the measures analysed here, the *Working Tax Credit* appeared in 2003,[7] the *Prime pour l'Emploi* in 2000, the *Revenu minimum d'activité* in 2004, and the *Contrato para personas desempleadas en situación de exclusión social* in 1995. All four thus have their roots in the second wave of reforms, although, in each case, the pace and particular processes of reform depended largely on national political events.[8] The first two

6 For more on this last point, see Gobin's concluding chapter in this volume.

7 The WTC replaced the Working Families Tax Credit introduced in 1999. However, wage supplements in the UK date back to 1971. See chapters by Ribeiro and Ruivo and Atzmüller on the UK case in this volume for a broader description.

8 See Atzmüller in this volume for a contextualisation of the Working Tax Credit in the labour market policies introduced under New Labour governments in the UK.

measures are all still in force, and the second two have been modified to different extents.

B. Characteristics of the Four Measures[9] *and Their Effects*

Two of the measures that are analysed in this chapter fit in the definition of wage supplements. At first glance, and from a technical point of view, the features of the *Working Tax Credit* (WTC) and the *Prime pour l'Emploi* (PPE) are very similar. Both consist of a means-tested payment granted to low income jobholders. The employment contract can be open-ended or fixed-term, and there is no time restriction on the payment of the benefit (jobholders can continue to claim for as long as they meet the income conditions). The amount of the benefit is deducted from the recipient's income tax (and NICs in the UK), and if it exceeds the latter, the difference is paid out in cash. During the period analysed, there was a minimum threshold for entitlement: 16 hours a week of paid work for families with children and workers with a disability for the WTC, and gross earnings corresponding to 0.3 times the full-time equivalent of the annual minimum wage (SMIC) for the PPE. Both measures were aimed at encouraging full-time employment, as the British model provided a bonus for recipients working more than 30 hours (still in effect), and in France the amount increased proportionately to the number of hours worked[10] (Urwin, 2003; Barbu and Khristova, 2004).

The other two measures are to be considered as wage subsidies. They have the same "activation" orientation as the tax credit systems, but here the resources are channelled to employers. The French *revenu minimum d'activité* (RMA) was a special kind of contract proposed to people who had been receiving the *revenu minimum d'insertion* (RMI) for at least two years, although take-up was not compulsory. It was a six-month contract signed for a minimum of 20 hours a week paid at least the SMIC hourly rate, and renewable no more than twice, its maximum duration being limited to 18 months. Workers on an RMA contract could, under certain conditions, continue receiving social assistance benefits (see Section II). The employer, who was under obligation to provide guidance (*tutorat*), personalised support (*accompagnement personnalisé*) and training for the employee, received a subsidy equivalent to the RMI for a single person (almost 60% of the SMIC) to cover a portion of the direct wage. This subsidised portion was exempt from employer social contributions, and workers were only entitled to social

9 Unless specified otherwise, the information presented here on the characteristics of these benefits corresponds to the measures in force in 2003-2004.

10 In France, employers also paid reduced social contributions on wages up to 1.8 times the minimum salary (SMIC).

security rights on the non-subsidised top-up financed by the employer. In June 2009, the RMI was merged with the *Allocation de parent isolé* (API, single parent allowance) and the *Allocation d'aide au retour à l'emploi* (support for a return to employment) and replaced by a single benefit, the *Revenu de Solidarité Active* (RSA, active solidarity income). The RMA was also abrogated in January 2010, and replaced by a new *Contrat unique d'insertion* (single contract for integration).

The Spanish *Contrato para personas desempleadas en situación de exclusión social* corresponds to a special employment contract intended to "improve the employability of people at risk of social exclusion" – that is, mainly unemployed persons receiving the guaranteed minimum income (*Renta Básica de Inserción*). The contract provides for a reduction in the employer's social contributions, which, in 2003-2004, amounted to a 65% reduction for a maximum of 24 months, regardless of the duration of employment. It thus differs from the French RMA in that the subsidy is not paid in cash to the employer, but corresponds to the tax resources transferred to the social security fund in order to cover the exempted portion of the employer's social contributions.[11] As in the case of the RMA, hired workers can, under certain conditions, continue receiving an income support benefit (see Section II). Unlike the RMA, however, the contract does not entail reduced social protection rights for the employee since the reductions in employers' contributions is compensated for by the state via the INEM budget.[12] Subsequently, in 2007, this kind of contract was limited to accredited "integration companies" (*empresas de inserción*) established by non-profit associations or foundations in order to promote the social integration of disadvantaged people. In 2009 a new regulation prohibited the re-hiring of workers who have already been hired on this contract, unless the worker's continued risk of exclusion has been established by a Public Social Service.

Table 1 compares the four measures on the basis of the variables presented in *Wage and Welfare* (Clasquin *et al.*, 2004). However, the original variable, *linkage*, has been split into two, in order to distinguish between the basis of entitlement to the resources and the conditions of entitlement. The common feature in all four cases is the emergence of a combination of a wage with tax-based resources, since employment is the pre-condition to initiating the transfer. A notable difference is that although the measures are oriented towards the activation of target

---

11 These tax resources were allocated to the INEM budget and counted as a transfer to the employer. This is still the case today.

12 The range of subsidised contracts that offer reductions in employers' social contributions for target populations has been always high in Spain (see López Andreu *et al.*, in this volume). However their "activation" dimension has been less strong since they were not designed to replace any "passive" measures.

populations by contributing to workers' income, the direct recipient of the resources changes depending on the type of scheme. In the case of wage supplements, the workers receive the benefit directly, whereas in the case of wage subsidies, they are only the indirect beneficiaries: the subsidies are directed at the employers, either to cover a portion of the direct wage (France) or to compensate for a reduction in their contributions (Spain).

Table 1: Comparison of the four "activation" measures

	Working Tax Credit (in force since 2003)	*Prime pour l'Emploi (in force since 2000)*	*Revenu minimum d'activité (in force from 2004 to 2010)*	*Contrato para personas desempleadas en situación de exclusión social (in force since 1995)*
Source of resources	Taxation	Taxation	Taxation	Taxation
Type of resources	Wage supplement	Wage supplement	Wage subsidy	Wage subsidy
Benefit Recipients	(Low paid) Workers	(Low paid) Workers	Direct recipients: Employers; Indirect recipients: (low paid) workers hired by the above	Direct recipients: Employers; Indirect recipients: (low paid) workers hired by the above
Basis of entitlement*	Being a job-holder	Being a job-holder	Being a job-holder	Being a job-holder
Conditions of entitlement	Means-tested on household income; minimum threshold of 16 hours worked per week	Means-tested on household income; minimum earnings of 0.3 times the SMIC	The hired workers have to have been receiving the guaranteed minimum income for at least two years	The hired workers have to be receiving the guaranteed minimum income

* Workers' resources being the focus of this table, the two variables related to "entitlement" concern the target populations only.

The different components of the income received by workers are represented in the formula below, where w_1 is the wage the worker receives from the employer. In the case of wage subsidies w_0 is the amount actually financed by the employer and s_e the subsidy received for hiring the worker. In the case of wage supplements s_w is the supplement the worker receives for being a job-holder.

Wage subsidy: Workers' Income $= w_1 = w_0 + s_e$

Wage supplement: Workers' Income $= w_1 + s_w$

The effects of wage subsidies (s_e) or wage supplements (s_w) on the employment relationship are clear: the low wages paid by employers are topped up with resources from taxation, thus producing a hybrid kind of wage. Linking entitlement to a tax-financed social allowance to being employed provides a means for channelling resources from taxation to replace part of the socialised wage.

II. What Do Wage Supplements and Subsidies "Activate"?

In order to assess the effects of these supplements and subsidies on workers, this section will present the characteristics of the schemes that would have been applied in the absence of these "activation" measures. This will enable us to analyse the differences in the type of benefit and status of the recipient linked to the transfer of resources, and thus to identify the changes in the institutional rationale. We will also be able to see what the differences mean for the individuals concerned.

In the United Kingdom, workers who loose their jobs have access to an unemployment benefit (contribution-based Jobseekers' Allowance) which is funded by National Insurance contributions (NICs) and payable for a maximum of 182 days. This benefit, however, is conditioned on claimants being available to work for at least 40 hours a week, actively looking for work, residing in the country, aged over 18 and under the State pension age, and having paid sufficient contributions over the last two tax years. After receiving the contribution-based Jobseekers' Allowance, workers can then claim the income-based Jobseekers' Allowance if their income falls below a minimum threshold; this allowance is funded by taxation, and has no time restriction (although workers have to be available for work and are obliged to sign an agreement with a placement service). Thus, once entitlement to the contribution-based benefit has been exhausted, a right linked to the wage is replaced by a social assistance allowance conditioned on the claimant being poor. The income-based Jobseekers' Allowance is also provided to the unemployed who have not paid enough contributions to be eligible for the contribution-based allowance. Unemployed people who are not capable of or available for work can only apply for the income support benefit.

In France, the unemployment benefit is funded by employer and employee contributions. In the period under analysis, it was payable for a maximum of 700 days,[13] and was administered by the ASSEDIC. In 2009, ASSEDIC was merged with the public employment service (ANPE) to form a new agency called *Pôle emploi*. Unemployed people

[13] For the unemployed between 50 and 56 years of age, the maximum was 1095 days (36 months), and for those aged 57 or older, the maximum was 1272 days (42 months) provided they had worked for 27 months during the previous 36 months.

who had exhausted their entitlements to this benefit then had access to the *allocation de solidarité spécifique* (ASS) for a further three years (if they had worked for at least 5 years during the previous 10 years). This allowance was financed by taxation and was means-tested. After this three-year period, unemployed people aged 25 or older whose income fell below a minimum threshold were entitled to the *Revenu minimum d'insertion* (RMI), which had no time restriction.

In Spain, as in France, the unemployment benefit is financed by employer and employee contributions; it is administered by the INEM (National Institute of Employment). The duration of entitlement corresponds to one-third of the period during which contributions were paid, up to a maximum of 720 days. After this period of entitlement, an unemployment assistance benefit (*subsidio de desempleo*), which is also administered by the INEM and financed by contributions, can replace the unemployment benefit under certain conditions. In the period analysed, it could be claimed by unemployed persons whose income fell below 75% of the minimum wage, on condition that they had paid contributions for a sufficient length of time;[14] this benefit was payable for 6 months, and could be renewed up to a maximum of 18 months. Thereafter, unemployed people only have recourse to the programmes providing a means-tested guaranteed minimum income, which, at the time, was of unlimited duration, financed by taxation and administered exclusively by the Autonomous Communities. The disparities between the amounts awarded by the various Autonomous Communities are relatively high, and in principle most of the measures have some kind of "activation" orientation – although in many cases this orientation is more formal than real. Only the *Renta activa de inserción* (active integration benefit), a specific measure for workers over 45 years old with dependants, has a national scope and is administered by the INEM.

A comparison of the systems for the period 2000-2005 in the UK, France and Spain reveals a similar three-phase graduation of the benefits available to unemployed people. In the first phase, the benefits in all three countries were contributory and of limited duration. In the second phase, provision was means-tested, financed by taxation in the UK and France and financed by contributions and conditioned on having a contributions record in Spain; it was of unlimited duration in the UK only. In the third phase, all benefits were of unlimited duration, financed by taxation, and clearly oriented towards avoiding poverty; recipients were not under obligation to be actively seeking a job – although the

[14] A minimum of 6 months for workers without dependants and 3 months for those with dependants.

idea of encouraging them to enter the labour market[15] was present in the French and Spanish measures.

In Table 2, the social assistance allowances that could be claimed for an unlimited period of time – the "passive" measures that are mostly likely to be "activated" – are broken down according to the same variables used in Table 1.

Table 2: "Passive" measures (with no time restriction)

	Income-Based Jobseekers' Allowance	*Revenu Minimum d'Insertion*	*Guaranteed Minimum Income Programmes*
Source of resources	Taxation	Taxation	Taxation
Type of resource	Allowance	Allowance	Allowance
Benefit Recipients	Low income unemployed people available for work	Low income unemployed people, who are encouraged to be available for work	Low income unemployed people, who are encouraged to be available for work
Basis of entitlement	Legal residence	Legal residence	Legal residence
Conditions of entitlement	Means-tested	Means-tested, minimum age: 25 years	Means-tested

This now makes it possible to compare these unlimited "passive" measures and the wage supplements and subsidies analysed in Table 1 in order to pinpoint their different logics and effects on the populations concerned. With regard to the source of the resource flows, it can be seen that this variable remains unchanged. The two tax credit systems (wage supplements) maintain the tax-financing of the *Income-based Jobseekers' Allowance* and the *Revenu minimum d'insertion*. However, in the case of the wage subsidies, the direct recipients of the transfers were no longer the unemployed but the employers. Moreover, in France, the RMA was associated with an exemption from employers' social contributions on the subsidised portion of the wage that was not compensated for. This kind of measure results in a reduction of the overall social protection resources and exerts a downward pressure on the social rights of all workers. In Spain, for the *contrato para personas desempleadas en situación de exclusión social*, tax resources are used to compensate for the reductions in employers' contributions, which means that the social rights linked to these jobs are financed by the taxes paid by the overall population.

---

15 See López Andreu *et al.* in this volume, for a follow-up of the changes presently affecting these measures.

With regard to the beneficiaries, the target populations remain the same: (former) low income unemployed people. In the case of the wage subsidies, the workers are not the direct recipients, but benefit indirectly via the subsidised contract. They can also, under certain conditions, continue to claim other social assistance allowances. In France, workers on an RMA contract could continue to collect the full RMI benefit during the first three months of employment; during the following nine months this allowance was reduced by an amount corresponding to 50% of the wage received from the employer. In Spain, being employed on a part-time *contrato para personas desempleadas en situación de exclusión* is compatible with the active integration benefit and some minimum income programmes, provided the total income is not above the eligibility threshold; under more restrictive conditions, workers can even continue to receive the unemployment assistance benefit. All four activation measures, however, mean that it is once again the workers as taxpayers who ultimately are paying for the measures (especially because of the weight of indirect taxes in the fiscal systems of the three countries concerned).

The most outstanding difference between the measures presented in Table 1 and those presented in Table 2 concerns the basis of entitlement. Legal residence is a sufficient condition for receiving a "passive" social assistance benefit, whereas access to all four "activation" measures is based on an additional criterion: being a job-holder.

The combination of tax-based and wage-based resources is a characteristic of the public resource regimes in Beveridgean countries, whereas the socialised wage regimes of the continental countries were traditionally based on an opposition between the employment relation and social assistance for the poor. With the implementation of the measures featured in Table 1 this distinction has thus been called into question. Both the "active" and the "passive" measures discussed here were designed for populations in a situation of poverty. But whatever their employment status, the proposed solution is one and the same: "Jobs, jobs, jobs". The unemployed poor (if able to work) are to be pushed into a job, while the working poor are to be maintained in employment by supplementing their wage with an allowance. In both cases, "activation" appears to be geared to turning the poor into "benefit-recipient wage-earners".

III. Consequences of Wage Supplements and Subsidies for Workers

A. 'Activation' and Recommodification

As we have seen, one of the main effects of the introduction of the "activation" measures analysed here is a shift in the status of means-tested benefit recipients, from jobless poor to working poor. At the same time, their right to a social assistance allowance based on a status of legal resident was replaced by a right to top up their wage with a tax-financed allowance based on their low-income job-holder status. The introduction of this linkage of tax-financed social assistance to an employment relation marks a profound transformation of workers' resources which, in the continental countries at least, were previously exclusively wage-based.

What are the consequences for workers of being pushed into this new status of "benefit-recipient wage-earners"? A closer look at the implications of activation measures shows that these go far beyond the discursive rhetoric focused on promoting employment. Indeed, if we understand a *discourse* as a "story-line", a generative sort of narrative that allows actors to give meaning to specific physical or social phenomena (Hajer, 1995; Mottier, 1999; Hajer and Versteeg, 2005; Kelly, 2009), it becomes clear that neo-liberal prescriptions are used to legitimate and justify employment and social policies[16] which have far deeper consequences for workers than the stated goal of improving the chances of the unemployed to find a job: they imply the dismantling of employment norms.

We have already seen that the neo-liberal arguments used to justify activation policies claim that employment rates can be increased thanks to a "market solution" that will improve economic performance. Since overregulation has resulted in distorted and therefore inefficient markets, the argument goes, the role of the state must be minimized in order to "liberate market forces". Deregulation, which in the context we are concerned with means abolishing labour regulations, is the prescribed path to achieving recommodification and the neoclassical ideal of a "pure market exchange". But this rationale overlooks the role of state intervention on which activation policies rest: (labour) markets may well be playing a far stronger role, but only thanks to the interconnected re-regulation of social assistance systems and employment norms. The comparison between our subsidised wage measures and the benefit schemes they were designed to "activate" (Tables 1 and 2) shows that activation introduces little change in the source of resources or the profile of recipients: the key difference is the target population being *out* or *in* the employment relation. It should be stressed that the provision of means-tested social benefits to job-holders is something that would have been unheard of thirty years ago in continental Europe, where employ-

[16] Barbier and Sylla (2004) in a pertinent discussion of the effects of these prescriptions at European level, point out that, nevertheless, they have not always been mechanically translated into political action, as policies are the result of the intervention and bargaining of many different actors.

ment was exclusively linked to the provision of social insurance, and social assistance was seen as a means to prevent the jobless from falling into absolute poverty. The new role played by social assistance exerts a downward pressure on social protection systems (which have already been made more contributory). Overall, these policies show that recommodification is the result of clear changes in the institutional rules governing the wage relation.

Authors as different as Boyer (1986), Marsden (1999) and Deakin (2002) stress the institutional character of the labour contract. This implies some form of state legislation, which can play a more or less explicit role in the rules governing the contract itself, depending on the national context. In many systems, as Deakin (2002, p. 191) points out,

> the State became the implicit third party to the contract, channelling the risks of insecurity throughout the workforce as a whole through the social insurance system, and using social security contributions and income tax to support the public provision of welfare services. The complex interaction of these different governance mechanisms was reflected in the juridical form of the contract of employment.

The wage supplements and subsidies presented in this chapter are a good example of how policy measures introducing a connection between an employment contract and a social assistance benefit (tutelary allowance) serve to re-regulate the wage relation and completely change its nature. For indeed, to use the expression employed by Marsden (1999, p. 5), these new regulations have partially changed the "rules of the game" (that is, the institutional forms governing employment relations) by linking entitlement to an allowance with claimants having a job. The state intervenes by establishing a logic of "first a job, and then a benefit" for the tax credit systems, or "first a benefit, and then a job" for the subsidised wage contracts we have reviewed. Furthermore, this change in the employment relation affects a specific class of workers: it is the low paid and presumably low skilled workers who are being pushed into a labour market under conditions that imply an "alteration in the nature of the relationship between control and degree of freedom" (De Nanteuil-Miribel and Nachi, 2004, p. 307). Needless to say, the current economic crisis has increased the number of workers in this situation, particularly in the case of women and young workers (Emmenegger *et al.*, 2011; Mascherini, 2011).

We can now see the end results for workers of this process of re-regulation: the terms of the exchange process between the buyers and sellers of labour power in the labour market have been modified, and this has amplified the power imbalance between employers and the new category of employees instituted by the "activation" measures. The former have seen their power strengthened thanks to their access to an increased supply of labour at lower cost, whereas the latter belong to the most vulnerable class of workers. Indeed, the process of recommodification has little to do with integrating target populations into a standard employment relation but serves instead, at least for the populations concerned, to dismantle the employment norm. The paradox is that despite prescriptions calling for a withdrawal of public intervention in order to strengthen the role of markets (recommodification), this goal is achieved not by less but by a new kind of state intervention which, by changing the basis of the entitlement to and the nature of resources, changes the nature of the employment relation.

B. *Tax credit Systems and Subsidised Wage Contracts: National Differences*

Thus far, the discussion has largely focused on comparing the internal logics of wage supplements and wage subsidies. This section will pay more attention to the societal context by examining some of the specific features of each country's activation measures.[17] The analysis of national differences and the variations they produce will enable us to assess the extent to which the change in the nature of the wage relation overrides specific national realities.[18]

One way of addressing national differences is to compare the centrality of the measures in each country during the period under analysis. In the case of tax credit systems, it is of interest to note that statistical data do not confirm the common assumption that this form of wage supplement would be more widespread in countries with a Beveridgean system (where many social protection resource flows come from taxation). In France, some 25% of fiscal households received the PPE during the period 2001-2005 (Barnau and Bescond, 2006; Stancanelli and Sterdyniak, 2004), while in the UK only around 13% of households received the Working and Child Tax Credits[19] during the first years of implementation (2003-2005) (HMRC, 2006b, 2007; Palmer, 2010).[20] Spain has never had measures equivalent to an in-work tax credit benefit, possibly because social assistance is the responsibility of the Auton-

---

17 See Barbier, Sylla and Eydoux (2006) for a comprehensive analysis of the activation systems of France, the UK, Germany and Denmark.

18 See Ribeiro and Ruivo and Atzmüller on the UK case in this volume for a broader description.

19 In the United Kingdom, eligibility for WTC and CTC is assessed jointly.

20 The figures for the UK are calculated as a percentage of total working-age households, while in France they are based on fiscal households. If working-age households were taken into account in France, the proportion would be even higher, as non-married couples are treated as independent fiscal households, thus increasing the base of the percentage.

omous Communities (while labour market policy remains the responsibility of the central government). However, the absence of a tax-credit system reflects the fact that Spanish labour market policies have focused more on reducing employers' labour costs than providing employment incentives for the jobless. This difference shows the preference given to demand-side over supply-side labour market policies in Spain.

The two subsidised wage contracts reviewed here were not particularly widespread in France or Spain, although the actual extent of the population affected is not easy to calculate. According to Paris (2008) only around 1% of RMI recipients (or 13,000 individuals) had an RMA contract in 2007, which corresponds to approximately 0.04% of the population of working age in that year. RMA beneficiaries who no longer collected the RMI were not presented in the official statistics, but it can be presumed that the numbers were small; this situation only occurred after nine months of employment, when the possibility of combining the two measures had been exhausted (it must be remembered that the RMA was a 6-month contract that could only be renewed twice). Information on the population affected by the *Contrato para personas desempleadas en situación de exclusión social* is even more difficult to access. In the official Spanish statistics on hiring, this subsidised contract is lumped together with five other types of contracts under the item "others", which represented 0.96% of contracts in 2005 (EPA, 2005). Given that the data on hiring is a percentage of all the contracts signed during a year (flux data), the proportion of the working-age population with this kind of contract (stock data) would be much lower. As for the new RSA, official statistics (Bourguignon 2011) show that the distribution of recipients of the RSA *socle* for the jobless (1.2 million households) remains relatively close to that observed for the RMI and API, while working recipients of the RSA *activité* (0.5 million households) constitute a new population.

While there are various other subsidised contracts in France and Spain that are far more widespread,[21] they are not targeted towards recipients of means-tested benefits. The very small percentage of the population concerned by contracts designed specifically for people collecting a social assistance benefit (i.e. contracts aimed at "activating" the recipients of these benefits) can be taken as an indication of the disconnection in these countries of means-tested measures from the main flows of social protection resources, which is consistent with their Bismarckian systems. However, the significant numbers affected by the *Prime pour l'Emploi* shows the extent of the changes that have progressively taken place in France. This trend has been amplified by the

---

[21] See López Andreu *et al.* in this volume.

economic crisis: the number of new households receiving the RSA is a sign of the role of means-tested measures in providing support to impoverished workers.

Another important aspect of these subsidised wage contracts is their interaction with the situation of workers in the national labour market. The *RMA* and the *Contrato para personas desempleadas en situación de exclusión social* both tend to create a vicious circle between activity and inactivity that has maintained workers in a situation of poverty. Given the limited duration of the subsidies, and the profile of the population concerned, these workers are most likely to return to unemployment once their contracts have expired. Thus "activation" here merely serves to create a subset of jobs that are disconnected from the standard wage relation, and as a result, to promote poor quality employment.[22]

Conclusion

This chapter has attempted to identify the consequences for workers' resources and status of the implementation of wage supplements and subsidies by analysing the connections these measures introduce between flows from the wage and taxation (social allowances).

The analysis has shown how tax resources traditionally allocated to workless households have been channelled into financing "active" labour market policies and used to subsidise employment by topping-up workers' low earnings (tax credits) or by covering a part of employers' labour costs (wage subsidies). The introduction of these devices intended to "activate" what are seen as "passive" expenditures implies a change in the origin of workers' resources that is particularly striking in the continental countries. The use of taxation to cover a part of the wage has blurred the traditional boundaries between the wage and social assistance that, in the Bismarckian systems, served to prevent the latter from exerting a downwards pressure on wages. Furthermore, some contracts are associated with reduced social contributions, which serves to disconnect employment from the socialised wage and thus to reduce the scope of the latter.

The measures analysed are also aimed at "activating" low-income target populations by pushing them into employment. The fact that entitlement to a tax-financed social assistance benefit is based on being a job-holder places individuals in a new situation in the labour market. In Bismarckian systems, the wage was the main origin of the resources

22 The 2009 reform of the *Contrato para personas desempleadas en situación de exclusión social* in Spain shows the policy makers' awareness of this problem, although it does not prevent the repeated use of this contract for rehiring workers who remain dependent on a minimum income allowance.

financing workers' social protection and time out-of-work, endowing the socialised wage resource regime with a remarkable liberating power (Friot, 2004). With the "activation" measures, the negative impact of the recommodification process in the continental countries stems from the fact that the return to the labour market does not imply a return to the standard employment relation, that is, the socialised wage relation. What has changed here, then, is the very meaning of employment, which is no longer centred on the socialised wage.

We have seen that the process of recommodification does not necessarily go hand in hand with deregulation, and that state regulations pushing recipients of means-tested benefits into the labour market change the "rules of exchange" for these workers. Since the measures examined base eligibility on being in subordinated employment, the targeted populations are placed in a particularly vulnerable situation, and the power imbalance between employers and employees is reinforced. In this sense, wage supplements and wage subsidies could be regarded as measures reinforcing labour market segmentation. Furthermore, the kind of re-regulation underpinning the subsidised employment measures analysed here does not produce "pure" market conditions; in many cases it implies that labour contracts have more complex implications and responsibilities for employees (and perhaps fewer for employers).

Regarding the change in workers' entitlements these measures produce, we have seen that, in the case of wage supplements, having an employment contract is a condition of access to resources coming from taxation. The combination of the wage with a social allowance means that resources once allocated to social assistance are being used to finance employment, and thus that the nature of the labour contract has been changed. This is particularly evident in the Bismarckian countries, where the resources to which jobholders are entitled were previously all channelled through the wage. In the Beveridgean countries, tax resources have traditionally been used to finance both social protection (partly) and social assistance. There is thus an attempt to import this model via the employment policies analysed here.

The effects of wage supplements and subsidies have been amplified with the present economic crisis. Activation policies have proved incapable of providing precarious workers with stable employment, with severe consequences in countries such as Ireland, Spain, Portugal, Lithuania or Denmark. These policies, together with the flexibilisation of labour markets, have also proved to be particularly ineffective tools in countries where the economy has been hit hardest by the downturn (Tangian, 2010).

However, all these changes must be placed in their national contexts. The scope of the measures analysed in this chapter as well as their effects on the articulation between employment and social protection systems differ according to the country. Although the logics of wage supplements and subsidies are closer to the Beveridgean than to the Bismarckian model, the population receiving wage supplements is larger in France than in the United Kingdom, and the resultant changes in the wage relation have thus been more far-reaching in France. It should be noted, in addition, that technically similar measures have different consequences depending on other elements of the societal reality that have not been dealt with here, such as the degree of flexibility in the labour market, unemployment levels, the informal support received by individuals or the level of collective bargaining. The impact of these measures at a societal level remains to be analysed. Nonetheless, the structural design of these measures appears fairly clear. Wage subsidies and wage supplements are good examples of the hybridisation of resources resulting from the subordination of social policy to employment policy. A direct outcome of this process is the weakening of the standard wage relation, even in the Beveridgean countries, which reinforces the power imbalance between employees and employers.

CONCLUSION

From "Wage-friendly" to "Employment-friendly" Growth

Looking Back on 44 Years of European Union History (1968-2012)

Corinne GOBIN

Senior Research Associate, Fonds National de la Recherche Scientifique, Université Libre de Bruxelles, Belgium

Since World War II, Western European societies have experienced uninterrupted overall economic growth, doubling the wealth produced every 30 to 40 years depending on the country. In other words, the means at our disposal today are considerably greater than they were in 1945, an era that saw the introduction of social security systems whose broader scope and more universal coverage far surpassed their earlier tentative versions. Yet – the paradox is striking – we are seeing a proliferation of discourses and analyses (echoed in government policies) that depict this same Western Europe as being on the brink of bankruptcy, "devastated" by a scarcity of resources that not only limits the possibilities of financing the social state (public services and social security) but also necessitates a sustained policy of budgetary austerity and wage restraint.

This masterful paradox has come to condition a large part of socio-political relations in Western Europe today. It owes its existence to the political and economic elites' adherence to a neo-liberal monetarist programme, which became so entrenched in the early 1980s that it effectively stifled democratic debate. The fall of the Berlin Wall served to reinforce the trend, favouring the emergence of an ideology "naturalising" the economy and presenting capitalism as the only possible path to development.

It is in this context that job creation emerged as a political watchword which, for over 20 years now, has met with a broad consensus across the European political class as well as among the majority trade unions united under the banner of the European Trade Union Confederation (ETUC). What this means is that economic growth is no longer expected to translate into wage growth encompassing the range of collective social rights to remuneration – as was the case from 1945 to

1975 – but into "employment growth" to the detriment of a wage-based redistribution. In other words, the post-war political programme that aimed at ensuring a more egalitarian distribution of wealth by reducing the gap between the highest and lowest wages as well as the share of wealth serving to remunerate capital has been replaced by its polar opposite. The result has been a widening gulf between low and high incomes and the massive transfer of collective resources to the financing of capital property, while the jobs created have served to spread the models of flexibility and precarious employment – part-time jobs, fixed-term contracts, and an increasing use of temporary agency workers.

This radical change did not stem from governments needing to adapt their economic policies to the constraints of a "properly functioning" economy. It corresponds to a political agenda that turns its back on all the values, principles, symbols and practices that, since the philosophical breech opened up by the Enlightenment, have contributed to imagining and implementing the democratic ideal of equality between all human adults.

If we are to understand the meaning of this change in course that has set European societies on a counter-democratic path, it is important to first take a look at the period which preceded it. This chapter will thus begin by tracing the major events of the late 1960s and early 1970s leading up to the move to restrain wage claims. It will then review the evolution of the approach to employment and wages within the dynamic of European construction, before analysing what lies behind the employment policy developed by the EU. The chapter will end with an examination of the major current trends and their implications.

I. 1968-1975: Wage Growth and Liberated Time

The eclipse of democratic debate on the redistribution of wealth grew out of the particular context of the 1970s. It is important to take a fresh look at this period since it provides many of the keys to understanding the political and social regression we are seeing today. In 1968, society reached boiling point. Living conditions had improved thanks to better wages and benefit entitlements and the expansion of public services, and this was accompanied by a broad understanding that continued productivity gains due to technological innovation and a more democratic spreading of knowledge would permit a constant deepening of democracy.[1] The two together fuelled a rejection of social relations that remained strongly marked by the expression of political domination (in the factory, particularly for the so-called "unskilled" workers trapped

1 The overriding feeling in the 1960s was that children would grow up to enjoy a better social situation than that of their parents.

in assembly line jobs; in the family, with the power of fathers and/or husbands over their wives and children; in school, where the "school-master" would progressively be transformed into a teacher; in asylums, in the city, and so forth).

In the beginning, after their initial reaction of fear and firm discourses on the urgency of the situation, European governments responded to this social upheaval with a grand "We have understood you", and deployed a discourse on the quality of life. This, in particular, took the concrete form of an agreement to improve and develop socio-cultural infrastructures by increasing public intervention not only in the social and cultural spheres, but in the economic sphere as well.

The case of Belgium can be taken as an example. On 26 January 1973, the new socialist Prime Minister Edmond Leburton, in presenting his governmental programme before Parliament, announced his agenda: "We pay homage to the preceding governments who changed the face of this country by providing it with an economic and technological infrastructure. We think that the time has come to make the same kind of concrete effort in the social and cultural sector". In addition to this decision to increase state intervention, other important measures were adopted. The law of 17 August 1974 granted all adults residing in Belgium the unconditional right to a minimum income (*minimum de moyens d'existence*) anchored to the social security system. Social Security rose from 17% of GDP in 1970 to 22% in 1975. Then, thanks to a strong tradition of "social planning" that had permitted free wage bargaining between the Belgian social representatives since 1960, a cross-sectoral minimum wage was introduced in 1975. The system of automatic wage indexation that had been introduced in 1950 was refined in 1968 on the basis of a comprehensive survey of household budgets. Social planning had also enabled trade unions to obtain regular pay increases through biennial cross-sectoral agreements, to ensure that workers would be the main beneficiaries of productivity gains. When post-1968 social discontent fuelled more politically-oriented demands for "worker control" and social transformation, the unions responded with what they knew best how to do, namely by negotiating significant pay rises at cross-sectoral level, the 40-hour work week, and an increase in social contribution rates. The real hourly wage of 4.6 for an hourly productivity of 5.1 during the period 1960-1969 rose to 9.2 for an hourly productivity of 7 during the period 1970-1975 (Boyer, 1986).[2] Thanks to the improved indexation system, workers' buying power was not affected when basic consumer prices climbed due to a knock-on effect of a

2 See p. 118. The real hourly wage is defined as the inflation-adjusted total wage bill divided by the total number of worker hours; hourly production is defined as value added divided by the number of hours worked.

world-wide hike in the prices of oil and numerous raw materials on the one hand, and the employer strategy to recuperate wage increases on the other.[3] This period saw an impressive drop – from 14% in 1961 to 3% in 1976 – in the share of capital income in net national income (De Keersmaecker, 1997). A new distribution of wealth going to wages and socialised resources (social security, civil service, public services) began to take shape. It resulted in a *de facto* marginalisation of the remuneration of capital, proving that the latter is based on relations of political domination, and that a democratised economy can function perfectly well without these.

The early 1970s saw a similar commitment on the part of the EEC Authorities to increase public intervention in the economy and all other societal dimensions. The European Commission drafted a number of proposals in response to the decision to enhance the social and trade-union dimension of Europe adopted by the Heads of State and Government at the Paris Summit of October 1972. The idea was to develop a social action programme, and a preparatory document of February 1973[4] included proposals to set up bipartite committees (with equal representation of labour and employer organisations) in all sectors of the economy to negotiate European framework agreements; to develop a proactive policy debate within the new Standing Committee on Employment (created in 1970) as soon as risks for employment were spotted; and to strengthen union presence in companies operating within the EEC. The Commission's "Guidelines for a social action programme" of 18 April 1973 included 32 points to be integrated into the *acquis communautaire*[5] between 1974 and 1976;[6] the document emphasised the importance of increasing the participation of the social representatives in all Community decision-making procedures, and not only those limited to social issues. Finally, a complete programme of 41 proposals was adopted on

3 The inflation rate rose from 4% in 1970 to 13% in 1975.

4 SEC(73) 597 final of 20 February 1973.

5 The cumulative body of Community laws which form part of the legal order of the European Union.

6 COM(73)520 final. The Commission took the view that social policy could not be approached as a by-product of economic measures but should become a central reference point integrated into the full range of Community policies. Some of the politically boldest and most innovating proposals were: to set up a permanent body to organise collaboration with national employment services; to organise Community information on the distribution of wealth and incomes in order to ensure a more equitable distribution, and examine the questions of equal pay for men and women and minimum wages; to undertake concerted studies with a view to contributing to the goal of abolishing assembly line work; and to set up a tripartite committee on security at work.

24 October 1973 for submission to the Council.[7] The programme established the principle of developing Community directives – and thus binding norms – in the social field and suggested that the Council rapidly adopt certain measures such as applying the 40-hour work week across the EEC by 1975. The first decisions in application of the programme were adopted by the Council at the Brussels Tripartite Conference of 16 December 1974.[8]

This progressive alignment of the European political class with trade union programmes came as a shock to the employer world and provoked a strong reaction. A few months after the Council decided to adopt the first European social directives, UNICE, the European private sector employers' organisation,[9] brought out a document detailing the positions it would defend at the upcoming Tripartite Conference of 1975. It demanded that the new policies of wage distribution be stopped, and spelled out the political stakes: accumulated pay hikes in Europe were beginning to change the nature of the politico-economic regime, it claimed, especially since these hikes exceeded productivity gains in several sectors – and in this case, how was capital to be "properly" remunerated?[10] Beginning in 1975-1976, public campaigns were launched relaying employer demands and programmes for a total overhaul of the economy. Key issues were the deregulation of the labour

---

7 Social Action Programme, COM(73) 1600 final of 24 October 1973. In addition to the noteworthy proposals for immediate action that would be adopted by the Council in 1974 (see foot note 8), the Commission also proposed "priority actions" such as extending the competence of the Standing Committee on Employment to include any issue having an impact on employment; the creation of a European Trade Union Institute; and a directive proposal to ensure improved protection of workers' interests in the case of company mergers. Its proposals for "complementary actions" included strengthening worker participation in the company, and possibilities for extending the joint committees.

8 Council Directive 75/117/EEC of 10 February 1975 relating to the application of the principle of equal pay for men and women. Council Directive 75/129/EEC of 17 February 1975 relating to collective redundancies. Regulation (EEC) No. 337/75 of the Council of 10 February 1975 establishing a European Centre for the Development of Vocational Training. Regulation (EEC) No. 1365/75 of the Council of 26 May 1975 on the creation of a European Foundation for the improvement of living and working conditions.

9 Renamed BusinessEurope in 2007.

10 The document, entitled "Economic and Social Tripartite Conference" and dated 13 November 1975, presented the positions UNICE intended to defend at the Tripartite Conference of 18 November. In addition to wage restraint, UNICE also called for the suppression of price control, decreased state intervention, a more flexible labour market, and policies to aid investment (by reducing social contributions and increasing fiscal aids) which it presented as securing job creation. Thus, in the autumn of 1975, the basic principles were already set out for what was to become the credo in economic and financial circles for the next thirty years.

market based on a reorganisation of working time, and the need for an austerity wage policy (reducing wages and social contributions).[11] The political world rapidly aligned with these new proposals: the President of the European Commission, François-Xavier Ortoli, backed the employer positions at the 1975 Tripartite Conference; French Premier Raymond Barre introduced his country's first austerity plan in 1976; at the 1978 European Tripartite Conference, West German Chancellor Helmut Schmidt pronounced his famous slogan, "Today's profits are tomorrow's investments and the day after tomorrow's jobs"; and in May 1979, Margaret Thatcher came to power and established neo-liberalism[12] as a full governmental programme in the UK. There is little doubt that the rapid emergence of this new alliance in favour of employer positions owed much to the development of influential think tanks bringing together key political, financial and economic leaders at the global level, and providing places for "neo-liberal socialisation" in response to the political and social effervescence that they viewed as a world-wide revolutionary threat (Davos Economic Forum, launched in 1971; the Trilateral Commission, formed in 1973).[13]

In contrast, the programme adopted by the ETUC at its London Congress of 1976 was poles apart from the employers' new proposals. It centred on the demand for a generalised reduction in working time to 35 hours without wage loss (via a European law or collective agreement), together with an extension of the time liberated from subordination to capitalist production (by increasing the number of days of paid leave, lowering the retirement age for all, and democratising education through broader access to higher education). With this demand, European trade unions expressed both a symbol of solidarity ("there are fewer jobs, so let productivity gains be used to redistribute existing jobs among all workers!"), and a symbol of social transformation (waged employment, while subordinated in a capitalist regime, must nonetheless work towards producing freed time and social emancipation). The attacks against this programme and national union actions that had either anticipated or were beginning to spread its message were impressive. The employer world refused to negotiate a reduction in working time, and in some cases completely blocked collective bargaining

[11] On Belgium, see Moden J. and Slover J. (1980).

[12] "Neo" here does not stand for "new", but indicates the return to the economic liberalism that had been the dominant doctrine among European elites in the second half of the 19th century.

[13] Keith Dixon (1998) shows how the philosophy of economic liberalism defended by von Hayek spread progressively throughout Europe after the end of World War II via the creation of think tanks. Clearly, people had been working on this return to economic liberalism for several decades.

rounds until the unions abandoned the demand.[14] Inflammatory comments claiming that a reduction of working time without wage loss was totally unrealistic were widely voiced in the press and certain academic circles. (Indeed, the rejection of this demand was – and remains – so strong that it would be of particular interest to undertake a scientific analysis of how this powerful bloc of opposition came to be constituted at European level.) At the same time, to counter the union demand, the employer side developed an antagonistic approach to the reorganisation of working time (favouring part time work, atypical employment contracts, flexible working hours, extending night work, the expansion of temporary work, etc.). The ideological offensive was such that in the space of twenty years the notion of a cross-sectoral reduction in working time[15] as a tool for social emancipation was transformed into its opposite: "part time" work with loss of wages, flexible hours, and an increased workload.

We have now touched on a crucial point regarding the political crisis (in the societal sense) that we have been experiencing since 1975. Labour victories led to a liberation of collective time, nourishing the possibility of imagining a society of equals and undermining the practices and logics of political domination. It is all there, in a nutshell. The widespread dissemination of knowledge means that there have never before been so many skilled people in the broad sense of the term (able to analyse, understand, be interested, and learn); greatly improved access to health care has enabled people to live longer while maintaining their intellectual and physical abilities; the continuous overall increase in wealth has opened up the possibility of eradicating poverty; and the invention of institutions such as social security, progressive income tax and public services has demonstrated the uselessness of the capturing of value by capital. In short, all this has made the possibility of achieving an increasingly real – and less purely formal – democracy greater than ever before.

This makes the paradox all the greater, for the discourse propagated by all kinds of experts, economic and financial circles, the political class and the media conjures up an image of a constrained society, handi-

---

14 In Belgium, the social planning process, thanks to which wages were consistently linked to productivity gains over a period of 15 years, was dropped in 1977. The process was restored in 1985, but in a completely modified form, with the government imposing an extremely strict control over the possibility of raising wages.

15 One of the lines of attack against the reduction of working time was precisely to crush its potential for social emancipation – which is clearly visible at the cross-sectoral level – by limiting it to a "technique" for managing flexibility on the basis of a "trade-off" within the company or sector, thereby changing the political thrust of the demand.

capped by a persistent scarcity of resources, a mass of deskilled workers, too many old people, an insufficiently adaptable labour force, technologies that are failing to enhance competitiveness... Clearly, a society that has finally achieved the capacity to produce emancipation and equality on a wide scale is a frightening prospect! The current offensive led by employers in Western Europe for a return to the 40-hour work week (or longer) is revealing of the centrality of the fight against liberated time. And it is all the easier to lead this offensive today given that, after over 25 years of progressive erosion, the main basis for the collective financing of time out of work and liberated activity – social contributions – has been severely amputated in the past 15 years.

II. The European Union's Counter-Offensive against the Wage and Social Emancipation

The widespread dissemination of government discourses, practices and policies concerning the reorganisation of working time, coupled with the policy of imposing an inflation rate close to zero, opened the way for launching a war on wages.

A. The Turning Point: 1975-1983

At EEC level, it was at the first European Summit of March 1975 that the Heads of State and Government agreed to make the fight against inflation the priority goal for their economic policies.[16] While at the time soaring oil prices provided a convenient pretext, it is interesting to note that what was initially introduced as a response to a specific situation has continued for over 30 years now to represent the major line of economic policy defended by the Community authorities.

At the Luxembourg Summit of March 1976, the fundamentals of the European economic policy agenda – which soon came to be viewed not as policy, but as "de-ideologised rationality" – were set out: "The European Council found that the Member States' governments should respect a certain discipline concerning money supply, budget deficits, production costs, including incomes, and payment balances in order to attain a high degree of convergence of economic policies." Thus, in 1976, for the first time, the idea of disciplining income appeared in the European Summit conclusions. The word "wage" was never used in these documents. The policy of restraint was advocated in a discreet manner, using the vaguer, multi-semantic notion of "income". Countries that had a sophisticated system for the automatic adaptation of wages to price trends were asked to remedy these: "The European Council also dis-

16 The discussion that follows is based on an analysis of the corpus of European Summit Conclusions presented by the Presidency of the Council.

cussed the effects caused by rigid systems of indexation of incomes and expressed the opinion that an adjustment of such mechanisms should be considered." (Maastricht Summit, March 1981). This of course would be done to the detriment of wage progression.

The term "competitiveness" made its first appearance in the Copenhagen Summit Conclusions of April 1978: "The European Council emphasized the need to restore the competitiveness of industries in distress. This remains the basic aim of national and Community policies in this field." We find it again in July 1978 (Bremen Summit), this time in association with the idea of the need for "structural change" (or, to use a more political term, might we not rather say a *regime* change?):

> The European Council concludes that preserving and improving the competitiveness of industry and increasing its innovativeness are important requirements for a higher level of economic growth and the creation of new jobs. Consequently, a greater readiness to undergo structural changes must be induced in firms and industries.

The topic of the organisation of working time was introduced by the Community authorities in 1979: "The European Council asked the Commission to submit a communication on the social and economic implications of concerted work-sharing*" (Paris European Summit, March 1979).

This marked the start of a new economic phase. Governments adopted a new approach to state "intervention" in the economy, and changed their discourses and practices accordingly. Instead of the goal being to increase and expand public services and the public economy with a view to improving their populations' quality of life, public intervention was redirected to helping close down the industries that had driven economic growth in the 1960s. Company directors were given public aid to disinvest from these old sectors, and society thus financed their conversion to new industries – which were presented as the source of future growth and therefore future jobs. In Belgium, for instance, the successive governments of this period embarked on a "New Industrial Policy" by creating the *Société nationale des secteurs nationaux*. Five sectors were targeted for "restructuring": coal, steel, shipbuilding, glass and textiles. The closure of the old industrial structures was socialised, with the state buying out these industries and financing social measures to accompany the shutdowns. From 1978 to 1982, Belgian governments paid out 279 billion Belgian francs in public aid to "downsize" these sectors and

* Translator's note: This is the term appearing in the English version of the Paris Summit Conclusions. It corresponds to the French "aménagement du temps de travail", which is now more commonly expressed as "organisation of working time" in EU documents.

finance industrial conversion (Escarmelle, 1986).[17] The idea was to mobilise all possible resources in order to "revitalise" industry. Thus, the Luxembourg Summit of December 1980 declared:

> The European Council is particularly concerned at the rapid increase in unemployment in the Member States of the Community. It reaffirms that the reduction of rates of inflation and improvements in the competitiveness of undertakings by suitable investments facilitating the necessary structural adjustments are the most appropriate ways of achieving improved growth and combating unemployment on a lasting basis.

Monetary discipline (the fight against inflation) was to be achieved by disciplining wages and budgetary expenditure in order to free up resources for increasing the competitiveness of firms – which translated into a *de facto* growth of the remuneration of profit-making property. Profits would explode, but investments lagged sadly behind (Husson, 2000). In fact, it was the meaning of "investment" that would change, and following popular English usage, come to focus essentially on financial investments (Deroubaix, 2003). A look at trends in the share of property income in Belgian national income speaks volumes: whereas in 1976, this share had dropped to a critical threshold of 3%, threatening the very existence of capitalism, by 1981 it had already climbed up to 16%, reaching 19% in 1986, 21% in 1989, and 24% in 1993 (whereas during the "golden sixties" the share of national income captured by property income had remained stable at around 13%) (De Keersmaecker, 1997).

The concept of competitiveness, after accompanying the theme of the liquidation of the old *national* growth sectors, was then almost immediately coupled with the argument for the need to comply with the rules of a *transnationalised* economy. It would be reflected in discourse by an unvarying declaratory ritual on the need to maintain the broad internal and external macroeconomic balance. Thus, for the Strasbourg European Summit of June 1979, "The struggle against inflation will continue. The major internal and external economic equilibria on which the competitiveness and growth of the economies of the Member States depend must be respected." This was then echoed at the Brussels Euro-

---

17 As a result of this policy, the Belgian budgetary deficit soared in a context of escalating interest rates. In the space of 10 years, one-third of State tax revenues would go to paying off the debt (essentially an internal debt to the major Belgian banks). This easy capture by the banks of a large share of public wealth served to root the country in the new neoliberal economic system. "Over 40% of the increase in public deficit from 4.9% of GDP in 1970-1973 to 15.5% in 1981 must be attributed to the increase in interest paid on public debt" (*Rapport sur l'exposé général du budget pour 1981-1982 fait par le Ministre belge au Budget*, Parliamentary document, p. 28).

pean Summit of March 1983: "The Council considers that the development of the productive capacity of European industry in the conditions required by international competitivity (*sic*) must constitute a major necessity for the Community".

B. From the Single Market (1985) to the Charter of Fundamental Rights (2000)

All of these orientations would be enshrined as a Community programme (and thus cease to be merely guidelines for intergovernmental coordination) with the 1985 Single Market agenda, which marked the beginning of the transfer of economic sovereignty from places where the economy could be controlled by national parliaments to a space where a collegial policy-making process would leave little room for the expression of opposition forces.

The entry into force of the Treaty of Maastricht, which opened the way for Economic and Monetary Union (EMU), marked a profound change in political regime. This is clearly revealed by the analysis of European Summit documents, which shows their evolution from texts listing a number of short, diverse recommendations, towards the presentation of what amounts to a highly developed and structured credo of mandatory economic behaviour. For example, the Summit Conclusions of December 1993 state the following:

> Meeting for the first time following the entry into force of the Treaty on European Union, the Heads of State and Government expressed their resolve to use to the full, immediately, the new possibilities offered by the Treaty to confront current problems and impart a further impetus to the Union [...].
>
> <u>ACTION TO BE UNDERTAKEN AT NATIONAL LEVEL – GENERAL FRAMEWORK</u>
>
> [...]. Member States should pay particular attention to the following measures:
>
> – improving education and training systems. Continuing training is, in particular, to be facilitated so as to ensure ongoing adjustment of skills to the needs of competitiveness and to combating unemployment;
>
> – improving flexibility within enterprises and on the labour market by removing excessive rigidities resulting from regulation as well as through greater mobility;
>
> – examination, at enterprise level, of economically sound formulas for the reorganization of work; such measures must not be directed towards a general redistribution of work, but towards internal adjustments compatible with improved productivity;

– targeted reductions in the indirect cost of labour (statutory contributions), and particularly of less-skilled work, in order to achieve a better balance between the costs of the various factors of production; fiscal measures possibly relating, inter alia, to the environment could be one of the means of offsetting a drop in social contributions, within a general context of stabilizing all statutory contributions and reducing the tax burden:

– better use of public funds set aside for combating unemployment by means of a more active policy of information, motivation and guidance of job-seekers through specialised agencies, whether public or private;

– specific measures concerning young people who leave the education system without adequate training [...].

The entry into force of the Treaty in 1993 also launched the annual ritual of setting the Broad Economic Policy Guidelines (BEPGs) adopted by the European Council. With the social chapter of the Treaty, the need to gear social policies to strengthening competitiveness was introduced for the first time in the history of the Community. Translated into an economic programme, this approach results in the orientations described at the beginning of the December 1993 Summit document: linking education and vocational training reforms to the goal of competitiveness; developing policies for flexibility[18] and mobility in work organisation, leading to a deregulation of the field; developing "individualised" and "targeted" measures for the distribution of employment; promoting an overall reduction in taxation and "targeted" cuts in social contributions (described as "indirect labour costs"); activating unemployment policies, etc.

The Treaty of Maastricht thus represents a decisive political step towards the complete transformation of the content and meaning of social policy in Europe. This systemic metamorphosis was rolled forward by the European political powers – that is the Heads of State and Government – as a mandatory European programme (and thus incorporated in the Treaty). It had been set in motion by the Single European Act which, in declaring that European social norms were to be restricted to setting minimum standards that must not impede the development of SMEs, had put limits on the long-time European political principle, dating from the European Coal and Steel Community and reiterated in the Treaty of Rome, of equalising working conditions in an upward direction. In 1991, the Treaty of Maastricht then clearly directed social policy towards serving the competitiveness of firms. And with the 1993 White Paper on "Growth, competitiveness and employment" produced by the

[18] The concept of the organisation of working time (mainly the expansion of part-time jobs) was broadened to include that of flexibility, which encompasses all aspects of the wage relation.

Delors Commission, employment policy became a vehicle for introducing profound reforms of the labour market and social security systems in order to strengthen competitiveness. In 1997, the Treaty of Amsterdam reinforced this instrumentalisation of employment, promoting the principles of adaptability, employability, flexibility, and "individual responsibility". The "stability" and "growth and employment" resolutions adopted at the Amsterdam Summit – continuing the process initiated by the Maastricht Treaty – sidelined public policy instruments such as direct taxation, social contributions, budgets promoting redistributive social policies, and the power to intervene in the creation of money, further delegitimising their use as tools for the decommodification of a wide range of social relations.

In March 2000, the Lisbon Summit further reinforced the subordination of all the social dimensions (education, pensions, health, etc.) to the goal of strengthening competitiveness. Social policy came to be viewed primarily as a productive factor geared to making Europe into the world's most competitive economy, and secondarily as a tool for "social inclusion" (meaning "integration into the new order"), and thus no longer as a tool for achieving equality. In December 2000, the Charter of Fundamental Rights of the European Union introduced the principle of "freedom of work" in the liberal sense of deregulation ("the right to engage in work"), and not in the labour sense of emancipation: the wage, excluded from Community competence, is ignored; and social benefits are not guaranteed as wage-based rights but as "aids".

III. What's Behind the EU's "Employment Policy"?

The discourses accompanying the policy constraints imposed on the management of the main resources flowing from production have led to a profound transformation of the notions of social policy and public authority.

A. From the Social State to the Tutelary State

The redistributive social state (1945-1975) had contributed to disseminating a universalising democratic imaginary (one person, one vote; equal pay for equal work; the collective origin and nature of rights to resources founded on a generalised wage-based solidarity; and legally binding collective agreements having primacy over the logics of civil law) (Gobin, 2002b). The current tutelary state whose role is to protect national solidarity for "target groups" defined as "problematic" and/or "poor" can no longer do this. On the contrary, it tends to develop a state discourse on guaranteeing what are called fundamental rights, and the use of the adjective "fundamental" helps to disconnect these rights from waged employment, since "everyone should benefit from them". This brings the public authorities to link them to the notion of "citizen", which leads in turn to the idea that they should be jointly financed by taxation (resources distributed to groups designated as "poor") and by the individual and/or enterprise (second and third pillars).

Furthermore, the forceful political discourse on the need to reduce the "tax burden" (social contributions) in order to increase the employment rate has produced such broad consensus that the trade unions have come to focus on seeking alternative, tax-based sources of financing. Preferably through a wealth tax, or by increasing direct taxation on all income, but not necessarily on a progressive basis; or by developing an "eco-tax" for companies or a "tax on speculation" for the financial sectors. This shift in focus towards diversified forms of taxation also contributes to disconnecting social security rights from the wage, and could, in the long run, serve to delegitimate union intervention in shaping policy in the field, with the unions' role being confined to negotiating the second and third pillars – and direct wages in a context of a strong policy of wage restraint. Subsidised employment also contributes to disconnecting pay from its wage-based source, in that it combines unemployment allowances, reduced wages, reduced or exempted social contributions and tax incentives for employers.

This move away from founding rights to resources on a solidarity between equals (via social contributions or progressive direct income tax) corresponds to a major goal of the current reform agenda. For indeed, if wage-earners collectively are recognised as being at the origin of the production of value and societal meaning, then it follows that the right to a wage should be consolidated as a universal, political right from adulthood on.[19] On the other hand, denying the political legitimacy of wage rights means reverting to the traditional justifications for rights to resources, where entitlement is contributory (the amount each person receives is based on what s/he has personally contributed) or based on a handicap (a person receives a remuneration because s/he is entitled to solidarity due to a "disadvantage" or an "abnormality"). And this is precisely what is happening. We are also seeing a growing trend to link the right to remuneration to the notion of personal merit.[20] The notion of rights is thus veering towards that of duties, although this would be inconceivable if wage rights were elevated to the status of a universal

---

[19] See Goblot, 2003. The tensions around the demand that the right to a wage be defined as a political right date back to the French Revolution. The categorisation of rights into "different generations", as asserted by classical legal orthodoxy, can be seen as part of the process fostering the declassification of social rights to remuneration.

[20] See the debates between Van Parijs, Schokhaert, Myles, Oksanen and Fornero in Journal of European Social Policy, 2003, 13 (3).

political right: preventing this from happening is *the* crucial issue for current reforms.

B. Pitting Jobs against Wages

The progressive rise to hegemony of the myth of the scarcity of resources has forced the trade unions to forgo pay bargaining and accept to "negotiate" on what was presented as "something else" to be redistributed, namely, jobs. But, disconnected from wage claims, employment can be turned into a weapon to combat wage rights. And as we have seen, the re-orientation of the social field to focus on "employment policy"[21] has led to a complete transformation of the notion of "social policy", turning it into a dimension of the single market.

Careful attention has been paid to "conceptualising"[22] an employment policy attuned to the "imperatives" of an economy supposedly characterised by ever more numerous and fluctuating markets, and thus necessitating flexible conditions of work and pay. From the beginning, the European Commission's reports on employment (the first appearing in 1989) developed, diffused and legitimated a battery of new instruments for "seeing, describing and deciding", such as a "labour market"[23] approach to work; introducing the concept of "employment rate" to replace those of "active population" and "unemployment rate"; inventing the notions of "target populations" or "target categories", "active" measures, "flexicurity", and so on. All these new notions have served to progressively depict employment as a "productive factor" primarily geared to improving the competitiveness of companies, and the population aged 15 to 64 years as human capital to be used for this purpose. The 1997 Amsterdam Summit declared this employment policy to be in the common interest and presented it as the central focus of the European Social Agenda – with the result that all the other components of social policy would be expected to contribute to strengthening the employment policy and would thus in turn, become "factors of production". Employment policy would in a way become a vehicle for tying

21 This notion of employment policy, although so widely accepted today, is a strange one. What is the point of creating jobs *per se*? However, when a state engages in societal development policies (environment, urban planning, health, education, culture, etc.), this necessarily creates jobs.

22 This change in the logic of perception of the social sphere and employment is not only produced in the framework of European expertise, but also in exchanges between experts at different political levels – the international (in particular OECD publications), Community and national levels. It can be argued that a transnational administrative governance exists.

23 This means that employment policy becomes a labour market policy, that is, a policy of adapting labour to the market.

the social dimension to the primary Community goal of improving competitiveness.

The new focus on "employment rate" was part of a general policy to "make work pay" by applying the recommendations set out in the monetary Stability Pact and the 1997 resolution on growth and employment. In other words, it was in line with a general policy to lower overall taxation and reduce social contributions. The notion of "employment rate" radically changes the previous model of work relations in several ways. It replaces the notion of "active population" and marginalises the usage of "unemployment rate",[24] for what is at stake here is that the largest possible number of people between the ages of 15 and 64 years be considered as employable, regardless of whether they are actually seeking work or not.[25] In this way, the unemployed become just one of the many categories of people that must be put back to work (young people, women, older workers, etc.), and this serves to undo the strong ties of solidarity that made an unemployed person a worker waiting to be employed and thus someone with wage rights. Moreover, categorising people into "target populations" justifies a "differentiated treatment" and thus "differentiated rights" that serve to undermine wage rights (lower hourly wages, reduced social contributions, reduction or elimination of social allowances, fiscal support from the state financing a part of the wage), and changes the perception of wage-earners collectively (who become administrative categories that are managed instead of a collective socio-political force). The idea that productive work, at least part-time, should become more frequent from the age of 15 also becomes more commonplace.[26] In a context of particularly high unemployment, the very fact of seeking to put people to work who are not looking for employment adds to the downwards pressure on wages

---

24 "[…] in many respects, [the employment rate] provides a more useful measure than the unemployment rate, since the latter does not take into account the considerable number of people who are not included in the active population because they are not actively seeking a job, but who would nonetheless like to work if given the opportunity to do so", Commission des Communautés européennes, *L'emploi en Europe*, Direction générale de l'emploi, des relations industrielles et des affaires sociales, 1994, p. 28 (our translation).

25 It also tends to imply that the notion of "inactive" corresponds to an abnormal situation, that is, that the fact of being disabled, in prison, sick, unemployed or studying should not exempt people from performing productive work which, in turn, serves to promote poorly paid, short-term jobs.

26 It thus undermines one of the most fundamental democratic rights: the right to compulsory education up to the highest possible age. The workfare ideology pushes children from the working classes into "vocational" tracks where the "training" provided is based on their unpaid part-time work in a company. The various student aids for higher education also tend to require that productive "work" be performed in exchange for the financial support provided.

(including social contributions), as well as serving to relax (or indeed eliminate) the safety net of "suitable employment". And this opens wide the door to the social production of increasing numbers of working poor.

"Lifelong learning" is another notion that goes hand in hand with that of "employment rate". Under cover of favouring vocational training, what is really being promoted here is a strategy to undermine the value of the professional qualification of workers. By playing on the image of an increasingly fluctuating and indeterminate market, employers have managed to portray workers as being perpetually ill-adapted and thus constantly needing to acquire new skills, which then immediately become outdated. Once again, we see the wage being undermined, and all the more easily so since the agenda is to focus on personalised training, which in turn favours the idea of a personalised wage. This strategy aims at defeating the key union combat to impose negotiations on pay scales strictly tied to qualification grids based on recognised skills and/or diplomas – that is, to stop the wage from once again becoming a "market price" as it was in the 19th century. This strategy also tends to transform the content of the notion of training, which instead of exclusively referring to the mastery of intellectual, practical and technical skills, increasingly includes references to aptitudes (the "ability to hold a job"). The term is voluntarily vague, and can refer to psychological aptitudes (not be depressive; be obedient and malleable?) or physical aptitudes or states (not fall ill frequently, not have AIDS, not be pregnant?).

C. A New Community Discourse on Wages

As we have seen, the word "wage" does not appear in the conclusions of the European summits drawn up by the Heads of State and Government. It was in the annual Broad Economic Policy Guidelines (BEPGs), which became mandatory with the entry into force of the Treaty of Maastricht in 1993, that a European political discourse on the wage began to be developed.

Our systematic analysis of the frequency of usage of the vocabulary relating to "wage" ("*salaire*", "*salarial*") in the French-language corpus of BEPG texts revealed that this is one of the major themes addressed in these documents.[27] The political message is highly concentrated: the EU asks the Member States to monitor wages with a view to restraining increases, in order to strengthen the competitiveness of European firms and monetary stability, and also to favour job creation. Alongside this general theme, particular attention is paid to low-skill low-wage jobs:

---

27 The lexical forms related to "*salaire*" occur 400 times, indicating their central place. See Gobin, part II in this volume for a more detailed presentation of this lexicometric study (corpus of the French language BEPGs from 1993 to 2005).

here, a generalisation of the practice of reducing social contributions is called for (this being presented as a means to increase wages!).

The gender wage gap appears as a topic in 2000, but as part of a more general discourse on the need for flexible pay and a greater differentiation in wage levels to reflect differences in regional competitiveness and local labour market conditions. Wage differentiation to "offset productivity gaps" is thus encouraged, and a finger pointed at the public sector where the civil service regime is claimed to entail wage "rigidity".

In an economic system where the central dynamic is entrusted to financial markets instead of remaining in the hands of national governments, the wage becomes the main adjustment variable. And this is why it would be excluded from EU legislative competence. Thus, in 1997, the Treaty of Amsterdam banished all pay-related questions from the range of topics that can be legislated at EU level.[28] The result would be the paradox reflected in the Charter of Fundamental Rights of 2000, which contains no provision for the overall protection of the right to a wage, but only mentions the principle of equal pay for men and women, this being the only issue falling within Community competence. Thus, in the EU, the wage ceases to be a political issue relating to the democratic question of how to define equality between human beings. It becomes a technical indicator that needs to be monitored in order to avoid a "drifting" that would be harmful to "maintaining the broad macro-economic balance".[29] Monitoring wages has become a priority goal for the European Central Bank and one of its tasks, even though the issue of wages does not fall within its mandate *stricto sensu* (Dufresne, 2004)

D. *A Pitfall for Euro-unionism*

Systemic European wage restraint could not, however, have been achieved without the – albeit involuntary – acquiescence of trade union leaders. In the particular political context of the EU, the conversion of social policy instruments into elements serving the free movement of business and capital has left the unions in an extremely paradoxical situation: their demand for a more social Europe has led them in fact to

---

28 Article 137, paragraph 6 of the Treaty of Amsterdam.

29 Thus, the fact that the wage is not a legislatable issue does not prevent the EU from dealing with it intensively (see Council Regulation (EC) No. 530/1999 of 9 March 1999 concerning structural statistics on earnings and on labour costs). With EMU, national statistics were reformed in order to be made useful for the EU. Thus, since 1995, the statistics produced by the Belgian National Bank no longer provide direct access to an overall table presenting the share of the different factors of production in the formation of national income. Only the share of employee earnings in national income is now accessible… and monitored.

legitimate the pursuit of regressive political reforms aimed at the transformation of the social field, and to contribute to disseminating and popularising regressive notions at national level (the three "pillars" for pensions, "lifelong learning", "social cohesion", "employment rate", "equal opportunity", etc., etc.).

ETUC resistance to neo-liberalism was swept away at the beginning of the 1990s (Gobin, 2000). This can be explained by a combination of factors: the shock created by the fall of the Berlin Wall and in its wake, the proclaiming of capitalism as the only possible horizon; the unions' fear of finding themselves totally isolated by an ever more hostile political world won over to neo-liberalism; the renewal of trade union leadership (the rise of the post-war generations and white collar leaders, with more centrist ideological positions); and political pressure from the European ruling class pushing the unions into becoming "partners" in the new policy orientations. As regards the last factor, the social dialogue procedure introduced at EU level by Pierre Bérégovoy (then French Minister of Social Affairs) in 1984 and by Jacques Delors[30] in 1985 played a decisive role in acclimatising the unions to drawing closer to employer and governmental positions. This procedure had indeed been designed as a vehicle for a new political culture of partnership, that is, political relations based on mutual understanding and cooperation rather than on an acknowledgement of social conflict.

The demand for this new form of union responsibility (as an actor in a partnership instead of conflict) is a repeated theme in EU documents. To cite just a few examples:

> The Social Partners are urged to continue the impressive contribution they have made over the past five years to wage moderation which has contributed so much to the improved economic outlook and improved prospects for new job creation. (European Commission, Special Forum, Summit on Employment, Employment and Social Affairs – Forum, published by the DGV, 1997)

> Economic and monetary union has helped to create a more cooperative industrial relations climate based on shared macro-economic objectives. (European Commission, Industrial Relations in Europe, 2000)

> For wage developments to contribute to an employment-friendly policy mix, social partners should continue to pursue a responsible course and conclude wage agreements in Member States in line with the general principles set out in the broad economic policy guidelines. (BEPGs, 2001)

> An ambitious, proactive social dialogue must therefore play a key role in meeting these challenges as a flexible, efficient, non-confrontational means

30 On taking office as President of the European Commission.

> for making adjustments and overcoming the obstacles to modernisation. (European Commission, COM (2002) 341 final of 26.6.2002)

Confronted with these numerous European constraints ("systemic", political, and moral), and having to function within a dynamic that had reached an all-time political low, the most the union actors could achieve was to attempt to work towards building a minimum basis of agreement at the level of a few countries (Doorn Group) or sectors (European coordination of sectoral wage bargaining) to limit wage dumping, by setting a theoretical wage standard which they would not drop below in their national pay bargaining rounds (Dufresne *et al.*, 2006). Just like the first worker coalitions setting up "*sociétés de maintien de prix*" in the 19th century. Some 180 years later, they are back at this same basic starting point!

IV. Flexicurity *versus* the Social State…and Austerity *versus* Democratic Sovereignty (2005-2012)

All the reforms of the past twenty years are converging today towards the move to "modernise the employment contract". From the late 1970s on, multiple forms of flexible work organisation began to be tested at national level before being socialised at EU level. The trend flourished to such an extent that in 2005 the European Commission announced its intention to initiate a far-reaching revision of labour law in order to tidy things up. Thus, in presenting the Social Agenda for 2006-2010, the Commission declared:

> In a dynamic economy, new forms of work emerge, for example economically dependent work and fixed-term work. […] Accordingly, the Commission intends to adopt a Green Paper on the development of labour law. In this Green Paper, the Commission will analyse current trends in new work patterns and the role of labour law in tackling these developments, by providing a more secure environment encouraging efficient transitions on the labour market. The discussion that this document will produce could lead to proposals for a whole range of measures to modernise and simplify the current rules.[31]

The reforms would go on to target the two ends of the employment relation that had been formalised in the model of the social state: on one hand, the *contract of employment* – governed by collectively negotiated public policy provisions which can only be derogated from to the benefit of employees; and on the other, the primacy of these *overriding mandatory provisions* over economic freedoms, as guaranteed by the state commitment to ensure the primacy of a collective order over individual

[31] Communication from the Commission on the Social Agenda, COM (2005) 33 final, p. 7.

economic wills. The very foundations of labour law would thus come under attack: eliminating the public policy provisions ensuring a hierarchy of norms, or at least reducing them to a bare minimum, while liberating individual initiative in the establishing of the employment contract, boils down to restoring the pre-eminence of civil and commercial law over labour law.[32] In view of this, "modernising" labour law could end up looking more like moving towards its abolition. The process was essentially set in motion by two EU interventions: the 2006 Green Paper on "Modernising labour law to meet the challenges of the 21st century" (followed by two Communications from the Commission in 2007),[33] and the regulation concerning the law applicable to contractual obligations adopted by the EU Authorities in 2008.[34] These texts call into question the rules governing the employment contract, and at the same time propose a new form of regulation said to be favourable to employers and employees alike: flexicurity.

With the Green Paper and the Community interventions that followed, the open-ended contract guaranteeing the stability of employment and wages and validating professional experience and qualification grids was challenged as the standard norm, and this served to destabilise the employment contract. However, the mushrooming of too many atypical contracts gave rise to segmented labour markets, thereby limiting the mobility of workers sought by the Commission. The next step, which served to further erode the open-ended contract, was to make it easier for employers to dismiss workers: this amounts to making the fixed-term contract the new employment norm. It was claimed that workforce turn-over would be offset by enhancing the action of national employment services in order to ensure that dismissed workers would find a new job rapidly and thus be able to maintain a relatively high level of replacement income. However, in this new employment system, recognition of the worker's professional qualification or skills has

---

32 In Great Britain and Ireland, due to the common law model, the current chipping away at protective labour legislation is less visible than in the continental political systems (where destabilisation of the labour code in favour of a civil law logic can be clearly seen); but the general trend pushed by the EU today towards undermining social norms so that they will cease to be seen as elements of public policy and, as such, superior to the will of the market and the contractual wills of individuals, will of course have negative consequences for wage-earners everywhere, whatever their national legal orders.

33 Communication from the Commission, June 2007, "Towards Common Principles of Flexicurity: More and better jobs through flexibility and security" and Communication from the Commission, "Outcome of the Public Consultation on the Commission's Green Paper, Modernising labour law to meet the challenges of the 21st century" (COM/2007/0627) of October 2007.

34 Regulation (EC) No. 593/2008 adopted on 17 June 2008.

entirely disappeared. The market, it is held, constantly requires "new competencies" that will have to be acquired from scratch each time, in a never-ending process of "lifelong learning". Workers are reduced to human capital that is kept continually on the move and thus continually deskilled. The wage loses its political, collectively negotiated attributes, to become a price that is set individually, as workers move incessantly from job to job. By instituting flexicurity as an employment system, the European elites have broken the only model that makes it possible to progress towards an emancipated society: that of the worker-as-producer. This individualising nomadism has blown apart workers' existence as a collective social force, making it possible to impose the idea that they are no longer the source of the production of wealth. And this allows companies to appropriate the political status of producer of societal resources and to arrogate staggering power for themselves.

The flexicurity strategy has been accompanied by the adoption of a new European regulation concerning the law applicable to contractual obligations, in the event of conflicts between different national legal regimes. This regulation is defined as applying to civil and commercial contracts, but its scope includes the employment contract – as if this were self-evident – thereby blurring the boundaries that had been established between civil law and social legislation. It concerns the hiring of workers who are of a different nationality to that of their employer – a situation that has become increasingly frequent due to the growth of outsourcing and the principle of free movement of services within the EU.

The autonomy conferred on the will of the parties is very broad, and is such that it might endanger a founding principle of social democracy, namely the requirement that general measures protecting employees override private wills. This regulation applying to work relations with a transnational dimension allows the law of reference governing the employment contract to be chosen by the parties concerned: it can be the law of any country in the world, and moreover apply to only part of the contract, since each clause can be subject to a different national legal regime. True, the text stipulates that the choice must not conflict with the "mandatory provisions that cannot be derogated from by agreement under the law that, in the absence of choice, would have been applicable". But this latter law is defined very broadly as the law of the country in which the employee habitually carries out his or her work (even if s/he is temporarily posted to another country). This means that in the case of a Polish employer hiring a Bulgarian worker for a worksite in Lithuania, a contract established under, say, Brazilian law cannot derogate from the overriding provisions of Bulgarian law. When the applicable law is difficult to determine, it will be that of the country where the employer's place of business is located, or of any country with which the contract is more closely connected. The regulation also stipulates that the directive on the transnational posting of workers[35] be applied: this requires compliance with the minimum social provisions of the host country, and includes a recommendation that the judge apply a restrictive interpretation of the notion of overriding mandatory provisions. What a legal mess this makes! The freedom granted both to the contracting parties and the judge to determine which general norms will be mandatory creates a truly fuzzy situation, whereas labour law, on the contrary, should be particularly clear and strict in order to provide maximum protection for the worker. Given the growing importance of outsourcing services transnationally, in a globalised economic context and an EU economic space of 27 countries with a statutory minimum wage gap of 1 to 11, this is clearly not a neutral regulation. The lack of clarity in the definition of mandatory provisions that should serve to limit pseudo individual freedoms in the field of employment relations has, moreover, been reinforced by four now famous judgments of the European Court of Justice delivered between December 2007 and June 2008 (the Laval, Rüffert, Viking and Luxembourg cases).[36]

In the first two judgments, the Court gave an extremely restrictive interpretation of the mandatory provisions applying to the employment contract of posted workers, limiting these to the specific provisions of the Posted Workers Directive, and thereby making the directive a *de facto* European labour code defining the norms governing working conditions. It further stated that only minimal provisions of general scope would apply (thus invalidating regional collective agreements in federal states, for instance). But the June 2008 ruling against the state of Luxembourg, in a case brought before the Court by the European Commission for failure to fulfil obligations, went a step further. Those basic mandatory public policy provisions, whether deriving from the Posted Workers Directive or determined by the Member State, were themselves radically called into question: the Court and the Commission considered that a Member State could not unilaterally determine what constitutes national public policy and that the four trade freedoms were to be interpreted in such a way that only a serious threat to the general interest of society could constitute a valid reason for restricting free trade. Finally,

[35] Directive 96/71/EC of the European Parliament and of the Council of 16 December 1996 concerning the posting of workers in the framework of the provision of services.

[36] Laval C-341/05, Rüffert C-346/06, and Luxembourg C-319/06. These judgments can be accessed at http://curia.europa.eu/jurisp/cgi-bin/form.pl?lang=en using the appropriate case number.

the ruling on the Viking case[37] clearly demonstrates that when the employer's freedom of establishment is given primacy, the right to strike and to collective action cannot be exercised. But how could things be otherwise when the collective imaginary is steeped in a civil law approach? When the employment relation is only perceived through the distorting liberal prism of a free, voluntary encounter between two equals signing a contract? In such a framework, striking workers can only be seen as irresponsible, "immature" people who do not honour their contractual commitments, and at the collective level, a strike represents an unacceptable obstacle to the freedom to do business.

With the banking crisis of 2008, the European Commission under President Barroso slightly modified its neo-liberal discourse, and even promised to introduce measures to control the banking sector's activities. But the change was short-lived. The speculative attacks on Greece's public debt at the beginning of 2010 served as a stepping stone for strengthening the control exerted by the Community over Member States' public policies through the surveillance of public finances, and for further pursuing policies to increase the flexibility of employment contracts as well as the general downward pressure on wages.

The new "European economic governance" that progressively took shape between 2010 and 2011 was not designed to re-regulate financial activities, but rather to dig deeply into the pockets of the majority of European populations via taxation and austerity programmes. Furthermore, with these austerity measures, the populations are made to pay a second time, since they are already footing the bill for state debts incurred to save the banks from bankruptcy in October 2008. The lame reaction from the majority of Europe's trade union leaders to this extensive public refinancing of the banking sector acted as a green light, enabling the European political class to enforce its austerity and new governance programmes.

According to the figures communicated by President Barroso in September 2011,[38] public expenditures on bailing out the banking sector in the EU between October 2008 and September 2011, totalled 4,600 billion euros (that is, about 13 times the annual GDP of Belgium, for example). Barroso's announcement that, in "compensation" for the efforts demanded of the people, a legal instrument was being prepared for 2014 permitting taxation of financial transactions, and expected to bring in an annual 55 billion euros, shows that political orientations

[37] Viking Case C-438/05.

[38] José Manuel Durão Barroso, President of the European Commission, *European renewal – State of the Union Address 2011*, SPEECH/11/607, European Parliament, Strasbourg, 28 September 2011, p. 6.

were clearly already no longer on the side of the people. For it seems that these tax revenues would correspond, in fact, to a "reimbursement" by the financial sector, which means a generous time-scale of 83 years, interest-free, if we take the 4,600 billion paid by European taxpayers over three years as reference.

True, the ETUC has never, in all its history, organised so many demonstrations – 10 European trade union actions between December 2008 and May 2012. But at the same time, using demonstrations to put pressure on governments has proved to be totally ineffective under current circumstances. For, indeed, the political class in power has transferred its duty of loyalty from the people to the banking world, and is far more concerned about its ratings and "financial credibility" than about the distress of its populations. Given this context, the new economic governance will serve to strengthen previous orientations aimed at destabilising the employment contract, the right to strike, attacking the wage, and putting the political system of the nation-state under outside supervision – and these attacks on the sovereignty of national public authorities will, in turn, serve to reduce popular sovereignty.

A brief glance at some of the key moments in European current affairs that have marked the last few years will suffice to illustrate that the trends analysed in the course of this chapter have not only continued, but have been exacerbated since the so-called "financial crisis". The latter development has only been possible due to the process of erosion undertaken in the previous decades.

As regards employment: in March 2010, the European Commission presented its Europe 2020 Strategy – a continuation of the Lisbon strategy – which calls for an increase in the employment rate of the population aged 20-64 from 69% (the 2010 target) to at least 75%.[39] The Commission also announced the strategy's aim to reduce school dropout rates and increase the numbers of university graduates, but in a context where school education is being increasingly reoriented towards teaching "useful skills" adapted to the job market, and universities are also coming under mounting pressure from this market utilitarianism (De Meulemeester, 2012).

The European Council of March 2011 unambiguously linked this policy of increasing the employment rate to pension reforms and stronger activation measures for the unemployed (based on cutting back their unemployment entitlements). The structural reforms advocated continue to boil down to budgetary austerity and the regression of wage rights: in

---

[39] See COM (2010) Europe 2020, A strategy for smart, sustainable and inclusive growth, p. 10.

short, governments must support economic growth by granting advantages to private capital.[40]

As regards the wage: At this same European summit, 23 Member States decided to adopt a "Euro Plus Pact", in order to go even further in applying the general reforms advocated by the Commission. They thus announced that steps would be taken to boost competitiveness by exercising strict control over wage trends, both at national level and for each major sector of activity, since "large and sustained increases may lead to the erosion of competitiveness, especially if combined with a widening current account deficit and declining market shares for exports".[41]

As regards the attack on democratic sovereignty and the people's right to be protected by a government that holds itself responsible for their well-being: the principles of the future European Stability Mechanism (ESM) were announced at the same European Council. This mechanism represents a total reversal of the social contract instituted at the end of World War II, since countries that are said to be "experiencing severe financing problems" will have to implement reforms imposed by a Troika consisting of the Commission, the European Central Bank, and the International Monetary Fund. Outside technocratic surveillance thus replaces the freedom of economic policy underpinned by the principle of universal suffrage. Putting state democratic sovereignty on hold in this way also means jettisoning popular sovereignty. A further illustration of this frontal attack on democratic sovereignty is provided by the budgetary control measures[42] which call on Member States to draw up three-year public budgets, thereby destabilising one of the driving principles of the democratic balance between parliament and government. It would seem that Article 4.2 of the Treaty of Lisbon is being applied to the letter: "It [the Union] shall respect their essential State functions, including ensuring the territorial integrity of the State, maintaining law and order and safeguarding national security. In particular, national security remains the sole responsibility of each Member State."

Finally, as regards the right to strike: on 21 March 2012, the European Commission presented a proposal for a Council regulation, also known as the "Monti II" proposal, which endorsed the main thrust of the case law established by the ECJ in its judgments of 2008. A decision by this same Court of Justice on 26 January 2012 concerning the Bianca Kücük case C-586/10, justified the employer's use of fixed-term con-

[40] European Council, Conclusions, Brussels, 25 March 2011, EUCO 10/11 CO EUR 6 CONCL 3, p. 3.

[41] *Ibid.*, p. 16.

[42] Adoption of the "European Semester" by EcoFin on 7 September 2010; vote by the European parliament in favour of the "Six Pack" on 28 September 2011, and of the "Two Pack" on 13 June 2012.

tracts in the event of a recurring – or even permanent – "need for replacement staff", and dismissed the case brought by a German employee who had been subjected to a succession of fixed-term contracts without interruption over a period of 11 years.

Conclusions

Too few people have as yet taken full measure of the scale of this change in political regime – at both "global" and European level – which has universalised the "laisser-faire, laisser-passer" ideology, that is, economic liberalism, as the only way of conceiving society. This chapter began with the paradox of a world that sees itself as suffering from a scarcity of resources when never before in history have we seen so many people with educational and technological skills producing such a vast quantity of wealth. Another paradox has followed close on its heels. The reformers of the 19th and 20th centuries had, with the invention of sociology and social legislation, demonstrated that economic liberalism is a societicidal doctrine which is incapable of imagining and inventing collective relations of social solidarity: bent as it is on defining individuals as free atoms who function in a rigid, mechanical way according to the laws of so-called rational choices, and whose only purpose in the world is to "consume", this doctrine develops a "counter-societal" imaginary that, given the scale of technological and military developments, is threatening humanity's survival. The current reforms claim to invent a new globalised society – but it is of the sort that destroys the very essence of human society by denying the reality of the interdependency and intermeshing of social relations, and thus of the necessity of social solidarity.

In keeping with the spirit of the present book, this overview of 44 years of EU history also seeks to provide a fresh occasion for reflecting on "social change". The political Left has long torn itself apart over that false "reform or revolution" alternative. But, indeed, the difference between these two terms only arises when people have a magical and somewhat violent vision of social change. This longstanding controversy has prevented many from seeing that even within capitalism, the complex dialectical interaction between the various progressive forces of change has been able to give birth to new institutions founding a truly counter-capitalist society. The model of the socialised wage is one of these.

The redistributive social state with its public services, and the imaginary and achievements of the socialised wage are stepping stones that can lead humanity towards social emancipation by creating the conditions of liberated work and by enshrining the rights to remuneration attached to the wage as universal political rights. And construct a "full wage" society instead of the current *impasse* of "full employment" based on precarious, deskilled jobs. It is because the socialised wage is the bearer of this strong message that the counter-reform movement launched in the wake of anti-1968 reactions has been so virulent, and is bent on eradicating all desire for autonomy *vis-à-vis* the totalitarian hold of the market. Marx stressed the fact that the new takes seed in the old. But not without the social forces able to understand and seize on the potentialities unleashed in the collective struggles and resistances of the moment.

European counter-reforms reduce the capacity for democratic control over the resources produced: all the tools, institutions, instruments and procedures that historically made it possible to institutionalise the capacity of democratic authorities to redistribute collective resources, notably through the use of public finances, have been brutally called into question. The current political control exercised over the Member States, imposing a policy of austerity on their public finances,[43] merely serves to highlight the loss of autonomy inflicted on all those institutions in a position to bring peoples further along the path towards the freedom to develop together what has meaning and what makes "society". The EU's new political system is collegial, but it is not formed by a community of states seeking to safeguard the sovereignty each derives from universal suffrage. It is formed by a college of governing individuals who have chosen to gradually subordinate the Member States to European institutions designed to serve profit-making property. The metaphor of a new empire consisting of subordinated provinces is beginning to take shape, and this new order is counter-democratic.

And yet it is within our grasp to turn this retrograde political construction around: by accepting to live to the full our role as free producers of society, and understanding that money, finances, the public budget, and the organisation of work are all political tools that can be used to further the goal of emancipation.

[43] With the Ecofin Council decision to launch the first "European Semester" in 2011 (introducing permanent budgetary control mechanisms). Preliminary to this decision, the IMF and the EU imposed measures in countries such as Greece and Romania which suspend national laws or collective agreements protecting workers and wages, to the benefit of enterprises; even a European law (on the limitation of working hours) was suspended in Romania.

References

Accardo A. (2006), *Introduction à une sociologie critique; lire Pierre Bourdieu*, Marseille, Agone, (first edition, le Mascaret 1991).

Accosstat (2011). "En 2010 les exonérations se stabilisent", No. 138, available at: http://gesd.free.fr/acoss138.pdf.

Adler M. (2004), "Combining welfare-to-work measures with tax credits. A new hybrid approach to social security in the United Kingdom", *International Social Security Review*, Vol. 57, No. 2.

Aglietta M., Berrebi L. (2007), *Désordres dans le capitalisme mondial*, Odile Jacob.

Althaler K.S., Dimmel N. (1993), "Sozialpolitische Handlungsfelder der experimentellen Arbeitsmarktpolitik. Aushandlungsformen, Kooperation und Konflikt zwischen Arbeitsmarktverwaltung, Ländern und Gemeinden", *Österreichische Zeitschrift für Politikwissenschaft*, 22, Issue 3, pp. 343-360.

Amable B. (2005), *Les Cinq Capitalismes. Diversité des systèmes économiques et sociaux dans la mondialisation*, Le Seuil, Collection Economie humaine, Paris.

Amable B., Demmou L., Ledezma I. (2009), "Stratégie de Lisbonne et réformes structurelles", *Revue de l'IRES*, No. 60, pp. 25-46.

Amable B., Gatti D., Schumacher J. (2006), *Welfare State retrenchment: the partisan effect revisited*, international conference "Etat et régulation sociale. Comment penser la cohérence de l'intervention publique?", pp. 11-13, September, Paris.

Arjona R., Ladaique M., Pearson M. (2002) "Protection sociale et croissance", *Revue économique de l'OCDE*, No. 35, 2002-2.

Atkinson A.B. (1995), *Incomes and the Welfare State*, Cambridge, Cambridge University Press.

Atzmüller R. (2006), *National report on Austria*. Part 1: Industrial relations and active labour market policies. Final report for RESORE (Employees' Resources and Social Rights in Europe), Vienna.

Atzmüller R. (2009), "Aktivierung statt Vollbeschäftigung. Die Entwicklung der Arbeitsmarktpolitik in Österreich", in Hermann C., Atzmüller R. (eds.), *Die Dynamik des "österreichischen Modells". Brüche und Kontinuitäten im Beschäftigungs- und Sozialsystem*, FORBA-Forschung Bd. 4, Edition Sigma, Berlin, Produktionsprozess, pp. 135-186.

Atzmüller R., Köchl S., Riesenecker-Caba T. (with the cooperation of Zingerle M.) (2006), *Wirtschaftliche und gesellschaftliche Bedeutung der Wiener sozialintegrativen Unternehmen*, FORBA Research Report No. 06/2006, Vienna.

Atzmüller R., Krenn M., Papouschek U. (2012), "Innere Aushöhlung und Fragmentierung des österreichischen Modells: Zur Entwicklung von Arbeitslosigkeit, prekärer Beschäftigung und Arbeitsmarktpolitik", in Scherschel K., Streckeisen P., Krenn M. (eds.), *Neue Prekarität. Die Folgen aktivierender Arbeitsmarktpolitik – europäische Länder im Vergleich*, Labour Studies, Band 2, Frankfurt/Main/New York, Campus, pp. 75-110.

Atzmüller R., Krischek C. (2010), National seminar – Austria national background paper, *Anticipating and managing restructuring in Austria*, A.R.E.N.A.S., VC/2008/0667, International Training Centre (ITC) ILO.

Auer, P., Efendioglu, Ü. and Leschke, J. (2008), *Active Labour Market Policies Around the World*, Genève, ILO.

Austin J.L. (1962), *How to do things with words*, Oxford, Oxford University Press.

Balme R., Chabanet D., Wright V. (eds.) (2002), *L'action collective en Europe. Collective action in Europe*, Paris, Presses de Sciences Po.

Banyuls J., Miguélez F., Recio A., Cano E., Lorente R. (2009), "The transformation of the Employment System in Spain: Towards a Mediterranean Neoliberalism?", in Bosch G., Lehndorff S., Rubery J. (eds.), *European Employment Models in Flux. A comparison of Institutional Change in Nine European Countries*. New York: Palgrave Macmillan.

Barbier J.-C. (2001), *Welfare to work policies in Europe: the current challenges of activation policies*, Document de travail du Centre d'Etudes de l'Emploi No. 11, November.

Barbier J.-C. (2007), "When Words Matter. Dealing Anew with Cross-National Comparison", in Barbier J.-C. and Letablier M.-T. (eds.), *Politiques sociales. Enjeux méthodologiques et épistémologiques des comparaisons internationales*. Brussels, PIE-Peter Lang.

Barbier J.-C. (2008), "Europe sociale: des enjeux culturels essentiels et mésestimés", *Lettre de la régulation*, No. 58, November, 7 p.

Barbier J.-C., Sylla N.S. (2004), *La stratégie européenne pour l'emploi: genèse, coordination communautaire et diversité nationale*. Rapport de recherche pour la DARES (Ministère de travail), January 2004.

Barbier J.-C., Sylla N.S., Eydoux A. (2006), *Analyse comparative de l'activation de la protection sociale en France, Grande-Bretagne, Allemagne et Danemark*. Rapport de Recherche, Noisy-le-Grand, Centre d'Études de l'Emploi.

Barbu R., Khristova A. (2004), *National Report for Deliverable 14/WP6 France*, Project "Employee's Resources and Social Rights in Europe", V[th] European Framework Programme.

Barnau L., Bescond G. (2006), "Analyse de l'évolution des bénéficiaires de la PPE", *Economie & prévision*, 173, pp. 163-170.

Biffl G. (2007), SOPREMI-Report on labour migration. Austria, Vienna, 2006-07 (http://www.wifo.at/wwa/jsp/index.jsp?fid=23923&typeid=8&id=30739&display_mode=2&language=2) Download August 2009.

Bilbao A. (1994), *Obreros y ciudadanos. La desestructuración de la clase obrera*, Madrid, Trotta.

Bilbao A. (1999), *Modelos económicos y configuración de las relaciones industriales*, Madrid, Talasa.

Bispinck R., Schulten T. (2011), "Trade Union Responses to Precarious Employment in Germany", *WSI-Diskussionspapier*, 178, December.

Bispinck R., Dribbusch H., Schulten T. (2010), "Allemagne. Erosion continue ou nouvelle stabilisation de la négociation collective de branche?", *Chronique internationale de l'IRES*, 126, September, pp. 39-56.

Bivand P. (2007), "How can we tell if the New Deal is working?", *Working Brief*, June 2007, Centre for Social Inclusion, pp. 20-22 (http://www.cesi.org.uk/working_brief/wb_back_issues/WB_2007/, accessed November 2009).

Blundell R. (2006), "Earned income tax credit policies: impact and optimality – The Adam Smith lecture, 2005", *Labour Economics*, 13, pp. 423-443.

Blundell R. and Meghir C. (2001), "Active labour market policies vs employment tax credits: Lessons from recent UK reforms", *Swedish Economic Policy Review*, 8, pp. 239-266.

Blundell R. and Reed H. (2000), "The employment effects of the working families tax credit", *Briefing Notes*, No. 6, Institute for Fiscal Studies.

Blundell R., Reed H., van Reenen J., Shephard A. (2003), "The impact of the New Deal for Young People on the labour market: a four year assessment", in Dickens R., Gregg P., Wadsworth J. (eds.), *The labour market under New Labour – The state of working Britain*, Houndsmills/Basingstoke, pp. 17-31.

Bonnefoy V., Robert-Bobée I. (2008), "La Prime pour l'Emploi en 2007: beaucoup de bénéficiaires pour des montants parfois faibles", *Solidarité Santé*, 5, 6-21.

Bosco A., Chassard Y. (1999), "A Shift in the Paradigm: Surveying the European Union Discourse on Welfare and Work", in Eurofound, *Linking Welfare and Work*, Luxembourg, Office for Official Publications of the European Communities, pp. 43-58.

Bourdieu P., Debons C., Hensche D., Lutz B. *et al.* (1998), *Perspektiven des Protests. Initiativen für einen europäischen Wohlfahrtsstaat*, Hamburg, VSA, 11-25.

Bourguignon F. (dir.) (2011), *Comité national d'évaluation du RSA. Rapport final*, Paris, Ministère des Solidarités et de la Cohésion Sociale.

Boyer R. (1986), *La flexibilité du travail en Europe*, Paris, La Découverte.

Boyer R. (2003), "Les institutions dans la théorie de la régulation", *Cahiers d'économie Politique*, 2003/1 No. 44.

Boyer R. (2004), *Théories de la régulation. Les fondamentaux*, La Découverte, Paris.

Boyer R. (2007), "Comment concilier solidarité sociale et efficacité économique à l'ère de la globalisation: une lecture régulationiste" in Paugam S. (dir.), *Repenser la solidarité. L'apport des sciences sociales*, Paris, PUF.

Brewer M. (2003), "The new tax credits", *Briefing Notes*, No. 35, Institute for Fiscal Studies.

Brewer M., Browne J. (2007), "The effect of the working families' tax credit on labour market participation", *IFS briefing note*, No. 69.

Brewer M., Duncan A., Shephard A. and Suárez M. (2006), "Did working families' tax credit work? The impact of in-work support on labour supply in Great Britain", *Labour Economics*, 13, pp. 699-720.

Brewer M., Francesconi M., Gregg P. and Grogger J. (2009), "Feature: In-work benefit reform in a cross-national perspective – Introduction", *The Economic Journal*, 119, February, F1-F14.

Brewer M., Muriel A., Philips D., Sibieta L. (2009), "Poverty and inequality in the UK", *IFS Commentary* C109, Institute for Fiscal Studies, http://www.ifs.org.uk/publications/4637, accessed November 2009).

Bundeskammer für Arbeiter und Angestellte (2004), *Die Lage der Arbeitnehmerinnen und Arbeitnehmer in Österreich 2004*, Vienna.

Bundesministerium für Arbeit und Soziales (BMAS) (1992), Die Effizienz der Arbeitsmarktverwaltung. Organisationsanalyse. *Forschungsberichte aus Sozial- und Arbeitsmarktpolitik*, Vienna.

Bundesministerium für Arbeit, Soziales und Konsumentenschutz (BMASK) (2012), *Dokumentation aktive Arbeitsmarktpolitik in Österreich 1994-2011. Maßnahmen, Instrumente, Programme und Politiken, Reformschritte, Monitoring, Evaluierung*, Wien.

Cahuc P. (2002), "À quoi sert la prime pour l'emploi?", *Revue Française d'Economie*, Vol. XVI, January, 3-61.

Castel N. (2009), *La retraite des syndicats: les raisons d'une impuissance*, Paris, La Dispute.

Cebulla A. (2005), "The road to Britain's New Deal", in Cebulla A., Ashworth K., Greenberg D., Walker R. (eds.), *Welfare-to-work: New Labour and the US Experience*, Aldeshot/Burlington, pp. 17-33.

CES (2005), *Memoria sobre la situación socioeconómica y laboral, Madrid*, Consejo Económico y Social.

Clasquin B. (2006), *Employees' Resources and Social Rights in Europe* HPSE-CT-2002-00104, RESORE final report, downloadable at: http://cordis.europa.eu/documents/documentlibrary/100123921EN6.pdf.

Clasquin B., Friot B. (eds.) (2001), *La Construction Sociale de l'Emploi*, Final Report of the TSER Network, contract ERB SOE-CT-97-3041.

Clasquin B., Moncel N., Harvey M., Friot B. (eds.) (2004), *Wage and Welfare – New Perspectives on Employment and Social Rights in Europe*, Brussels, PIE Peter Lang.

Cochard M., Junot-Mesqui B., Arnaud F. and Vermare S. (2008), "Les effets incitatifs de la prime pour l'emploi: une évaluation difficile", *Economie et Statistique*, 412, pp. 57-80.

Commission européenne (2007), *Vers des principes communs de flexicurité: des emplois plus nombreux et de meilleure qualité en combinant flexibilité et sécurité*, Office des publications officielles, Luxembourg.

Commission européenne (2010), "Initiative phare Europe 2020. Une Union de l'innovation", *Europe 2020 Flagship Initiative Innovation Union* SEC(2010)1161.

Commission of the European Communities (2005), *Green Paper Confronting demographic change: a new solidarity between the generations*, Brussels, March.

Coriat B., Petit P., Schméder G. (dir.) (2006), *The Hardship of Nations – Exploring the Paths of Modern Capitalism*, Edward Elgar.

Coron G. (2003), "Retraite par capitalisation et Union européenne: retour sur la directive IRP", *Revue de l'IRES*, No. 43, 2003/3, pp. 3-35.

Coron G. (2006), "Union européenne et système de retraite français, une perspective de sociologie du droit", Université Paul Verlaine de Metz, Thèse sous la direction de Jean-Yves Trépos.

Council Regulation (EU) No. 1177/2011 of 8 November 2011 amending Regulation (EC) No. 1467/97 on speeding up and clarifying the implementation of the excessive deficit procedure, *OJ L 306, 23.11.2011.*

Crespo E., Serrano Pascual A. (eds.) (2004), *Are Activation Policies converging in Europe? The European Employment Strategy for Young People*, Brussels, ETUI.

Cussó R., Gobin C. (2008), "Du discours politique au discours expert: le changement politique mis hors débat?", *MOTS. Les langages du Politique*, No. 88, pp. 5-11, Lyon, Ed. ENS.

Damon J. (2009), "Du RMI au RSA, en passant par le RMA", *Revue de droit sanitaire et social*, 46 (2): 213-22.

Daniel C. (1998), "Les politiques de l'emploi: une révolution silencieuse", *Droit Social*, No. 1, January, pp. 3-11.

DARES (2003), *Les politiques de l'emploi et du marché du travail*, Paris, La Découverte.

DARES (2004), *Plan National d'Action pour l'Emploi 2004, données statistiques*, document d'études. Accessed 2/06/2006 at: http://www.travail-emploi-sante.gouv.fr/IMG/pdf/DE_88.pdf.

Deakin S. (2002), "The evolution of the employment relation", in Auer P. and Gazier B. (eds.), *The Future of Work, Employment and Social Protection* (Symposium France/ILO), Geneva, ILO.

De Graaf W., Clasquin B. (2004), "Whither Social Rights and Societal Resources?", in Clasquin B., Moncel N., Harvey M. and Friot B. (eds.), *Wage and Welfare. New Perspectives on Employment and Social Rights in Europe*, Brussels, PIE-Peter Lang.

Dehousse R. (1998), *La cour de justice des communautés européennes*, Paris, Monchrestien, 2nd edition.

De Keersmaecker M.-L. (ed.) (1997), *Les inégalités sociales en Belgique, Vie ouvrière*, Brussels.

De Meulemeester, J.-L. (2012) "L'enseignement supérieur et la crise en Europe: quelques reflexions", No. 12-02, *Dulbea Working Papers*, ULB, Brussels, 12 January 2012, http://econpapers.repec.org/paper/dulwpaper/-2013_2f1074 18.htm.

De Nanteuil-Miribel M., Nachi M. (2004), "Flexibility and Security: What forms of Political Regulation", *Transfer*, 10 (2), pp. 300-318.

Deroubaix J.-C. (2003), "De l'AMI aux ABI. La libre circulation des capitaux en marche", in *MOTS*, Dossier Mondialisation(S), ENS Éditions, Lyon, No. 71, pp. 11-22.

Dickens R., Manning A. (2003), "Minimum wage, minimum impact", in Dickens R., Gregg P., Wadsworth J. (eds.), *The labour market under New Labour – The state of working Britain*, Houndsmills/Basingstoke, pp. 201-213.

Dimmel N. (2000), *Gemeinnützige Zwangsarbeit? Arbeitsmarktintegration zwischen Arbeitspflicht und innovativen Beschäftigungsmaßnahmen*, Wien, OEGB-Verlag.

Dixon K. (1998), *Les évangélistes du marché*, Paris, Raisons d'agir, 1998.

Dorfinger G. (2006), Experimentelle Arbeitsmarktpolitik einst und heute – Eine Analyse der Rolle von gemeinnützigen Akteuren in der experimentellen Arbeitsmarktpolitik, in Stelzer-Orthofer C. (Hg.), *Arbeitsmarktpolitik im Aufbruch. Herausforderungen und innovative Konzepte*, Linz, pp. 233-247, Mandelbaum.

Dufresne A. (2004), *Le discours de la banque centrale européenne concernant les aspects sociaux*, in Les Actes des 7e Journées internationales d'Analyse statistiques des Données Textuelles, Louvain-la-Neuve, pp. 373-381.

Dufresne A. (2006), *Les stratégies de l'euro-syndicalisme sectoriel. Etude de la coordination salariale et du dialogue social, Université Nanterre-Paris X and Université libre de Bruxelles*, doctoral thesis.

Dufresne A. (2009) "Les enjeux nationaux au cœur de la dimension transnationale du syndicalisme. Le cas du groupe de Doorn (1997-2007)", *Sociologies pratiques*, *Qui défend les salariés? Les territoires de l'action syndicale*, PUF 19, pp. 69-80.

Dufresne A. (2010), *L'Eurosyndicalisme et la défense du salaire*, Paris, La Dispute.

Dufresne A. (2011), *Le Salaire, un enjeu pour l'euro-syndicalisme. Histoire de la coordination des négociations collectives nationales*, Presses Universitaires de Nancy.

Dufresne A. (2012), "Le salaire, variable d'ajustement. Les indicateurs européens de 'coût du travail' au service de la modération salariale", *Actes des XIIIèmes journées internationales de sociologie du travail* (JIST), Presses universitaires de l'ULB.

Dufresne A., Degryse C., Pochet P. (eds.) (2006), *The European Sectoral Social Dialogue – Actors, developments and challenges*, Brussels, PIE-Peter Lang.

Dufresne A., Gobin C. (2007), "Vers une offensive syndicale européenne? Le 11e Congrès de la Confédération européenne des syndicats", *Chronique Internationale de l'IRES*, September 2007, No. 108, pp. 70-80.

DWP (Department for Work and Pensions) (2007), *Ready for work: Full employment in our generation*, http://www.dwp.gov.uk/policy/welfare-reform/legislation-and-key-documents/ready-for-work/ (accessed in November 2009).

DWP (Department for Work and Pensions) (2009a), *Transforming Britain's Labour Market. Ten years of the New Deal.* http://www.dwp.gov.uk/supplying-dwp/what-we-buy/welfare-to-work-services/flexible-new-deal/ (accessed in November 2009).

DWP (Department for Work and Pensions) (2009b), *Job seekers regime & Flexible New Deal, Phase 2 Launch events*, http://www.dwp.gov.uk/supplying-dwp/what-we-buy/welfare-to-work-services/flexible-new-deal/ (accessed in November 2009).

DWP (Department for Work and Pensions) (2011), *The work programme*, http://www.dwp.gov.uk/docs/the-work-programme.pdf (accessed in July 2012).

ECOTEC, Research and Consulting Limited (2002), *UK Contribution to the Evaluation of the European Employment Strategy*. http://www.lex.unict.it/eurolabor/en/documentation/altridoc/2002impact_evaluation.htm (accessed in April 2010).

Eichhorst W., Hemerijck A. (2008), "Welfare and Employment: a European Dilemma?", *Discussion Paper* Serie, IZA DP No. 3870, Bonn, December 2008, 36 p.

Eichmann H., Flecker J., Klambauer M. (2008), *Öffentliche Auftragsvergabe und prekäre Beschäftigung. Branchenanalysen zu Erwachsenenbildung, Architektur, Reinigung*, Final Report, Forba-Forschungsbericht No. 08/2008, Vienna.

EMF (2011), European Metalworkers Federation, *Coordination des salaires et crise économique en Europe*, Document adopté au 116e Comité exécutif de la FEM, Bruxelles, 23 et 24 November 2011.

Emmenegger P., Hausermann S., Palier B., Seeleib-Kaiser M. (eds.) (2011), *The Age of Dualization: The Changing Face of Inequality in De-industrializing Societies*, Oxford, Oxford University Press.

Employment Committee (2009), *Employment Guidelines (2008) – indicators for monitoring and analysis (endorsed by EMCO 24.06.09)* at http://ec.europa.eu/social/main.jsp?catId=115&langId=en (accessed in April 2010).

EPA (Encuesta de Población Activa) (2005), *Movimiento laboral registrado.* [on line] <http://www.ine.es> (accessed in January 2011).

Escarmelle J.-F. (1986), *L'État industriel dans les politiques de sortie de crise*, Cabay, Louvain-la-Neuve.

Esping-Andersen G. (1990), *The Three Worlds of Welfare Capitalism*, Cambridge, Polity Press.

Esping-Andersen G. (1999), *Social Foundations of Postindustrial Economies*, Oxford, Oxford University Press.

EUROFOUND (2003), *Flexibility and Social Protection*, Luxembourg, Office for Official Publications of the European Communities.

European Commission (2000), *Labour Market Policy Database. Methodology*, April, 2002 Edition.

European Commission (2003) *Private pension schemes, their role in adequate and sustainable pensions* – Joint report by the Commission and the Council, Luxembourg, Publications Office.

European Commission (2004), *Employment in Europe 2004*, Luxembourg: Office for Official Publications of the European Communities.

European Commission (2006), Labour Market Policy Database. Methodology. Revision of June 2006.

European Commission (2007), *EUR 23313 – EU Research on Social Sciences and Humanities – Employees' Resources and Social Rights in Europe – RESORE*, Luxembourg: Office for Official Publications of the European Communities, 2007, 150 p., ISBN 978-92-79-08220-7, http://cordis.europa.eu/documents/documentlibrary/100123921EN6.pdf (accessed in June 2009).

European Commission (2009), *Employment in Europe 2009*, Brussels, Office for Official Publications of the European Communities.

European Commission (2010), *Green Paper towards adequate, sustainable and safe European pension systems* SEC(2010)830 COM/2010/0365 final.

European Commission (2011), Recommendation for a COUNCIL RECOMMENDATION on the National Reform Programme 2011 of the United Kingdom and delivering a Council opinion on the updated Convergence Programme of the United Kingdom, 2011-2014, 7.6.2011, http://ec.europa.eu/europe2020/pdf/recommendations_2011/csr_uk_en.pdf (accessed March 2012).

Evaluation de la Stratégie Européenne pour l'Emploi (2002), France, January, http://www.lex.unict.it/eurolabor/en/documentation/altridoc/2002impact_evaluation.htm (accessed in April 2010).

Facing the Challenge (2004), *The Lisbon strategy for growth and employment*, Brussels, European Commission, Report from the High level Group chaired by Wim Kok.

Fargion V. (2001), "Des réformes négociées: le cas de l'Italie", in Daniel C. and Palier B. (eds.), *La protection sociale en Europe, le temps des réformes*, La Documentation Française, pp. 231-246.

Fehr-Duda H., Lechner F., Neudorfer P., Reiter W., Riesenfelder A. (1996), *Die Effektivität arbeitsmarktpolitischer Beschäftigungsmaßnahmen in Österreich – Ergebnisse einer Wirkungsanalyse der "Aktion 8000"*, AMS Studie, Herausgegeben vom AMS Österreich, Vienna, Wissenschaftsverlag.

Feurstein G. (1998), "Die Bewährungsprobe des Arbeitsmarktservices", in Khol A., Ofner G., Stirnemann A. (eds.), *Österreichisches Jahrbuch für Politik*, Vienna/Munich, Böhlau, pp. 515-527.

Ferrera M. (2005), *The Boundaries of Welfare*, Oxford, Oxford University Press.

Ferrera M. (2008), "Solidarity beyond the nation-state? Reflections on the European experience", *URGE Working Paper*, No. 2/2008, Milano, 16 p.

Ferrera M., Hemerijck A. (2003), "Recalibrating Europe's welfare regimes", in Zeitlin J., Trubek D. (eds.), *Governing work and welfare in the new economy: European and American experiments*, Oxford, Oxford University Press, pp. 88-128.

Field F., White P. (2007), "Welfare isn't working. The New Deal for Young People", REFORM, http://www.reform.co.uk/Research/Welfare/Welfare Articles/tabid/111/smid/378/ArticleID/629/reftab/72/Default.aspx Accessed November 2009.

Fink M. (2006), "Arbeitsmarkt- und Beschäftigungspolitik im Vereinigten Königreich und Dänemark: unterschiedliche Pfade zum Erfolg?", in Stelzer-Orthofer C. (ed.), *Arbeitsmarktpolitik im Aufbruch. Herausforderungen und innovative Konzepte*, Wien, Mandelbaum Verlag, pp. 97-135.

Fink M. (2006b), "Zwischen 'Beschäftigungsrekord' und 'Rekordarbeitslosigkeit': Arbeitsmarkt und Arbeitsmarktpolitik unter Schwarz-Blau/Orange", in Talos E. (ed.), *Schwarz-Blau. Eine Bilanz des "Neu-Regierens"*, Politik und Zeitgeschichte Band 3, edited by Talos E. und Fink M., Berlin LIT-Verlag, pp. 170-187.

Fitoussi J-P., Pisani-Ferry J., Le Cacheux J. (2003) "L'évaluation des politiques économiques en débat. Débat sur la prime pour l'emploi du 16 juin 2003", *Revue de l'OFCE*, 87, October, 255-280.

Fischer G., Talos E. (1987), „Materielle Versorgung bei Arbeitslosigkeit", in Talos, Emmerich/Wiederschwinger, Margit (eds.), *Arbeitslosigkeit – Österreichs Vollbeschäftigungspolitik am Ende?*, Vienna, Veralg für Gesellschaftskritik, pp. 231-253.

Fravega E., Queirolo Palmas L. (2005), *Mutations dans les relations entre emploi et protection sociale. Une lecture à travers des mesures phares dans 8 pays européens*. Deliverable 35, WP6. Employees' Resources and Social Rights in Europe (HPSE-CT-2002-00104).

French NAPE (2003), *National Action Plan for Employment, France*, 2003, http://www.lex.unict.it/eurolabor/en/documentation/altridoc/politiche_occupazione.htm (accessed in April 2010).

Freyssinet J. (2002), "Les normes d'emploi et les normes de protection sociale: l'impact de la diversification des temps de travail – des tendances en Europe occidentale", in Sarfati H. and Bonoli G. (eds.), *Mutations du marché du travail et protection sociale dans une perspective internationale: voies parallèles ou convergentes?*, Bern, Peter Lang, pp. 155-172.

Freyssinet J. (2009), "Flexibilité et sécurité: quelles stratégies d'acteurs", *Travail et Emploi*, No. 118, April-June, pp. 113-121.

Friot B. (1998), *Puissances du salariat: emploi et protection sociale à la française*, Paris, La Dispute.

Friot B. (1999), *Et la cotisation sociale créera l'emploi*, Paris, La Dispute.

Friot B. (2004), "Resource regime reforms and worker status", chapter 3 in Clasquin *et al.* (eds.), *Wage and Welfare*, Brussels, PIE Peter Lang.

Friot B. (2004), *Libération ou subordination du travail dans les conflits sur le financement de l'emploi de la protection sociale: l'intérêt d'une analyse des régimes de ressources*, Utrecht Workshop Paper, Project "Employee's Resources and Social Rights in Europe", Vth European Framework Programme.

Friot B. (2006), "Le salariat: pour une approche en termes de régimes de ressources", in Vatin F. (ed.), *Salariat: théorie, histoire, enjeux*, Paris, La Dispute.

Friot B. (2008), "Régimes de ressources et statut des salariés: l'exemple des pensions de retraites", in Guillemard A.-M. (ed.), *Où va la protection sociale?* Paris, PUF, 2008, coll. Le lien social.

Friot B. (2010), *L'enjeu des retraites*, Paris, La Dispute.

Friot B. (2012), *L'enjeu du salaire*, Paris, La Dispute

Friot B. (2012b), *Puissances du salariat; emploi et protection sociale à la française*, Paris, la Dispute (nouvelle édition).

Gafsi I., L'Horty Y. and Mihoubi F. (2005), "Réformer les exonérations de cotisations sociales sur les bas salaires", *Revue Française d'Economie*, Vol. XIX, No. 3, pp. 91-116.

Gatti D., Glyn A. (2006), "Welfare States in hard times", *Oxford Review of Economic Policy*, Vol. 22, No. 3.

Gazier B. (2003), *Tous "Sublimes". Vers un nouveau plein-emploi*, Paris, Flammarion.

Gazier B. (2008), "Flexicurité et marchés transitionnels du travail: esquisse d'une réflexion normative", *Travail et Emploi*, No. 113, January-March, pp. 117-128.

Glassner V., Keune M. (2010), "Negotiating the crisis? Collective bargaining in Europe during the economic downturn", *DIALOGUE Working Paper 10*. Geneva: International Labour Office.

Glassner V., Pochet P. (2011) "Why trade unions seek to coordinate wages and collective bargaining in the Eurozone: past developments and future prospects", *ETUI Working paper* 3 Brussels.

Gobin C. (1997), *L'Europe syndicale*, Bruxelles, Labor.

Gobin C. (2000), "L'Europe syndicale au risque de la mondialisation", *Les Temps modernes*, No. 607, Paris, pp. 159-177.

Gobin C. (2002), "Le discours programmatique de l'Union européenne: d'une privatisation de l'économie à une privatisation du politique?", *Sciences de la Société*, No. 55, Toulouse, Presses Universitaires du Mirail, pp. 156-169.

Gobin C. (2002b), "De l'Union européenne à ...l'européanisation des mouvements sociaux", *Revue Internationale de Politique Comparée*, Vol. 9, No. 1, Brussels, De Boeck Université, 2002.

Gobin C. (2005), "La démocratie, le syndicalisme et la gouvernance de l'Union européenne: la mémoire du conflit démocratique en péril?", in Maximos Aligisakis (ed.), *L'Europe et la mémoire. Une liaison dangereuse?*, pp. 41-70, Geneva, Collection Europa, Institut européen de l'Université de Genève.

Gobin C. (2007), "Coût salarial et non salarial", in Durand P. (ed.), *Les Nouveaux Mots du Pouvoir. Abécédaire critique*, Brussels, Aden, pp. 107-110.

Gobin C., Dufresne A. (2010), "Union Europea: El Derecho Civil contra el Derecho Salarial" in *Revista latinoamericana de Estudios del Trabajo, Proteccion, Empleo y Prevision Social*, Universidad de Carabobo, Bárbula, Venezuela, II Epoca Año 15, No. 23/24, 43-60.

Goblot J.-J. (2003), *Le droit au travail. Passé, présent, avenir*, Syllepse, Paris, 2003.

Gollbach J. (2000), *Grenzüberschreitende Tarifpartnerschaften in der Metallindustrie. Ein Ansatz zur europäischen Koordinierung gewerkschaftlicher Tarifpolitik*, Essen, Klartext Verlag.

Gray A. (2004), *Unsocial Europe – Social Protection or Flexploitation?* London/Ann Arbor, Pluto Press.

Grimshaw D., Rubery J. (2012), "The end of the UK's liberal collectivist social model? The implications of the coalition government's policy during the austerity crisis", *Cambridge Journal of Economics*, Vol. 36, pp. 105-126.

Grover C. (2011), "Cutting social security and tax credit spending", *Journal of Poverty and Social Justice*, Vol. 19, No. 3, pp. 235-248.

Hajer M. (1995), *The Politics of Environmental Discourse*, Oxford, Oxford University Press.

Hajer M., Versteeg W. (2005), "A decade of discourse analysis of environmental politics: Achievements, challenges, perspectives", *Journal of Environmental Policy & Planning*, 7(3): 175-184.

Hall P.A., Soskice D. (eds.) (2001), *Varieties of capitalism: The Institutional Foundations of Comparative Advantage*, Oxford, Oxford University Press.

Handler, Joel F. (2004), *Social citizenship and workfare in the United States and Western Europe: the paradox of inclusion*, Cambridge, Cambridge University Press.

Hantrais L. (2009), *International comparative research: Theory, methods and practice*, London, Palgrave Macmillan.

Haque R. (2011), "Universal credit briefing", *Working Brief*, Issue 221, pp. 6-8.

Harvey M., Maier R. (2004), "Rights over Resources", in Clasquin B., Moncel N., Harvey M. and Friot B. (eds.), *Wage and Welfare. New Perspectives on Employment and Social Rights in Europe*, Brussels, PIE-Peter Lang.

Harvey M., Urwin P. (2006), *The Working Tax Credit and other In-Work Benefits in the UK*, UK contribution in response to the "ultimate questionnaire" for WP 6, RESORE (Employee's Resources and Social Rights in Europe).

Heidenreich M., Zeitlin J. (eds.) (2009), *Changing European Employment and Welfare Regimes: The Influence of the Open Method of Coordination on National Reforms*, EUI Studies in the Political Economy of Welfare, London, Routledge.

Hege, A. (2005), "Le retour improbable à la normalité de la négociation collective, ou les dilemmes du mouvement syndical", *Chronique Internationale de l'IRES*, No. 92, January 2005.

Héritier P., Maurice J. (2010), "Salaires et crise", *Revue de l'IRES*, No. 64.

Higelé J.-P. (ed.) (2009), *Les transformations des ressources des travailleurs. Une lecture de l'emploi et des droits sociaux en France*, Nancy, Presses Universitaires de Nancy.

Higelé J.-P., Khristova A. (2005), *Prime pour l'emploi et exonérations générales de cotisations*. National report for Deliverable 29, WP6. Working document. "Employees' Resources and Social Rights in Europe" (HPSE-CT-2002-00104.

Higelé J.-P., Khristova A. (2007), "Politiques menées au nom de l'emploi et mutation des ressources des travailleurs: une comparaison européenne", *Revue de l'IRES*, No. 53, 2007/1, pp. 139-167.

Hilal, N. (2005), "*La naissance d'une coordination syndicale européenne: les mobilisations sociales dans le secteur des transports ferroviaires et routiers*", doctoral thesis, Sciences-Po, Paris.

HM Treasury (2002), The Child and Working Tax Credits – The modernisation of Britain's Tax and Benefit System, *Number Ten*, April.

HM Treasury (2005), Tax Credits: Reforming Financial Support for Families – The Modernisation of Britain's Tax and Benefit System, *Number Eleven*, March.

HM Treasury (2008), Tax Credits: improving delivery and choice – a discussion paper; The modernisation of Britain's tax and benefit system, *Number Twelve*, March.

HMRC (2006), CTC and WTC Statistics, April.

HMRC (2006b), *Child Tax Credit and Working Tax Credit Take-up rates 2003-04*, London, Tax Credits Analysis Team.

HMRC (2007), *Child Tax Credit and Working Tax Credit Take-up rates 2004-05*, London, Tax Credits Analysis Team.

HMRC (2011a), *CTC and WTC Statistics*, April.

HMRC (2011b), CTC and WTC Statistics-Finalised annual awards, May.

HMRC (2012), http://www.hmrc.gov.uk/rates/taxcredits.htm (accessed in March 2012).

Hochrainer K., Potmesil S., Zauner M. (2011), "Die österreichische Arbeitsmarktpolitik in der Wirtschaftskrise", *WISO*, Vol. 34, No. 2, 34-47.

Howarth C., Kenway P. (2004), *Why worry any more about the low paid?*, London, New Policy Institute, http://www.npi.org.uk/reports/low%20pay.pdf (Download October 2005).

Hoynes H., Blundell R. (2001), "Has 'in-work' benefit reform helped the labour market?", *NBER Working Paper Series*, WP 8546, October.

Husson M. (2000), "Le modèle européen des années 90", in Lamotte B. and Mounier A. (eds.), *Transformations du travail et croissance économique*, Paris, L'Harmattan.

Husson M. (2010), "Le partage de la valeur ajoutée en Europe", *Revue de l'IRES*, No. 64, 1, pp. 48-91.

Inland Revenue (2002a), The New Tax Credits: A Regulatory Impact Assessment, July 2002, United Kingdom.

Inland Revenue (2002b), Working Families' Tax Credit Statistics Quarterly Enquiry, November 2002, United Kingdom.

Inland Revenue (2003), Child and Working Tax Credits Quarterly Statistics, London, ONS, July.

Inland Revenue (2004), Child and Working Tax Credits Quarterly Statistics, London, ONS, April.

INSEE (2002), *L'Economie Française*, Edition 200-3, INSEE, 205-218.

Institut für Policy Research (1992), „Effektivität und Effizienz der österreichischen Arbeitsmarktverwaltung", in Bundesministerium für Arbeit und Soziales: Die Effizienz der Arbeitsmarktverwaltung, Organisationsanalyse, *Forschungsberichte aus Sozial- und Arbeitsmarktpolitik*, No. 45, Vienna, pp. 1-100.

International Labour Organisation (ILO) (2011), *Report on the High Level Mission to Greece*, Athens, 19-23 September.

International Labour Organisation (ILO) (2011), Global Wage Report 2010/2011, *Wage policies in times of crisis*, Geneva.

IRES (2006), *La chronique internationale*, special issue, "Les salaires minima, enjeu international" 103, November.

Jacobsson K. (2009), "Achievements and Non-achievements of the European Employment Strategy", in Morel N., Palier B., Palme J., pp. 119-130.

Jessop B. (2002), *The future of the capitalist state*, Cambridge/Oxford/Malden, Polity.

Jessop B. (2003), "From Thatcherism to New Labour: Neo-Liberalism, workfarism, and labour market regulation", in Overbeek H. (ed.), *The Political Economy of European Unemployment: European Integration and the Transnationalization of the Employment Question*, London, Routledge.

Jobs, jobs, jobs. Creating more employment in Europe (2003), Report of the Employment Taskforce, chaired by Wim Kok, November.

Kelly M. G. E. (2009), *The political philosophy of Michel Foucault*, New York, Routledge.

Keune, M. and Pochet, P. (2008), "Flexiseguridad: utilidad, desventajas y alternativas", *Gaceta Sindical*, No. 11, pp. 133-152.

Keune M., Pochet P. (2009), "Flexicurité en Europe: une approche critique", *Revue de l'IRES*, No. 63.

Khristova A. (2012), *Rapport salarial et intégration européenne: enjeux pour la théorie de la régulation*, Communication à la conférence co-organisée par l'AFEP, l'AHE et l'IIPPE Political Economy and the Outlook for Capitalism, 5-7 July 2012, Paris.

Khristova A., Moncel N. (2004), Deliverable 15/WP6, *Cross national studies on Subsidised Employment and Active Labour Market Policies: State of the Art*, "Employee's Resources and Social Rights in Europe", Vth European Framework Programme.

Klammer U. (2005), "Flexicurity schemes" in *Reconciling Labour Flexibility with Social Cohesion. Facing the Challenge*, part II, pp. 157-189; Trends in social cohesion No. 15, Council of Europe Publishing.

Kuhnle S. (ed.) (2000), *Survival of the European Welfare State*, London, Routledge/ECPR Studies in European Political Science.

Lallement M. (2003), "Raison ou trahison? Éléments de réflexion sur les usages de la comparaison en sociologie", in Lallement M. and Spurk J. (eds.), *Stratégies de la comparaison internationale*, Paris, CNRS Editions.

Lechner F., Reiter W., Riesenfelder A. (1996), Anforderungsgerecht – Ergebnisse der Evaluierung des Beschäftigungsprogrammes "Aktion 8000", in Arbeitsmarktservice Österreich: Ergebnisse der innovativen Arbeitsmarktpolitik, AMS Report, Vienna, Wissenschaftsverlag.

Legendre F., Lorgnet J.-P., Mahieu R. and Thibault F. (2004), "La prime pour l'emploi constitue-t-elle un bon instrument de soutien aux bas revenus?", *Revue de l'OFCE*, No. 88, January, 43-58.

Leigh A. (2005), "Optimal design of earned income tax credits: evidence from a British natural experiment", Australian National University, Centre for Economic Policy Research, *Discussion Paper 488*.

Lefresne F. (2005), "Les politiques d'emploi et la transformation des normes: une comparaison européenne", *Sociologie du travail*, Vol. 47, No. 3405-420.

Lefresne F. (2008), "Regard comparatif sur l'indemnisation de chômage: la difficile sécurisation des parcours professionnels", *Chronique internationale de l'IRES*, No. 115, November.

Lefresne F., Sauviat C. (2011) "Les modèles sociaux européens et américain confrontés à la crise", *Economie et Travail*, No. 33, August.

Leonardi L., Martin Artiles A., Molina O., Calenda D., Carrasquer P. (2011), "¿Es exportable la flexiguridad? Un estudio comparado de Italia y España", *Cuadernos de Relaciones Laborales*, Vol. 29, No. 2, pp. 417-443.

Leschke J. (2009), "The segmentation potential of non-standard employment: A four-country comparison of mobility patterns", *International Journal of Manpower*, 30(7), pp. 692-715.

Lewis J. (1992), "Gender and the Development of Welfare Regimes", *Journal of European Social Policy*, Vol. 2(3), pp. 159-73.

L'Horty Y. (2006), "Dix ans d'évaluation des exonérations sur les bas salaires" *Connaissance de l'Emploi* (Le 4 pages du Centre d'Etudes de l'Emploi), No. 24, January.

Lowell T. (1996), "The Europeanisation of Labour: structure before action", *European Journal of Industrial Relations*, 2, 3, pp. 325-344.

Low Pay Commission (2005), *National minimum wage*, Low Pay Commission report 2005, (London, www.lowpay.gov.uk/lowpay/report/pdf/DTi-Min_Wage.pdf (Download October 2005).

Low Pay Commission (2006), *National minimum wage*. Low Pay Commission report 2006, London, http://www.lowpay.gov.uk/lowpay/rep_a_p_index.shtml (Download May 2006).

Low Pay Commission (2007), *National Minimum Wage: Low Pay Commission's 2007 Report*, London.

Low Pay Commission (2008), *National minimum wage*. Low Pay Commission report 2008, London, http://www.lowpay.gov.uk/lowpay/ rep_a_p_index.shtml (Download October 2009).

Low Pay Commission (2012), *National minimum wage*, Low Pay Commission report 2012, London, http://www.lowpay.gov.uk/lowpay/report/pdf/2012 (Download July 2012).

Lutz H., Mahringer H. (2007), "Wirkt die Arbeitsmarktförderung in Österreich? Überblick über die Ergebnisse einer Evaluierung der Instrumente der Arbeitsmarktförderung in Österreich", *WIFO-Monatsberichte*, No. 3, pp. 199-218.

Mairhuber I. (2002a), Report on Austria in *Report for the EU Group of Experts "Gender and Employment"*, co-ordinated by Jill Rubery and the UMIST co-ordinating team for the Equal Opportunities Unit, DG V, Commission of the European Union. Vienna.

Mairhuber I. (2002b), *Council's Recommendation 2002*, Report on Austria, Vienna.

Mairhuber I. (2009), "Entwicklung der österreichischen Alterssicherung seit den 1980er Jahren", in Hermann C., Atzmüller R. (eds.), *Die Dynamik des österreichischen "Modells". Brüche und Kontinuitäten im Beschäftigungs- und Sozialsystem*, Berlin, Edition Sigma, pp. 177-198.

Marry C. (2003), "Pour le mélange des genres dans les comparaisons internationales", in Lallement M. and Spurk J. (eds.), *Stratégies de la comparaison internationale*, Paris, CNRS Editions.

Marsden D. (1999), *A theory of employment systems. Micro-Foundations of Societal Diversity*, Oxford, Oxford University Press.

Mascherini M. (2011), *Young people and NEETs in Europe: first findings*, Dublin, Eurofound. http://www.eurofound.europa.eu/pubdocs/2011/72/en/1/EF1172EN.pdf [accessed in May 2012].

Math A. (2001), Réformes des retraites et concurrence. Une analyse des rôles et stratégies des acteurs au niveau communautaire, *Document de travail*, No. 01.04, October.

Maurice M., Sellier F., Silvestre J. (1982), *Politique d'éducation et organisation industrielle en France et en Allemagne*, Paris, PUF.

Melis, Africa (2005), "Expenditure on Labour Market Policies, 1998-2003", *Statistics in Focus*, 17/2005, Eurostat.

Metcalf D. (2008), "Why has the British National Minimum Wage had little or no impact on employment?", *Journal of Industrial Relations*, Vol. 50, No. 3, pp. 489-512.

Mikol F., Vicard A., Bonnefoy V. and Mirouse B. (2008), "La Prime pour l'Emploi, un dispositif bien connu dans son principe, peu dans ses modalités", *Solidarité Santé*, 5, pp. 22-30.

Millar J. (2008), "Making work pay, making tax credits work: An assessment with specific reference to lone-parent employment", *International Social Security Review*, Vol. 61, 2/2008.

Mitterauer L., Reiter W., Riesenfelder A. (1999), *Evaluation der BESEB 1997, Endbericht*, Vienna, L&R Sozialforschung.

Moden J. and Sloover J. (1980), *Le patronat belge. Discours et idéologies 1973-1980*, Brussels, Crisp.

Moncel N., Ruivo M. (2002), "L'impact des politiques d'emploi sur la socialisation des ressources des travailleurs dans cinq pays européens", *Sociologia del Lavoro*, No. 85, pp. 195-206.

Moncel N., Ruivo M., Fravega E. (2004), "Work-Welfare Nexus at the Heart of the Social Construction of Employment: New Perspectives on Labour Markets Changes and Social Exclusion", in Clasquin B., Moncel N., Harvey M. and Friot B. (eds.), *Wage and Welfare. New Perspectives on Employment and Social Rights in Europe*, Brussels, PIE-Peter Lang.

Morel N., Palier B., Palme J. (2009), "What Future for Social Investment?", *Research Report 2009/2*, Institute for Future Studies, Stockholm, 193 p.

Morel N., Palier B., Palme J. (2012), *Towards a social investment welfare state? Ideas, Policies and Challenges*, Bristol, Policy Press.

Mottier V. (1999), "Narratives on National Identity: Sexuality, Race and the Swiss 'Dream of Order'", *ECPR Joint Sessions Working Paper*.

National Action Plan for Employment 2003, Maßnahmen die Österreich beschäftigen. Eine Offensive der Bundesregierung. http://ec.europa.eu/social/main.jsp?catId=101&langId=en (Last Access: December 2010).

Noel A. (1995), "The politics of Workfare", in Evans, Patricia M., Sayeed, Adil, *Workfare: Does it Work? Is it fair?*, Montreal, Institute for Research.

Obinger H., Talos E. (2006), *Sozialstaat Österreich zwischen Kontinuität und Umbau. Eine Bilanz der ÖVP/FPÖ/BZÖ-Regierung*, Verlag für Sozialwissenschaft, Wiesbaden.

OECD (1998), Employment Outlook – *Towards an employment-centered social policy*, Paris, OECD Publications.

OECD (2006), *Boosting Jobs and Incomes. Policy Lessons form Researching the OECD Jobs Strategy*, Paris, OECD.

OECD (2010), OECD Employment Outlook 2010, OECD Publishing.

Offe C. (1984), *"Arbeitsgesellschaft" – Strukturprobleme und Zukunftsperspektiven*, Frankfurt/New York. Campus.

OJEC (2000) – Official Journal of the European Communities, 21.03.2000.

OJEC (2001) – Official Journal of the European Communities, 24.01.2001.

OJEC (2002) – Official Journal of the European Communities, 01.03.2002.

OJEC (2003) – Official Journal of the European Communities, 05.08.2003.

OJEC (2005) – Official Journal of the European Communities, 06.08.2005.

OJEC (2010) – Official Journal of the European Communities, 24.11.2010.

Ordonnance No. 2006-344 du 23 mars 2006 relative aux retraites professionnelles supplémentaires, JORF, 24 March.

Ourliac B. and Nouveau C. (2012), "Les allègements de cotisations sociales patronales sur les bas salaires en France de 1993 à 2009", *Documents d'Etudes – Dares – 2012*, No. 169, February.

Paris H. (2008), "Produire des données statistiques dans un environnement décentralisé: le cas particulier du RMI", *Recherches et Prévisions*, 91, pp. 136-144.

Palier B. (2008), "Comparer les transformations des systèmes de protection sociale de l'Europe continentale", *Revue française des affaires sociales*, No. 1, pp. 139-150.

Palmer G. (2010), *The impact of devolution. Indicators of poverty and social exclusion*, Joseph Rowntree Foundation, www.jrf.org.uk (accessed in January 2011).

Peck J. (2001), *Workfare States*, New York/London, Guilford Press.

Peer Review (2000), *Tax and Benefit Reform in the UK*, Executive Summary, December.

Peters M., Dorenbos R., Van der Ende M., Versantvoort M. and Arents M. (2004), *Benefit Systems and their Interaction with Active Labour Market Policies – Final Report*, Employment and Social Affairs, European Commission, 423 p.

Pierson P. (ed.) (2001), *The New Politics of the Welfare State*, Oxford, Oxford University Press.

Ramaux C. (2012), *L'Etat Social*, Paris, Fayard.

Ramos, F. (2010), "Les polítiques actives d'ocupació", in AAVV, *Manual per a la gestió de politiques de promoció econòmica i desenvolupament local*, Barcelona, COLPIS and Departament Economia i Finances Generalitat de Catalunya.

République Française (2005), National Reform Programme for Economic and Social Growth, Working Document, October 2005, http://www.sgae.gouv.fr/actualites/docfiles/traductionENPNR.pdf (accessed in June 2009).

République Française (2006), *2006 Progress Report on the 2005-2008 National Reform Programme for Economic and Social Growth*, Courtesy translation, 28 September, http://www.sgae.gouv.fr/actualites/htmlpages/pnr/rapport/ (accessed in June 2009).

République Française (2007), *2007 Progress Report on the 2005-2008 National Reform Programme*, Courtesy translation, 15 October, http://www.sgae.gouv.fr/actualites/docfiles/French-progress-report-2007-courtesy.pdf (accessed in June 2009).

République Française (2012a), Projet de loi de finances 2012. Évaluation des voies et moyens. Tome II. Dépenses fiscales, Version of 03/10/2011 at 23:00:36, http://www.performance-publique.budget.gouv.fr/farandole/2012/pap/pdf/VMT2-2012.pdf.

République Française (2012b), Projet de loi de financement de la Sécurité Sociale, Annexe 5, Présentation des mesures d'exonération de cotisations et contributions et de leurs compensations, http://www.securite-sociale.fr/IMG/pdf/annexe5_plfss_2012.pdf (accessed in March 2012).

Rist G. (2002), *Les mots du pouvoir, Sens et non-sens de la rhétorique internationale*, Nouveaux Cahiers de l'IUED, No. 13, Collection Enjeux, Paris-Genève, PUF.

Rodgers G. (1992), "El debate sobre el trabajo precario en Europa Occidental", in Rodgers G. and Rodgers J. (eds.), *El trabajo precario en la regulación del mercado laboral*, Madrid, Ministerio de trabajo y seguridad social.

Ruivo M., Dias Da Silva A. (2004), *Subsidised Employment and Labour Market Policy in Portugal*. National report for Deliverable 9, WP6. Working document, "Employees' Resources and Social Rights in Europe" (HPSE-CT-2002-00104).

Salais R., Whiteside N. (eds.) (1998), *Governance, Industry and Labour Market in Great-Britain and France*, London, Routledge.

Santos Ortega A. (2003), "La invasión de la ideología empresarial en los márgenes del mercado de trabajo: inseguridad laboral, paro e inserción", in *Cuadernos de Relaciones Laborales*, Vol. 21, No. 1, pp. 107-128.

Sarfati H., Bonoli G. (eds.) (2002), *Mutations du marché du travail et protection sociale dans une perspective internationale: voies parallèles ou convergentes?*, Bern, Peter Lang.

Scharpf F.-W. (2000), "The Viability of Advanced Welfare States in the International Economy: Vulnerabilities and Options", *Journal of European Public Policy*, 7:2, pp. 190-228.

Scharpf F.-W. (2000b), *Gouverner l'Europe*, Paris, Presses de Sciences Po.

Schmid G. (2002), "Une assurance-emploi pour gérer les transitions critiques tout au long de la vie", in Auer P. and Gazier B. (ed.), *L'avenir du travail, de l'emploi et de la protection sociale – Dynamique du changement et protection des travailleurs*, Compte-rendu de symposium, OIT, pp. 71-92.

Schmidt K. (1991), *Geschichte der Arbeitsmarktverwaltung Österreich von ihren Anfängen an*, Salzburg, Arbeiterkammer.

Schulten T., Bispinck R., Schäfer. C. (2006), *Minimum wages in Europe*. Brussels, ETUI-REHS.

Schulten, T. (2009), Minimum wages in Europe: new debates against the background of economic crisis, *ETUI Policy Brief*, No. 2.

Schulten, T. (2012), Minimum wages in Europe under austerity, WSI Minimum Wage report 2012, *ETUI Policy Brief*, No. 5.

Schweighofer J. (2003), Ist die "europäische Beschäftigungsstrategie" nach 5 Jahren am Ende? Zur Evaluierung des Luxemburg-Prozesses 1998-2002, *Materialien zu Wirtschaft und Gesellschaft*, No. 84, Vienna, Kammer für Arbeiter und Angestellte.

Sebastián C. (1995), "El desequilibrio en el mercado de trabajo", *Papeles de Economía Española*, No. 62, pp. 344-360.

Sefton T., Sutherland H. (2005), "Inequality and poverty under New Labour", in Hills J., Stewart K. (eds.), *A more equal society? New Labour, poverty, inequality and exclusion*, Bristol, The Policy Press, pp. 231-249.

Segura J., Durán F., Toharia L. and Bentolila S. (1991), *Análisis de la contratación temporal en España*, Madrid, Ministerio de Trabajo y Seguridad Social.

Serrano A. (2003), "Towards convergence of European activation policies?", in Foden D. and Magnusson L. (eds.), *Five years' experience of the Luxembourg employment strategy*, Brussels, ETUI.

Serrano A. (2005), "Del desempleo como riesgo al desempleo como trampa: ¿Qué distribución de las responsabilidades plantea el paradigma de la activación propuesto por las instituciones europeas?", *Cuadernos de Relaciones Laborales*, 23 (2), pp. 219-246.

Serrano Pascual A. (2009), "Batailles d'idées dans l'espace européen: la lutte contre le chômage et le combat pour le nommer", *Revue de l'IRES*, No. 60, pp. 47-64.

Serrano Pascual A., Magnusson L. (2007), *Reshaping Welfare States and Activation Regimes in Europe*, Brussels, PIE Peter Lang.

Spreitzer H. (1999), *Die dunklen Seiten des österreichischen Arbeitsmarktes*, Diss. Univ. Vienna.

Stancanelli E., Sterdyniak H. (2004), "Un bilan des études sur la Prime pour l'Emploi", *Revue de l'OFCE*, January, pp. 17-41.

Statistik Austria (2007), Arbeitsmarktstatistik. Jahresergebnisse 2006, Mikrozensus-Arbeitskräfteerhebung, Vienna (http://www.statistik.at/web_de/ dynamic/statistiken/arbeitsmarkt/publikationen?id=3&webcat=3&nodeId=64& frag=3&listid=3).

Stiglbauer, A. (2010), Der österreichische Arbeitsmarkt in der großen Rezession: Entwicklungen und wirtschaftspolitische Maßnahmen, in: *Geldpolitik & Wirtschaft*, No. 3, 27-47 (Download July 2012: http://www.oenb.at/de/ img/gewi_2010_q3_analyse02_tcm14-209645.pdf).

Strickland P. (1998), Working Families Tax Credit and Family Credit, *Research Paper*, 98/46, April, House of Commons Library.

Streeck W. (1995), "From market making to state building? Reflections on the political economy of European social policy" in Leibfried S. and Pierson P. (eds.), *European Social Policy. Between fragmentation and integration*, Washington D.C., The Brookings institute.

Surel Y. (2010), "Le poids des organisations internationales dans les réformes des politiques sociales", *Informations sociales*, No. 157, pp. 36-43.

Talos E. (1987), "Arbeitslosigkeit und beschäftigungspolitische Steuerung: Problemwahrnehmung/Problemartikulation, Zielsetzungen, Strategien und Maßnahmen in Österreich seit Mitte der siebziger Jahre", in Talos E., Wiederschwinger M. (eds.), *Arbeitslosigkeit – Österreichs Vollbeschäftigungspolitik am Ende?*, Vienna, Verlag für Gesellschaftskritik, pp. 91-166.

Talos E., Kittel B. (2001), *Gesetzgebung in Österreich – Netzwerke, Akteure und Interaktionen in politischen Entscheidungsprozessen*, Vienna, WUV.

Talos E., Wörister K. (1998), "Soziale Sicherung in Österreich", in Talos, E. (Hg.), *Soziale Sicherung im Wandel – Österreich und seine Nachbarstaaten – Ein Vergleich*, Vienna, Böhlau, pp. 209-288.

Talos E., Wörister K. (1994), *Soziale Sicherung im Sozialstaat Österreich. Entwicklung – Herausforderungen – Strukturen*, Baden-Baden, Nomos.

Tangian A. (2010), Not for Bad Weather: Macroeconomic Analysis of Flexicurity with Regard to the Crisis, Brussels, *ETUI Working Paper*, 2010.06.

Taylor-Gooby, P. (2012), Root and branch restructuring to achieve major cuts: The social policy programme of the 2010 UK Coalition Government, in: *Social Policy & Administration*, Vol. 46, No. 1, pp. 61-82.

Théret B. (2010), "La protection sociale comme lien territorial: une solution d'avenir pour l'Europe?", *Finance & Bien commun*, No. 37-38, pp. 45-83.

Todorov T. (2006), *L'Esprit des Lumières*, Paris, Robert Laffont, paperback edition.

Traxler, F. (2002), *Considérations relatives au programme politique de négociation collective*, Paper presented to the ETUC, November 2002, Florence.

Traxler F., Brandl B. (2009), "Towards Europeanization of Wage Policy. Germany and the Nordic Countries", *European Union Politics*, 10, pp. 177-201.

Tritremmel W. (1998), "Ausgliederung der Arbeitsmarktverwaltung. Eine erste Bilanz", in Khol A., Ofner G., Stirnemann A. (Hg.), *Österreichisches Jahrbuch für Politik*, Vienna/München, Böhlau, pp. 529-544.

Turner L. (1996), "The Europeanisation of Labour: structure before action", *European Journal of Industrial Relations*, Vol. 2, issue 3, pp. 325-344.

UK NAPE (2003), *National Action Plan for Employment, United Kingdom*, 2003: http://www.lex.unict.it/eurolabor/en/documentation/altridoc/politiche_occupazione.htm (accessed in April 2010).

Unger B. (1999), "Österreichs Wirtschaftspolitik: Vom Austro-Keynesianismus zum Austro-Neoliberalismus?", in Karlhofer F., Talos E. (eds.), *Zukunft der Sozialpartnerschaft: Veränderungsdynamik und Reformbedarf*, Vienna, Signum, 165-190.

Urwin P. (2003), *National Report for Deliverable 9/WP6. United Kingdom*, Project "Employee's Resources and Social Rights in Europe", Vth European Framework Programme.

Vasapollo L. (2006), "Trabajo atípico y precario como elemento determinante estratégico del capital en el paradigma del devenir postfordista", in Bel J. (*et al.*), *Miradas sobre la precariedad*, Barcelona, El Viejo Topo.

Verd J.M. (2004), *Deliverable 12/WP4. Employee's nature of resources and social rights and their entitlement conditions*, Project "Employee's Resources and Social Rights in Europe", Vth European Framework Programme.

Wagner E., Lassnigg L. (2005), *Arbeitsstiftungen als Instrument im Strukturwandel*, Projektbericht, Vienna.

Watt A. (2003), *Reform of the European Employment Strategy after five years: a change of course or merely of presentation?*, Speech presented in the Seminar "The territorial dimension of the EES", IES, Córdoba.

Weiler (1981), "The Community System: the Dual Character of Supranationality", *Yearbook of European Law*, pp. 267-306.

Wessels W. (1997), "An Ever Closer Fusion? A Dynamic Macropolitical View on Integration Processes", *Journal of Common Market Studies*, Vol. 35, No. 2, June, pp. 267-299.

White Paper, An agenda for adequate, safe and sustainable pensions, February 2012, COM(2012) 55 final.

WIFO (Wirtschaftsforschungsinstitut, Austrian institute for economic research) (2006), *Das Wifo-Weißbuch. Mehr Beschäftigung durch Wachstum auf Basis von Innovation und Qualifikation*, Aiginger K., Tichy G., Walterskirchen E. (project coordination), Wien.

Wilk M. (1991), "Die Entwicklung der Arbeitsmarktpolitik in Österreich unter besonderer Berücksichtigung der aktiven Arbeitsmarktpolitik in Österreich von 1980-1984", in Stelzer-Orthofer C. (ed.), *Arbeitsmarktpolitik in Österreich*, Mandelbaum Linz.

Wilkinson F. (2001), "The theory and practice of wage subsidisation: some historical reflections", *Radical Statistics* 77, http://www.radstats.org.uk/no077 (accessed in May 2004) (Download October 2005).

Wilthagen T. and Tros F. (2004), "The concept of 'flexicurity': a new approach to regulating employment and labour markets", *Transfer*, 2/04, pp. 166-186.

Zauner H. (2006), "Entwicklungen und Maßnahmen der aktiven Arbeitsmarktpolitik in Österreich. Standortbestimmung aus Sicht eines Netzwerks von Non-Profit-Organisationen in der aktiven Arbeitsmarktpolitik", in Stelzer-Orthofer C. (ed.), *Arbeitsmarktpolitik im Aufbruch. Herausforderungen und innovative Konzepte*, Linz, Mandelbaum, pp. 204-216.

"Work & Society"

The series "Work & Society" analyses the development of employment and social policies, as well as the strategies of the different social actors, both at national and European levels. It puts forward a multi-disciplinary approach – political, sociological, economic, legal and historical – in a bid for dialogue and complementarity.

The series is not confined to the social field *stricto sensu*, but also aims to illustrate the indirect social impacts of economic and monetary policies. It endeavours to clarify social developments, from a comparative and a historical perspective, thus portraying the process of convergence and divergence in the diverse national societal contexts. The manner in which European integration impacts on employment and social policies constitutes the backbone of the analyses.

Series Editor: Philippe Pochet, General Director ETUI-REHS (Brussels) and Digest Editor of the Journal of European Social Policy

Recent Titles

No.75 – *The Wage under Attack. Employment Policies in Europe*, Bernadette CLASQUIN & Bernard FRIOT (eds.), 2013, 978-2-87574-029-8

No.74 – *Quality of Employment in Europe. Legal and Normative Perspectives*, Silvia BORELLI & Pascale VIELLE (eds.), 2012, 978-90-5201-888-1

No.73 – *Renewing Democratic Deliberation in Europe. The Challenge of Social and Civil Dialogue*, Jean DE MUNCK, Claude DIDRY, Isabelle FERRERAS & Annette JOBERT (eds.), 2012, 978-90-5201-875-1

No.72 – *Democracy and Capabilities for Voice. Welfare, Work and Public Deliberation in Europe,* Ota DE LEONARDIS & Serafino NEGRELLI (eds.), 2012, 978-90-5201-867-6

No.71 – *Trajectoires des modèles nationaux. État, démocratie et travail en France et en Allemagne*, Michèle DUPRÉ, Olivier GIRAUD et Michel LALLEMENT (dir.), 2012, ISBN 978-90-5201-863-8

No.70 – *Precarious Employment in Perspective. Old and New Challenges to Working Conditions in Sweden*, Annette THÖRNQUIST & Åsa-Karin ENGSTRAND (eds.), 2011, ISBN 978-90-5201-730-3

No.69 – *Europe 2020: Towards a More Social EU?*, Eric MARLIER & David NATALI (eds.), with Rudi VAN DAM, 2010, ISBN 978-90-5201-688-7

No.68 – *Generations at Work and Social Cohesion in Europe*, Patricia VENDRAMIN (ed.), 2009, ISBN 978-90-5201-647-4

No.67 – *Quality of Work in the European Union. Concept, Data and Debates from a Transnational Perspective*, Ana M. GUILLÉN & Svenn-Åge DAHL (eds.), 2009, ISBN 978-90-5201-577-4

No.66 – *Emerging Systems of Work and Welfare*, Pertti KOISTINEN, Lilja MÓSESDÓTTIR & Amparo SERRANO PASCUAL (eds.), 2009, ISBN 978-90-5201-549-1

No.65 – *Building Anticipation of Restructuring in Europe*, Marie-Ange MOREAU (ed.), in collaboration with Serafino NEGRELLI & Philippe POCHET, 2009, ISBN 978-90-5201-486-9

No.64 – *Pensions in Europe, European Pensions. The Evolution of Pension Policy at National and Supranational Level*, David NATALI, 2008, ISBN 978-90-5201-460-9

No.63 – *Restructuring in the New EU Member States. Social Dialogue, Firms Relocation and Social Treatment of Restructuring*, Marie-Ange MOREAU & María Esther BLAS LÓPEZ (eds.), 2009, ISBN 978-90-5201-456-2

No.62 – *Jobs on the Move. An Analytical Approach to "Relocation" and its Impact on Employment*, Béla GALGÓCZI, Maarten KEUNE & Andrew WATT (eds.), 2008, ISBN 978-90-5201-448-7

No.61 – *Les nouveaux cadres du dialogue social, Europe et territoires*, Annette JOBERT (dir.), 2008, ISBN 978-90-5201-444-9

No.60 – *Transnational Labour Regulation. A Case Study of Temporary Agency Work*, Kerstin AHLBERG, Brian BERCUSSON, Niklas BRUUN, Haris KOUNTOUROS, Christophe VIGNEAU & Loredana ZAPPALÀ, 2008, ISBN 978-90-5201-417-3

No.59 – *Changing Liaisons. The Dynamics of Social Partnership in Twentieth Century West-European Democracies*, Karel DAVIDS, Greta DEVOS & Patrick PASTURE (eds.), 2007, ISBN 978-90-5201-365-7

No.58 – *Work and Social Inequalities in Health in Europe*, Ingvar LUNDBERG, Tomas HEMMINGSSON & Christer HOGSTEDT (eds.), SALTSA, 2007, ISBN 978-90-5201-372-5

No. 57 – *European Solidarities. Tensions and Contentions of a Concept*, Lars MAGNUSSON & Bo STRÅTH (eds.), 2007, ISBN 978-90-5201-363-3

No. 56 – *Industrial Relations in Small Companies. A Comparison: France, Sweden and Germany*, Christian DUFOUR, Adelheid HEGE, Sofia MURHEM, Wolfgang RUDOLPH & Wolfram WASSERMANN (eds.), SALTSA, 2007, ISBN 978-90-5201-360-2